Study Guide

for

Siegel's

Criminology
Ninth Edition

Study Guide

for

Siegel's

Criminology
Ninth Edition

Eugene E. Bouley Jr.
Georgia College and State University

THOMSON
─────✦─────™
WADSWORTH

Australia • Canada • Mexico • Singapore • Spain • United Kingdom • United States

Printed in the United States of America
1 2 3 4 5 6 7 09 08 07 06 05

Printer: Darby Printing

ISBN 0-495-00095-7

Cover art: © Margaret Carsello/Images.com

For more information about our products, contact us at:
Thomson Learning Academic Resource Center
1-800-423-0563

For permission to use material from this text or product, submit a request online at
http://www.thomsonrights.com.
Any additional questions about permissions can be submitted by email to **thomsonrights@thomson.com.**

Thomson Higher Education
10 Davis Drive
Belmont, CA 94002-3098
USA

Asia (including India)
Thomson Learning
5 Shenton Way
#01-01 UIC Building
Singapore 068808

Australia/New Zealand
Thomson Learning Australia
102 Dodds Street
Southbank, Victoria 3006
Australia

Canada
Thomson Nelson
1120 Birchmount Road
Toronto, Ontario M1K 5G4
Canada

UK/Europe/Middle East/Africa
Thomson Learning
High Holborn House
50–51 Bedford Road
London WC1R 4LR
United Kingdom

Latin America
Thomson Learning
Seneca, 53
Colonia Polanco
11560 Mexico
D.F. Mexico

Spain (including Portugal)
Thomson Paraninfo
Calle Magallanes, 25
28015 Madrid, Spain

Table of Contents

Student Introduction

Student Introduction

This study guide was designed and written to introduce students to the study of criminology by helping them master the important concepts and principles presented in Larry Siegel's *Criminology*, 9th edition, and to further stimulate their interest in studying the issue of crime. The following is a brief description of how you can best make use of this study guide in learning the materials in the text and in preparing yourself for your examinations.

I suggest that you take the following steps to achieve the maximum benefits from this study guide. First, you should read the **Learning Objectives** to familiarize yourself with the key issues that will be addressed in the chapter. Second, you should spend time reviewing and studying the **Keywords and Definitions** to assist you in understanding the key terms and concepts that are contained in the chapter. The page numbers listed in the study guide for each keyword are the page numbers where the word is first used in the textbook. Third, you should read the **Chapter Outline** and the **Chapter Summary** to obtain a general idea of the chapter's contents. Fourth, you should diligently read the chapter in the text and in addition, I recommend that you highlight the significant points in the chapter.

The last step is to complete the **Test Bank** without using the text for reference. If you have problems completing some of the questions, you should review the text until you can complete most of the answers. After completing the test bank, you can evaluate your accuracy by turning to the **Answer Key** at the end of the chapter. Note that there are no answers to the **Essay Questions**, but the essay questions do show the page numbers in the textbook containing the material that will answer the question. If you do not do as well on the sample questions as you anticipated, you may wish to spend more time studying the textbook and conduct a further review of the study guide.

The study guide also provides you with **Student Exercises** which will give you some practical applications of what you have studied in the chapter. Your professor may assign these exercises as homework or extra credit work. The study guide also contains **Criminology Web Links** which are designed to acquaint you with web sites that will provide you with crime-related material that will be of value to you in doing research for this course and for your other criminal justice courses.

I hope you enjoy this study guide and find it helpful in your mastering the material in the textbook. I also wish you success in this course and in all your academic pursuits. A special thanks and my gratitude are extended to my wife, Terry, for her contributions to the preparation of this study guide.

Eugene E. Bouley, Jr., Ph.D.
Georgia College & State University
Milledgeville, Georgia

Study Guide

for

Siegel's

Criminology
Ninth Edition

Chapter 1

Crime, Criminology, and the Criminal Law

LEARNING OBJECTIVES

1. Discuss what is meant by the field of criminology.

2. Discuss the historical context of criminology.

3. Identify the differences among the various schools of criminological thought.

4. Explain the differences among the various schools of the criminological enterprise.

5. Discuss how criminologists define crime.

6. Explain the concepts of criminal law.

7. Discuss the difference between evil acts and evil intents.

8. Describe the various defenses to crime.

9. Describe the changes criminal law is undergoing.

10. Discuss the ethical issues facing criminology.

KEYWORDS AND DEFINITIONS

Criminologists: Use objective research methods to pose research questions (hypotheses), gather data, create theories, and test their validity. (page 1)

Criminology: An academic discipline that makes use of scientific methods to study the nature, extent, cause, and control of criminal behavior. (1)

Interdisciplinary science: A field of study that involves several disciplines; criminologists have been trained in diverse fields such as sociology, criminal justice, political science, psychology, economics, and the natural sciences. (1)

Decriminalized: Making a criminal act legal. (2)

Utilitarianism: The philosophy that behavior occurs when the person believes it is useful, purposeful, and reasonable. (6)

Classical criminology: The theory that holds that people have free will to choose criminal activity or lawful solutions to meet their needs; criminal solutions may be more attractive than lawful ones; a person's choice of criminal solutions may be controlled by fear of punishment, and the more severe, certain, and swift the punishment is, the better it is able to control criminal behavior. (6)

Positivism: The belief that human behavior is a function of forces beyond a person's control and that the scientific method can be used to solve problems. (7)

Criminal anthropology: The field of study that believes that serious offenders inherit criminal traits. (8)

Atavistic anomalies: The physical characteristics (enormous jaws and strong canine teeth) of criminals that show they are throwbacks to more primitive times. (8)

Biological determinism: The view that criminality is the result of inherited physical traits. (8)

Biosocial theory: The theory that holds that there is a link among physical and mental traits, the social environment, and behavior. (8)

Anomie: Norm or role confusion; describes the chaos and disarray accompanying the loss of traditional values in modern society. (9)

Chicago School: Pioneered by Robert Ezra Parks, Ernest W. Burgess, and Louis Wirth, it refers to the scholars who taught at the University of Chicago and the unique style of their research. (9)

Social ecology: The idea that social forces operate in urban areas and create criminal interactions causing some neighborhoods to become "natural" areas for crime. (9)

Socialization: The interactions people have with the various individuals, organizations, institutions, and processes of society that help them mature and develop. (10)

Criminological enterprise: The broader arena of criminology that consists of criminal statistics, sociology of the law, theory construction, criminal behavior systems, penology, and victimology. (11)

Ex post facto laws: A law that makes a behavior criminal after it was committed or makes a penalty applicable retroactively. (13)

White collar crime: Term developed by Edwin Sutherland and used to describe economic crime activities. (14)

Crime typology: Research on the links between different types of crimes and criminals. (14)

Penology: The study of the correction and control of known offenders in order to formulate strategies for crime control. (14)

Consensus view: The perspective that crimes are behaviors believed to be repugnant to elements of society. (14)

Substantive criminal law: The written code that defines crimes and their punishments. (14)

Social harm: Behaviors that are harmful to other people and society in general must be controlled; it is what sets strange, unusual, or deviant behavior – or any other action that departs from social norms - apart from criminal behaviors. (15)

Deviant behavior: Strange, unusual behavior or any other action that departs from social norms. (15)

Conflict view: The perspective that depicts society as a collection of diverse groups who are in constant and continuing conflict. (15)

Interactionist view: The perspective that holds that (1) people act according to their own interpretation of reality, through which they assign meaning to things; (2) they observe the way others react, either positively or negatively; and (3) they reevaluate and interpret their own behavior according to the meaning and symbols they have learned from others. (16)

Moral entrepreneurs: Those who use their influence to shape the legal process in the way they see fit. (16)

Crime: A violation of societal rules of behavior as interpreted and expressed by a criminal legal code created by people holding social and political power. Individuals who violate these rules are subject to sanctions by state authority, social stigma, or loss of status. (17)

Common law: Early English law and its use of precedents that became the basis of American law. (18)

Mala in se: Crimes that are considered inherently evil and depraved. (18)

Mala prohibitum: Crimes defined by the legislature, which reflect existing social conditions. (18)

Inchoate offenses: Incomplete or contemplated crimes such as attempt, conspiracy, or solicitation. (18)

Felony: Any crime punishable by incarceration for one year or more, or death. (19)

Social control function: The ability of the criminal law to control, restrain, and direct human behavior through its sanctioning power. (19)

Actus reus: The guilty act committed by the accused. (20)

Mens rea: The criminal intent to commit the act; referred to as a guilty mind. (20)

Strict liability crimes: Those crimes for which the law states that a person accused is guilty simply by doing what the statute prohibits; intent does not enter the picture. (21)

Justification: A legal defense in which the individual usually admits to having committed the criminal act but maintains that he or she should not be held criminally liable because the act was justified. (21)

CHAPTER OUTLINE

I.   What is criminology?
    A.   Criminology and criminal justice
        1.   Criminology – the scientific approach to studying criminal behavior
            a.   Includes the processes of making laws, of breaking laws, and of reacting to the breaking of laws
            b.   Most important areas
                1)   Development of criminal law and its use to define crime
                2)   Cause of law violation
                3)   Methods to control criminal behavior
            c.   Refers to verified principles – implies scientific method should be used in criminology
            d.   It is an interdisciplinary science
            e.   Explains the origins, extent, and nature of crime in society
        2.   Criminal justice scholars
            a.   Engaged in describing, analyzing, and explaining the behavior of justice agencies
            b.   Identifying effective methods of control
        3.   Both fields overlap
            a.   Criminologists must know how agencies of justice operate
            b.   Criminal justice experts must understand the nature of crime
    B.   Criminology and deviance
        1.   Deviance – behavior that departs from social norms
        2.   Not all crimes are deviant
        3.   Not all deviant acts are illegal or criminal
        4.   Criminologists study how deviant acts are criminalized and how criminal acts are decriminalized
        5.   Criminologists are concerned with the concept of deviance and its relationship to criminality

II.   A brief history of criminology
    A.   Classical criminology
        1.   Prior to the 18th century, those who violated social norms or laws were believed to be witches or possessed by demons

2. 18th century
   a. Brought the concept of utilitarianism
   b. Utilitarianism emphasizes that behavior occurs when a person believes it is useful, purposeful, and reasonable
3. Cesare Beccaria
   a. People seek pleasure and avoid pain
   b. Crimes provide people pleasure
   c. To deter crime, pain of punishment must outweigh the pleasure of crime
   d. Beccaria and his followers form the core of classical criminology
4. Classical criminology
   a. People have free will and choose their behavior
   b. Crime is attractive because it requires less work than legal behaviors and it has a greater payoff
   c. Crime can be controlled by fear of punishment
   d. The more severe, certain, and swift the punishment, the greater the control
5. Classical perspective influenced the judicial philosophy of the 18th and 19th centuries

B. Nineteenth-century positivism
   1. The scientific method took hold in Europe
   2. People began using careful observation and analysis of natural phenomena to understand the workings of the world
   3. Auguste Comte
      a. The father of sociology
      b. Applied scientific methods to sociology
      c. He and his followers became known as positivists
   4. Two elements of positivism
      a. Human behavior is a function of forces beyond the person's control
      b. The use of the scientific method to solve problems
   5. Positivist criminology
      a. Physiognomists – studied facial features of criminals to determine their association with antisocial behavior
      b. Phrenologists – studied the link between the shape of the skull and bumps on the head and antisocial behavior
      c. Concept of psychopathic personality
   6. Biological determinism and Cesare Lombroso
      a. Serious offenders inherit criminal traits
      b. Born criminals have atavistic anomalies – throwbacks to more primitive times

C. Foundations of sociological criminology
   1. Traced to the works of Adolphe Quetelet and Emile Durkheim
   2. Quetelet
      a. Began the use of data and statistics in criminological research
      b. Uncovered the relationship of age, sex, season, climate, population composition, and poverty to criminality
   3. Durkheim
      a. Crime is a normal and necessary social event
      b. Impossible to imagine a society without crime
      c. Crime paves the way for social change
      d. Crime calls attention to social ills
      e. Coined the term anomie – norm and role confusion

D. The Chicago School and beyond
   1. Pioneered research in social ecology
      a. Found some neighborhoods are "natural areas" for crime due to social forces
      b. Poverty leads to a critical breakdown in social institutions, such as schools and family
      c. Crime is a reaction to an inadequate environment
      d. Studied the influence of poverty levels on crime rates
      e. Crime is a function of where one lives
   2. Socialization view
      a. Sutherland – people learn criminal attitudes
      b. Reckless – crime occurs when children develop an inadequate self-image
E. Conflict criminology
   1. 1960s brought an antiestablishment counterculture movement, the civil rights movement, the women's movement
   2. Sociologists applied Marxist principles to the study of crime
   3. Economic system produces conditions that support a high crime rate
F. Contemporary criminology
   1. Choice theorists – criminals are rational and decide if crime is worthwhile
   2. Deterrence theory – choice is structured by fear of punishment

III. What criminologists do: The criminological enterprise?
   A. Criminal statistics
      1. To create valid and reliable measurements of criminal behaviors
      2. To establish accurate indicators of the true number of criminal acts
   B. Sociology of law – concerned with
      1. The role social forces play in shaping the criminal law
      2. The role of criminal law in shaping society
   C. The nature of theory and theory development
      1. Social theory
         a. Systematic set of interrelated statements or principles that explain some aspect of social life
         b. Serves as a model or framework for understanding human behavior
      2. Grand theories – try to explain the structure of human behavior and the forces that change or alter its content and direction
   D. Criminal behavior systems
      1. Subarea of criminology
      2. Involves research on specific criminal types and patterns
      3. Involves research on the links between different types of crimes and criminals (crime typology)
   E. Penology
      1. The correction and control of known criminal offenders
      2. Formulates strategies for crime control
      3. Involves rehabilitation and treatment
   F. Victimology
      1. Victim behavior is often a key determinant of crime
      2. Victims' actions may precipitate crime
      3. Study of crime not complete unless the victim's role is considered
      4. Studying the victim's role
         a. Actual costs of crime to the victim
         b. Probabilities of victim risk

       c.   Victim culpability or precipitation of crime
       d.   Victim services

IV. How criminologists view crime
    A.   The consensus view of crime
       1.   Crimes are behaviors believed to be repugnant to all elements of society
       2.   Substantive criminal law reflects values, beliefs, and opinions of society's mainstream
       3.   Consensus or general agreement among a majority on what behaviors should be illegal and viewed as crimes
       4.   Criminal law is applied uniformly to all
       5.   Faith in the concept of an ideal legal system
       6.   Crime linked to the concept of social harm
       7.   Behaviors that are harmful to other people and society in general must be controlled
       8.   Many deviant acts are not criminal
    B.   The conflict view of crime
       1.   Criminal law reflects and protects established economic, racial, gendered, and political power and privilege
       2.   Society is a collection of diverse groups who are in constant and continuous conflict
       3.   Groups use the law and criminal justice system to advance their economic and social position
       4.   Criminal law protects the haves from the have-nots
       5.   Definition of crime controlled by those with wealth, power, and position
       6.   "Real" crimes are human rights violations, unsafe working conditions, inadequate child care, etc.
    C.   The interactionist view of crime
       1.   Antecedents found in the symbolic interaction school of sociology
       2.   Characteristics of the position
           a.   People act according to their own interpretation of reality
           b.   They observe the ways others react, either positively or negatively
           c.   They reevaluate and interpret their own behavior according to the meaning and symbols they have learned from others
       3.   There is no objective reality
       4.   Good and evil is interpreted by the evaluator
       5.   Crime reflects the preferences of those in power
       6.   Criminals are those society chooses to label
       7.   The deviant is the one to whom the label has been successfully applied
       8.   Criminal law conforms to the beliefs of moral entrepreneurs
       9.   Crime has no meaning unless people react to it negatively
    D.   Defining crime – an integrated definition
       1.   Violation of societal values
       2.   As interpreted and expressed by a legal code
       3.   Created by people holding social and political power
       4.   Individuals who violate the rules are subject to sanctions
       5.   By state authority, social stigma, or loss of status

V. Crime and criminal law
    A. Common law
        1. Based on the English system of law
            a. Royal judges published their decisions in local cases
            b. Judges used these written decisions as a basis for the decision making
            c. Precedent – new rule successfully applied in a number of cases
        2. Types of crimes
            a. Mala in se
            b. Mala prohibitum
    B. Contemporary criminal law
        1. Crimes are divided into two types
            a. Felonies
            b. Misdemeanors
        2. Goals of criminal law
            a. Enforce social control
            b. Discourage revenge
            c. Express public opinion and morality
            d. Deter criminal behavior
            e. Punish wrongdoing
            f. Maintain social order
    C. The criminological enterprise: The elements of criminal law
        1. State must show that the accused
            a. Committed the guilty act – actus reus
            b. Had the criminal intent or guilty mind – mens rea
        2. Actus reus
            a. Guilty actions must be voluntary
            b. Failure to act can be a crime
                1) If there is a relationship between the parties based on status
                2) If imposed by statute
                3) If there is a contractual relationship
        3. Mens rea
            a. Criminal intent exists if the results of the action are certain to occur
            b. Strict liability – crimes defined by statute that do not require intent
        4. Criminal defenses
            a. Deny the actus reus
            b. Deny the mens rea
            c. Justification
    D. The evolution of criminal law
        1. Criminal law is constantly evolving to reflect social and economic conditions
        2. May change because of shifts in culture and in social conventions

VI. Ethical issues in criminology
    A. What is to be studied?
    B. Who is to be studied?
    C. How are studies to be conducted?

CHAPTER SUMMARY

Criminology is the scientific approach to studying criminal behavior. It deals with the processes of making laws, of breaking laws, and of reacting to the breaking of laws. Research in criminology is characterized by the use of the scientific method. Criminal justice refers to describing, analyzing, and explaining the behavior of justice agencies. Although the two fields are different, they do overlap. Criminologists must know how criminal justice agencies operate and criminal justice experts must understand the nature of crime.

Classical criminology developed in the 19th century. Cesare Beccaria argued that people have free will and choose their behavior. Therefore, crime can be controlled by fear of punishment, if is severe, certain, and swift. Positivism followed classical criminology. It began with biological determinism and Cesare Lombroso who argued that serious offenders had inherited criminal traits. The foundations of sociological criminology developed with Adolphe Quetelet and his use of data and statistics in criminological research. Emile Durkheim followed with the idea that crime is a normal and necessary social event. He coined the term "anomie" to describe norm and role confusion. In the United States, the Chicago School pioneered research in social ecology and found that some neighborhoods are "natural areas" for crime because of poverty and broken social institutions. The socialization view followed, proposing that people learn criminal attitudes or develop an inadequate self-image. The 1960s and 1970s brought conflict criminology that applied Marxist principles to the study of crime. In contemporary criminology we find choice theorists, who propose that criminals are rational and decide if crime is worthwhile, and deterrence theorists, who argue that crime is structured by the fear of punishment.

The criminological enterprise has six major subareas. First, there is criminal statistics which tries to describe and measure crime. Next is the sociology of the law which analyzes how society shapes the law and the law shapes society. Third is theory and theory development which focus on crime causation. Next is criminal behavior systems which focuses on crime typology. Fifth, there is penology which deals with corrections, rehabilitation, and treatment. Lastly, there is vicitmology which focuses on the role of victims in crime.

There are three perspectives from which criminologists view crime. The first is the consensus view which holds that the substantive criminal law reflects the values, beliefs, and opinions of society's mainstream and that there is a consensus or general agreement among a majority of citizens on what behaviors should be illegal. The second perspective is the conflict view which holds that society is a collection of diverse groups who are in constant and continuous conflict. Those groups who achieve power use the law and the criminal justice system to advance their economic and social position so that they become the haves and control the have-nots. The third perspective is the interactionist view of crime. Under this view, people act according to their own interpretation of reality. They observe how others react positively or negatively. They reevaluate and interpret their own behavior according to the meaning and symbols they have learned from others. Therefore, good and evil in interpreted by the evaluator.

Our system of criminal law is based on English common law and the use of precedents. We view crimes as being of two types: 1) mala in se and 2) mala prohibitum. We also classify crimes according to the punishments allowed in the law: 1) felonies are the most serious and 2) misdemeanors are the lesser crimes. There are two components in every crime: 1) the guilty act or actus reus and 2) the guilty mind or mens rea. Consequently, there are three basic criminal defenses: 1) deny the actus reus, 2) deny the mens rea, or 3) provide justification for the act.

Criminology is a discipline that involves several ethical issues that fall into three categories. First, what is to be studied? Second, who is to be studied? Third, how are the studies to be conducted?

STUDENT EXERCISES

Exercise 1

Make a list of five deviant acts that are not criminal. Make a list of five criminal acts that are not deviant. Compare your list with those compiled by your classmates. Why do you think that there is not complete agreement among you and your classmates?

Exercise 2

Make a list of 15 crimes. Ask 5 or 6 classmates of yours (who are not in your criminology class) to rank the 15 crimes from most serious to least serious. How do the rankings provided by your classmates compare? Overall, is there general agreement or complete disagreement? Criminologists from what perspective of crime would have predicted this result?

CRIMINOLOGY WEB LINKS

http://cj.wadsworth.com/siegel_crim9e
This website is designed exclusively for your textbook. Take a look around the website to familiarize yourself with it. Also keep in mind that it will always have an up-to-date list of weblinks contained in the textbook.

http://www.criminology.fsu.edu/cjlinks/
This is an outstanding website of maintained by Dr. Cecil Greek. It contains a wealth of information pertaining to criminology-related web sites.

http://www.ncjrs.org/
This is the website containing a wealth of information pertaining to crime and justice. It provides you access to a wealth of government documents on every aspect of crime.

This web site maintains the Bureau of Justice Statistics (BJS) Federal Justice Statistics Program (FJSP) database, which contains information about suspects and defendants processed in the Federal criminal justice system. Using data obtained from Federal agencies, the FJSP compiles comprehensive information describing defendants from each stage of Federal criminal case processing.

TEST BANK

FILL-IN THE BLANKS

1. Criminology is a discipline that makes use of the _____ _____ to study the nature, extent, cause, and control of criminal behavior.

2. Criminal justice refers to the study of _____ social control that handle criminal offenders.

3. The earliest "scientific" studies examining human behavior were _____ oriented.

4. The Chicago School pioneered research on the _____ _____ of the city of Chicago.

5. Criminal statistics involves measuring the amount and trends of _____ _____.

6. A criminologist's choice of orientation or perspective depends, in part, on his or her _____ of crime.

7. The _____ view of crime traces its antecedents to the symbolic interaction school of sociology.

8. Inherently evil crimes are often referred to as _____ _____ _____.

9. To satisfy the requirements of actus reus, guilty actions must be _____.

10. _____ _____ _____ are crimes defined by statute that do not require mens rea, as the person is guilty simply by doing what the statute prohibits.

TRUE/FALSE QUESTIONS

1. T/F Criminology is an interdisciplinary science.

2. T/F Criminologists study how criminal acts are decriminalized.

3. T/F Deviance refers to the study of behavior that departs from the law.

4. T/F Classical criminology believes people's choice of crime may be controlled by his or her fear of punishment.

5. T/F Positivism holds that criminals are not responsible for their crimes.

6. T/F Atavistic anomalies means that criminals are degenerates.

7. T/F Durkheim argued that crime is not useful and it is unhealthy for society.

8. T/F The Chicago School sociologists and their contemporaries focused on the functions of social institutions.

9. T/F Conflict criminology applies Marxist principles to the study of crime.

10. T/F The sociology of law is a subarea of the criminological enterprise.

11. T/F Penology is the study of the links between different types of crimes and criminals.

12. T/F Substantive criminal law is the written code that defines crimes and their punishments.

13. T/F The consensus view of crime links illegal behavior to the concept of social harm.

14. T/F According to the conflict view of crime, "real" crimes include murder, rape, and torture.

15. T/F Criminal law has a social control function.

MULTIPLE CHOICE QUESTIONS

1. Emphasizing that behavior occurs when the actor considers it useful, purposeful, and reasonable is called:
   a. determinism
   b. hedonism
   c. utilitarianism
   d. classicism

2. Which is NOT a subarea in the field of criminology?
   a. Identifying the nature of crime
   b. Explaining the behavior of justice agencies
   c. Explaining the cause of crime
   d. Describing the extent of crime

3. The most famous classical criminologist is:
   a. Cesare Beccaria
   b. Cesare Lombroso
   c. Adolphe Quetelet
   d. Emile Durkheim

4. To control criminal behavior, punishment must be:
   a. swift
   b. severe
   c. certain
   d. all of the above

5. Those who study the shape of the skull and bumps on the head to determine whether their physical attributes were linked to criminal behavior are called:
   a. physiognomists
   b. phrenologists
   c. classical criminologists
   d. positivists

6. Lombroso held that born criminals suffer from:
   a. mental illness
   b. disease
   c. atavistic anomalies
   d. all of the above

7. The assumed link among physical and mental traits, the social environment, and behavior is called:
   a. positivism
   b. biological determinism
   c. biosocial theory
   d. criminal anthropology

8. The person who instigated the use of data and statistics in performing criminological research is:
   a. Emile Durkheim
   b. Adolphe Quetelet
   c. Robert Ezra Park
   d. Ernest W. Burgess

9. The cartographic school of criminology made extensive use of:
   a. social statistics
   b. the law
   c. skull measurements
   d. psychology

10. The interactions people have with the various individuals, organizations, institutions, and processes of society that help them mature and develop are called:
    a. cartography
    b. social ecology
    c. anomie
    d. socialization

11. Which of the following is a subarea of the criminological enterprise?
    a. penology
    b. criminal behavior systems
    c. sociology of law
    d. all of the above

12. The subarea of criminology concerned with the role social forces play in shaping criminal law is called:
    a. criminal behavior systems
    b. penology
    c. vicitimology
    d. the sociology of the law

13. The study of criminal behavior that involves research on the links between different types of crimes and criminals is known as:
    a. crime categorization
    b. crime typology
    c. victimology
    d. penology

14. The position that crimes are behaviors believed to be repugnant to all elements of society called:
    a. consensus view
    b. interactionist view
    c. conflict view
    d. criminological view

15. What sets deviant behavior apart from criminal behavior is:
    a. society's attitude
    b. the law
    c. social harm
    d. precedent

16. Depicting society as a collection of diverse groups is the position of:
    a. consensus view
    b. interactionist view
    c. conflict view
    d. criminological view

17. Those who say that those who hold social power impose their definition of right and wrong on the rest of the population hold the:
    a. consensus view
    b. interactionist view
    c. conflict view
    d. criminological view

18. The basis for the U.S. legal system is found in the:
    a. Mosaic Code
    b. Code of Hammurabi
    c. Napoleonic Code
    d. English Code

19. Which of the following pertains to common law?
    a. English parliament could not enact legislation to supplement judge-made law.
    b. Precedents would be commonly applied in all cases.
    c. The only crimes are mala in se.
    d. All of the above.

20. The unlawful touching of another with the intent to cause injury is called:
    a. assault
    b. battery
    c. rape
    d. solicitation

21. For a crime to occur, the state must show the accused had the intent to commit the act. The intent to commit the act is commonly called:
    a. mala in se
    b. actus reus
    c. mala prohibitum
    d. mens rea

22. If a child is sick, the parents must seek medical aid. The failure to act in this case is considered a crime for which of the following reasons?
    a. imposition by statute
    b. contractual relationship
    c. relationship of the parties based on status
    d. biological determinism

23. By arguing that they were falsely accused and that the real culprit has yet to be identified, the accused is:
    a. denying the actus reus
    b. denying the mens rea
    c. arguing justification
    d. denying the mala in se

24. Criminal law can change because of which of the following?
    a. social conditions
    b. economic conditions
    c. shifts in culture
    d. all of the above

25. A major ethical issue in criminology is that too often criminologists focus their attention on:
    a. white males
    b. poor and minorities
    c. prisoners
    d. juveniles

ESSAY QUESTIONS

1. List and describe the subareas of the criminological enterprise.

2. Explain the conflict view of crime.

3. Explain the interactionist view of crime.

4. Discuss the social goals the government hopes to achieve by outlawing unacceptable behaviors.

5. List and describe the three major categories of ethical issues in criminology.

MATCHING

1. _____ Deviance
2. _____ Interdisciplinary
3. _____ Emile Durkheim
4. _____ Code of Hammurabi
5. _____ Criminological Enterprise
6. _____ Anomie
7. _____ Social Theory
8. _____ Criminal Law
9. _____ Bourgeoise
10. _____ Substantive Criminal Law

A. A condition produced by normlessness.
B. Criminologists have been trained in diverse fields most commonly sociology, but also criminal justice, political science, psychology, economics, and the natural sciences.
C. Written code that defines crimes and their punishments.
D. Owners of the means of production.
E. Systematic set of interrelated statements or principles that explain some aspect of social life.
F. Behavior that departs from social norms.
G. Most famous set of written laws of the ancient world preserved on basalt rock columns.
H. Has a social control function.
I. Crime is normal.
J. Subareas within the broader arena of criminology.

CHAPTER 1 ANSWER KEY

Fill in the Blank Answers

1. scientific methods
2. agencies
3. biologically
4. social ecology
5. criminal behavior
6. definition
7. interactionist
8. mala in se
9. voluntary
10. strict liability crimes

True/False Answers

1.	T	6.	F	11.	F
2.	T	7.	F	12.	T
3.	F	8.	T	13.	T
4.	T	9.	T	14.	F
5.	F	10.	T	15.	T

Multiple Choice Answers

1.	C	11.	D	21.	D
2.	B	12.	D	22.	C
3.	A	13.	B	23.	A
4.	D	14.	A	24.	D
5.	A	15.	C	25.	B
6.	C	16.	C		
7.	C	17.	B		
8.	B	18.	A		
9.	A	19.	B		
10.	D	20.	B		

Essay Questions

1. Pages 11-14
2. Pages 15-16
3. Pages 16-17
4. Pages 19-20
5. Pages 22-24

Matching Answers

1.	F	6.	A
2.	B	7.	F
3.	I	8.	H
4.	G	9.	D
5.	J	10.	C

Chapter 2

The Nature and Extent of Crime

LEARNING OBJECTIVES

1. Be familiar with the various forms of crime data.

2. Know the problems associated with collecting valid crime data.

3. Be able to discuss recent trends in the crime data.

4. Be familiar with the factors that influence crime rates.

5. Be able to discuss patterns in the crime rate.

6. Recognize age, gender, and racial patterns in crime.

7. Be able to discuss the association between social class and crime.

8. Describe the various positions on gun control.

9. Be familiar with Wolfgang's pioneering research on chronic offending.

10. Be able to discuss the influence of the chronic offender on criminology.

KEYWORDS AND DEFINITIONS

Self-report survey: Type of survey in which participants describe their recent and lifetime criminal activity. (page 30)

Victimization survey: Type of survey in which people describe their experience as crime victims. (30)

Sampling: Selecting for study a limited number of subjects who are representative of entire groups sharing similar characteristics. (30)

Population: An entire group sharing similar characteristics. (30)

Cross-sectional survey: A type of survey that is representative of all members of society. (30)

Cohort: A group of people who share like characteristics over time. (30)

Retrospective cohort study: Looking back into the early life experiences of an intact group of people who share like characteristics. (31)

Uniform Crime Report (UCR): Data collected from local law enforcement agencies by the Federal Bureau of Investigation and published yearly. (31)

Meta-analysis: Gathering data from a number of previous studies. (32)

Systematic review: Collecting the findings from previously conducted scientific studies that address a particular problem, appraising and synthesizing the evidence, and using the collective evidence to address a particular scientific question. (32)

Index crimes: The eight most serious crimes that are reported by the Federal Bureau of Investigation in the Uniform Crime Reports; the crimes include murder and nonnegligent manslaughter, forcible rape, robbery, aggravated assault, burglary, larceny, arson, and motor vehicle theft. (33)

Part I crimes: The major unit of analysis of the Uniform Crime Report; the crimes include murder and nonnegligent manslaughter, forcible rape, robbery, aggravated assault, burglary, larceny, arson, and motor vehicle theft. (33)

Part II crimes: All other crimes that are not included in the Part I offenses of the Uniform Crime Reports. (33)

Cleared crimes: Crimes are cleared 1) when at least one person is arrested, charged, and turned over to the court for prosecution; or 2) by exceptional means, when some element beyond police control precludes the arrest of an offender. (33)

National-Incident-Based Reporting System: A new program that is attempting to provide more detailed information on individual criminal incidents by using a uniform, comprehensive program. This program requires local police agencies to provide at least a brief account of each incident and arrest within 22 crime patterns, including the incident, victim, and offender information. (35)

National Crime Victimization Survey: A national survey sponsored by the Bureau of Justice Statistics of the U.S. Department of Justice. Households are asked to report on the frequency, characteristics and consequences of criminal victimization for such crimes as rape, sexual assault, robbery, assault, theft, household burglary, and motor vehicle theft. (36)

Instrumental crimes: Those crimes committed for the purpose of obtaining desired goods and other services that cannot be obtained through conventional means. (48)

Expressive crimes: Crimes that are committed as a means of expressing rage, frustration, and anger against society. (48)

Aging out: The process by which offenders reduce the frequency of their offending behavior as they age. (53)

Masculinity hypothesis: The view that women who commit crimes have biological and psychological traits similar to men. (54)

Chivalry hypothesis: The view that female criminality is hidden because of the culture's generally protective and benevolent attitude toward women. (54)

Liberal feminist theory: The theory that suggests that the traditionally lower crime rate for women could be explained by their "second class" economic and social position. (54)

Career criminal (or chronic offender): The small group of criminal offenders that accounts for a majority of all criminal offenders. (60)

Early onset: The exposure to a variety of personal and social problems at an early age that makes on most at risk to repeat offending. (60)

Persistence (or continuity of crime): The origination of delinquent careers early in life, committing of crime throughout adolescence, and continuing into adulthood. (60)

Three strikes and you're out: The policy that requires people convicted of three violent felony offenses to serve a mandatory life sentence without parole. (61)

CHAPTER OUTLINE

I. How criminologists study crime
    A. Survey research
        1. Used to measure attitudes, beliefs, values, characteristics, and behavior
        2. Also used to analyze the relationship between two or more personal factors
        3. Types of surveys
            a. Self-report surveys
            b. Victimization surveys
            c. Cross-sectional surveys
        4. Surveys are excellent and cost-effective techniques for measuring the characteristics of large numbers of people
            a. Questions and methods are standardized
            b. With good samples can generalize findings from small groups to large populations
            c. Questions can measure subjects at a single point in time, on prior behavior, and on future goals and aspirations
    B. Cohort research: longitudinal and retrospective
        1. Difficult, expensive, and time consuming to follow a cohort over time
        2. Sometimes researchers do retrospective cohort studies

C. Official record research
   1. Uniform Crime Report
      a. Crimes reported to local law enforcement
      b. Number of arrests by police agencies
   2. Can use official data to focus on social forces that affect crime
D. Experimental research
   1. True experiments have three elements
      a. Random selection of subjects
      b. Control or comparison group
      c. An experimental condition
   2. Quasi-experimental design if it is impossible to randomly select subjects or manipulate conditions
   3. Criminological experiments
      a. Relatively rare because they are difficult and expensive to conduct
      b. Ethical and legal roadblocks to manipulating subjects' lives
      c. Require long follow-up to verify results
E. Observational and interview research
   1. Sometimes researchers focus on a relatively few subjects
   2. Sometimes they observe criminals firsthand to gather insight into their motives and activities
   3. Sometimes they bring subjects into a laboratory setting to observe how they react to a predetermined condition or stimulus
F. Meta-analysis and systematic review
   1. Meta-analysis
      a. Gathers data from a number of previous studies
      b. Compatible information and data are extracted and pooled together
      c. When analyzed, more powerful and valid indicator of results than a single study is
   2. Systematic review
      a. Collect findings from previous studies addressing a particular problem
      b. Appraise and synthesize the evidence
      c. Use collective evidence to address a particular scientific question

II. Measuring crime trends and rates
   A. Official data: The Uniform Crime Report
      1. FBI tallies and annually publishes the number of reported offenses in U.S.
      2. Part I crimes – murder and nonnegligent manslaughter, forcible rape, robbery, aggravated assault, burglary, larceny, arson, and motor vehicle theft
      3. Part II crimes
         a. All offenses not included in Part I crimes
         b. Only data on arrests collected for these crimes
      4. Compiling the UCR
         a. Data reported by law enforcement agencies monthly to the FBI
         b. Unfounded or false reports are eliminated from the count
         c. Cleared crimes reported monthly
         d. Also reported
            1) Data on the number of clearances involving the arrest of juvenile offenders
            2) Data on the value of property stolen and recovered in connection with Part I crimes

             3)   Detailed information on homicides
        e.   Methods of expressing crime data
             1)   Raw figures on crimes reported and arrests made
             2)   Rates per 100,000 people computed
             3)   Changes in the number and rate of crime over time
    5.   Validity of the UCR – three main concerns
        a.   Reporting practices
             1)   Not all crimes are reported
             2)   Victim surveys indicate less than 40 percent are reported
        b.   Law enforcement practices
             1)   Changes in how reporting is done
             2)   Law enforcement interpretation of the definitions of index crimes
             3)   Systematic errors
             4)   Some may deliberately alter their reports to improve image
             5)   Boosting efficiency may increase crime rates
             6)   Higher crime may result from improved technology or better-qualified personnel
        c.   Methodological issues
             1)   No federal crimes are reported
             2)   Reports are voluntary and vary in accuracy and completeness
             3)   Not all police departments submit reports
             4)   The FBI uses estimates in its total crime projections
             5)   If an offender commits multiple crimes, only the most serious is recorded
             6)   Each act is listed as a single offense for some crimes but not for others
             7)   Incomplete acts are lumped together with completed ones
             8)   Important differences exist between the FBI's definition of certain crimes and those used in a number of states
    6.   NIBRS: The future of the UCR
        a.   National Incident-Based Reporting System – a program that collects data on each reported crime incident
        b.   Includes a brief account of each incident and arrest
        c.   Information provided on 46 specific offenses
        d.   Hate and bias crime information provided
        e.   Twenty-two states have implemented NIBRS
B.   Victim surveys: The National Crime Victimization Survey
    1.   Designed to address non-reporting issue
    2.   Large nationally representative sample
    3.   People report victimization experiences
    4.   High completion rate
    5.   Considered relatively unbiased, valid estimation of victimizations
    6.   Validity of the NCVS
        a.   Overreporting due to misinterpretation of events
        b.   Underreporting due to embarrassment, fear, or forgetfulness
        c.   Inability to record the personal criminal activity of those interviewed
        d.   Sampling errors
        e.   Inadequate question format that invalidates responses
C.   Self-report surveys
    1.   Helps illuminate the "dark figures of crime"

2. Most self-report studies focus on delinquency and youth crime
   a. School setting makes it convenient
   b. School attendance is universal, so the survey represents a cross-section of the community
   c. Juveniles have the highest reported crime rates
3. Validity of self-reports
   a. Responses accurately reflect their true life experiences
   b. Critics disagree
      1) Can't expect them to candidly admit illegal acts
      2) May exaggerate criminal acts, forget, or be confused
      3) A lot of trivial offenses in self-reports
   c. "Missing cases" phenomenon is a problem
   d. Reporting accuracy differs among racial, ethnic, and gender groups
D. Evaluating crime data sources
   1. Uniform Crime Reports
      a. Strengths
         1) Contains data on number and characteristics of people arrested
         2) Arrest data can provide a measure of criminal activity
         3) Sole source of data on homicide
         4) Standard upon which most criminological research is based
      b. Weaknesses
         1) Omits those crimes not reported to the police
         2) Subject to the reporting caprices of the police
   2. National Crime Victimization Survey
      a. Strengths
         1) Includes unreported crimes
         2) Includes important information on the personal characteristics of victims
      b. Weaknesses
         1) Limited sample
         2) Relies on personal recollections
         3) Does not include data on important crime patterns
   3. Self-report surveys
      a. Advantage – can provide information on personal characteristics of offenders
      b. Weakness – rely on the honesty of participants
   4. All three
      a. Not all in sync
      b. Crime patterns and trends are similar
      c. Problems in each source consistent overtime

III. Crime trends
   A. Explaining crime trends
      1. Trends
         a. 1880 – WWI: number of reported crimes decreased
         b. WWI – 1930: Crime rates declined until 1930
         c. 1930 – 1960: crime rates increased gradually
         d. 1960s – 1981: crime rate growth had a greater rate of increase
         e. 1981 – 1984: began a consistent decline
         f. 1984 – 1991: crime rate increased
         g. 1991 – 2003: crime rate declined

2. Reasons for crime trend
   a. Age
      1) Graying of America
      2) Declining birthrate
   b. Economy – strong economy helps lower crime rates
   c. Social malaise
      1) Increase in social problems related to rising crime rates
      2) Racial conflict may increase crime rates
   d. Abortion
      1) Availability of abortion related to reduced crime rates
      2) Selective abortion by women most at risk to have children
      3) Better maternal, familial, or fetal care due to having fewer children
   e. Guns
      1) Availability of guns
      2) More teens with guns
   f. Gangs
      1) Gang members more likely to possess guns
      2) Crime associated with gangs
      3) "Younger brother syndrome" – younger brothers avoid gangs after seeing what happened to older brothers
   g. Drug use
      1) Relationship between violent crime rate and crack epidemic
      2) Decrease in crack and a decrease in violence
   h. Media
      1) Violent theme media
      2) Violence on TV correlated to aggressive behaviors
   i. Medical technology
      1) Quality of healthcare significantly reduces murder rates
      2) Fluctuations in murder rates linked to availability of emergency medical services
   j. Justice policy
      1) Increase in the number of police on the streets
      2) Aggressive police tactics
      3) Tough laws and lengthy prison terms
   k. Crime opportunities
      1) Market conditions and the low price of pilferable items
      2) Improved home and commercial security devices
B. Trends in violent crime
   1. Decrease in the number and rate of murders
   2. Eleven percent decline in the total number of violent crimes
C. Trends in property crime
   1. Drop in the property crime rate
   2. Not as dramatic as for violent crime rate
D. Trends in victimization data (NCVS findings) – confirms UCR's view is accurate
E. Self-report findings – self-reports indicate crime rates are more stable than UCR says

IV. What the future holds
   A. Fox predicts a significant increase in teen violence
   B. Steffensmeier and Harer predict a moderate increase in crime
   C. Technology has created a new class of crimes in e-commerce

V. Crime patterns
- A. The ecology of crime
  - 1. Day, season, and climate
    - a. Most crimes occur during the warm summer months of July and August
    - b. Murders and robberies occur frequently during December and January
    - c. Crime rates are higher on the first day of the month
  - 2. Temperature
    - a. Association between temperature and crime resembles an inverted U-curve
    - b. Crime rates rise with rising temperatures
    - c. Crime rates decline around 85 degrees
  - 3. Regional differences
    - a. Large urban areas have the highest violence rates
    - b. Exceptions to this trend are large transient or seasonal populations
    - c. "Southern subculture of violence"
- B. Use of firearms
  - 1. Play a dominant role in criminal activity
  - 2. Zimring and Hawkins argue that the proliferation of handguns and the high rate of lethal violence they cause separate the U.S. crime problem from the rest of the world
  - 3. Kleck and Gertz maintain may be a more effective deterrent to crime
- C. Social class and crime
  - 1. Crime rates highest in the inner city, high-poverty areas
  - 2. Prisoners were members of the lower class, unemployed, or underemployed before incarceration
  - 3. Alternative explanation – function of law enforcement practices
    - a. Police devote more resources to poor areas and apprehension rates are higher there
    - b. Police more likely to arrest and prosecute lower class citizens
  - 4. Class and self-reports
    - a. 1950s – no relationship between social class and youth crime
    - b. Little support for the idea that crime is primarily a lower-class phenomenon
    - c. Many self-report instruments include trivial offenses
    - d. If only serious offenses are considered, a significant association can be observed
  - 5. Class-crime controversy
    - a. If crime is related to social class, then economic and social factors cause crime
    - b. Why the uncertainty – methods to measure social class vary widely
    - c. Possible that the association between class and crime is more complex than a simple linear relationship
  - 6. Does class matter?
    - a. Official crime is more prevalent among the lower class
    - b. Less serious crime is spread more evenly throughout the social structure
    - c. Lower class more likely to suffer psychological abnormalities that may promote crime
- D. Age and crime
  - 1. Age is inversely related to crime
  - 2. Younger people commit crime more often than do their older peers
  - 3. Relationship has been stable since 1935

4. Aging out of crime
    a. Agnew – the peak in criminal activity can be linked to essential features of adolescence in modern, industrial societies
        1) A reduction in supervision
        2) An increase in social and academic demands
        3) Participation in a larger, more diverse, peer-oriented world
        4) An increased desire for adult privileges
        5) A reduced ability to cope in a legitimate manner and increased incentive to solve problems in a criminal manner
    b. Wilson and Hernstein – aging out is a function of the natural history of the human life cycle
E. Gender and crime
    1. All three types of crime data confirm male crime rates are higher than those of females
    2. In self-reports, males report criminal behavior more than females, but not to the degree suggested by official data
    3. Explaining gender differences: traits and temperament
        a. Early criminologists pointed to emotional, physical, and psychological differences to explain crime rate differences
        b. Masculinity hypothesis
        c. Chivalry hypothesis
    4. Explaining gender differences: socialization and development
        a. Girls socialized to avoid being violent and aggressive
        b. Girls supervised more closely
        c. Research shows most girls develop moral values that strongly discourage antisocial behavior
        d. Gender-based differences in human development that help shape behavior choices
            1) Cognitive differences
            2) Socialization differences
            3) Gender schema theory – different expectations for males and females
    5. Explaining gender differences: feminist views
        a. Liberal feminist theory – traditionally lower crime rates for women could be explained by their "second-class" economic and social position
        b. As women's social roles changed and their lifestyles became more like men's, it was believed that their crime rates would converge
        c. Self-report studies seem to indicate that the pattern of female criminality is quite similar to that of male criminality
    6. Is convergence likely?
        a. Female crime rates seem to be increasing at a faster pace than men's
        b. Females joining teen gangs in record numbers
F. Race and crime
    1. Minorities involved in a disproportionate share of criminal activity
    2. Responsible for a disproportionate number of Part II arrests
    3. Possible reasons
        a. Data reflect racial differences in the crime rate
        b. May reflect police bias in the arrest process
    4. Research – no relationship between race and self-reported delinquency
    5. Racism and discrimination
        a. Economic deprivation

28

  b. Legacy of racism and discrimination
  c. Black crime may be a function of the socialization process
 6. Institutional racism
 7. Economic and social disparity
 8. Family dissolution
 9. Convergence possible – if economic and social obstacles can be removed
G. Criminal careers
 1. Most offenders commit a single criminal act and discontinue after arrest
 2. Small group of offenders (career criminals or chronic offenders) account for a majority of all criminal offenses
 3. Wolfgang, Figlio, and Sellin
  a. 6 percent of total sample were arrested 5 or more times
  b. Responsible for 51.9 percent of all offenses
 4. Early onset
 5. Persistence – the continuity of crime
  a. Children who are disruptive at age 5 or 6 most likely to persist in crime
  b. Apprehension and punishment have little effect
  c. Best predictor of future behavior is past behavior
 6. Implications of the chronic offender concept
  a. Chronic offender is the central focus of crime policy
  b. Three strikes and you're out

CHAPTER SUMMARY

Criminologists study crime by using survey research, cohort research, official research, experimental research, observational and interview research, and meta-analysis and systematic reviews. Survey research includes three types: self-report surveys, victimizations surveys, and cross-sectional surveys. Most experimental research in criminology is quasi-experimental, as "true" experiments are difficult and expensive to conduct. There are also ethical and legal roadblocks to manipulating subjects' lives and they require long follow-up to verify results.

Criminologists measure crime trends and rates using the Uniform Crime Report (UCR), the National Crime Victimization Survey (NCVS), and self report surveys. The Federal Bureau of Investigation publishes the UCR which contains the data provided by law enforcement agencies across the country. The data, once compiled, is reported as Part I and Part II crimes. Part I crimes include murder and nonnegligent manslaughter, forcible rape, robbery, aggravated assault, burglary, larceny, arson, and motor vehicle theft. Part II crimes are all other offenses not included in Part I. Crime data in the UCR are expressed as raw figures and arrests made, rates per 100,000 people, and changes in the number and rate of crime over time. The main weaknesses concerning the validity of the UCR are that not all crimes are reported, law enforcement practices distort the reporting, and methodology issues. The FBI is looking to eventually replace the UCR with the National Incident-Based Reporting System (NIBRS) which collects information on 46 specific offenses and includes more comprehensive information than the UCR does.

The National Crime Victimization Survey (NCVS) is designed to overcome the problems of the UCR by including crimes not reported to the police. It includes information from a large nationally representative sample and it reports the victimization experiences of the participants. The NCVS has some weaknesses, especially underreporting and overreporting. Self-report surveys help to illuminate the "dark figure of crime." Most of these studies focus on delinquency and youth crime. The main weaknesses of self-report surveys are 1) a lot of trivial offenses are included in self-reports; 2) participants may exaggerate, be confused, or forget; and 3) they may not candidly admit illegal acts. Although the data from the UCR, the NCVS, and self-report surveys are not completely in sync, the crime patterns and trends are similar. In addition, the problems in each of these data sources are consistent over time.

Crime rates have risen and fallen over the many years our nation has been in existence. Several factors affect crime trends, including the age distribution of the population, the economy, social malaise, abortion, the availability of guns, gangs, drug usage, the media, medical technology, justice policy, and crime opportunities. The violent crime rate has been decreasing as the rate of property crime, although it has not been as dramatic as the violent crime trend. These trends are apparent in the UCR and are confirmed by the NCVS. Self-report surveys, however, indicate that crime rates are more stable than the UCR says. The projections for the future are mixed.

Crime has followed several predictable patterns over the years. Most crimes occur during the warm summer months of July and August. Murders, however, are most frequent in December and January. The association between crime and temperature is like an inverted U-curve with crime rising with temperature, but beginning to decline around 85 degrees. Crime rates are also highest in urban areas and in the southern and western United States. Although crime rates are highest in the inner city, high poverty areas, criminologists have never shown a strong correlation between crime and social class. One main reason may be that the methods used to measure social class vary widely and a second may be that the relationship between the two may be more complex than a simple linear relationship.

Age is inversely related to crime; younger people commit more crime than their older peers do. The aging out process refers to the process by which offenders reduce the frequency of their offending behavior as they age. This may be due to a reduction in supervision or it may be a function of the natural history of the life cycle.

All three types of crime data confirm that male crime rates are higher than those of females. Over the years a variety of reasons have been given for this phenomenon such as the masculinity hypothesis, the chivalry hypothesis, socialization and development, and liberal feminist theory. Self-report studies indicate that the pattern of female criminality is similar to that of male criminality. Recent data also indicates that female crime rates are rising faster than men's, and that females are joining gangs in record numbers.

Minorities involved in a disproportionate share of criminal activity. However, research indicates no relationship between race and self-reported delinquency. Some of the reasons for high minority levels of criminal activity may be racism, discrimination, and institutional racism (economic disparity, social disparity, and family dissolution). If social and economic obstacles are removed, convergence of majority and minority crime rates is possible.

Most offenders commit a single crime and discontinue after arrest. Nevertheless, as

Wolfgang, Figlio, and Sellin found, there is a small group responsible for the majority of all crimes. The offenders in this group are called chronic offenders or career criminals. The chronic offender has been the central focus of crime policy and such programs as three strikes and you're out.

STUDENT EXERCISES

Exercise 1

Take a look at your local newspaper or any other paper that is in your university library or online. Look at ten to fifteen articles dealing with different crimes. Make notes concerning the demographic characteristics of the victims and the offenders. What did you find out? How do your findings compare with the information provided in the textbook? Give reasons for any differences.

Exercise 2

Go online to http://www.ojp.usdoj.gov/bjs/pub/ascii/cv03.txt and scan the article concerning criminal victimization in 2003. Write a summary of your findings.

CRIMINOLOGY WEB LINKS

http://www.fbi.gov/ucr/ucr.htm
This website is designed to provide information on the Uniform Crime Reports. Check out the website to see the wealth of information that is contained there.

http://www.ojp.usdoj.gov/bjs/cvict.htm
This website contains information concerning the National Crime Victimization Survey. Check out the variety of links to see for yourself the amount of information that is available.

http://www.albany.edu/sourcebook/
This website contains statistics from a wide variety of sources (more than 100). It is under the auspices of the Bureau of Justice Statistics. Look at the site for you may find information that you will be able to use in this and other classes.

This publication from the National Institute of Justice is entitled *Research on Women and Girls In the Justice System: Plenary Papers of the 1999 Conference on Criminal Justice Research and Evaluation—Enhancing Policy and Practice Through Research,* Volume 3. It contains three articles on women and the criminal justice system.

TEST BANK

FILL-IN THE BLANKS

1. Criminologists conduct _____ when they want to measure attitudes, beliefs, values, characteristics, and behavior.

2. _____ is the process of selecting for study a limited number of subjects who are representative of entire groups sharing similar characteristics.

3. _____ research involves observing a group of people who share a like characteristic over time.

4. _____ _____ are more likely to be solved than property crimes because police devote more resources to serious acts.

5. The National Crime Victimization Survey confirms that many crimes go _____ to the police.

6. Some experts believe that the presence and quality of _____ can have a significant impact on murder rates.

7. Most reported crimes occur during the months of _____ and _____.

8. The term used to describe the resorting to theft and other illegal activities to obtain desired goods and services the person is unable to obtain legitimately is _____ _____.

9. There is general agreement that _____ is inversely related to criminality.

10. The perspective which holds that much female criminality is hidden because of the culture's generally protective and benevolent attitude toward women is called _____.

TRUE/FALSE QUESTIONS

1. T/F Taking an intact cohort of known offenders and looking back into their early life experiences by checking their educational, family, police, and hospital records is called a longitudinal cohort study.

2. T/F Experimental research is very common in criminology.

3. T/F When some element beyond police control precludes the physical arrest of an offender, the case is considered by the Uniform Crime Report to be cleared by exceptional means.

4. T/F Higher crime rates may occur as departments adopt more sophisticated computer technology and hire better-educated, better-trained employees.

5. T/F National Crime Victimization Survey data are considered a relatively unbiased, valid estimate of all victimizations for the target crimes included in the survey.

6. T/F Most self-report studies have focused on juvenile delinquency and youth crime.

7. T/F There is strong evidence that the reporting accuracy in self-report surveys is similar among racial, ethnic, and gender groups.

8. T/F Crime experts view change in the population age distribution as having the greatest influence on crime trends.

9. T/F As the level of social problems increases, crime rates decrease.

10. T/F The drop in property crime rates in recent years has been more dramatic than the decline in violent crime rates.

11. T/F Large urban areas have by far the highest violence rates.

12. T/F There is a very strong correlation between social class and crime.

13. T/F Aging out is caused by the physical inability to commit crime.

14. T/F The masculinity hypothesis argues that a few "masculine" females were responsible for the handful of crimes women commit.

15. T/F Racial differentials in crime rates may also be tied to economic disparity.

MULTIPLE CHOICE QUESTIONS

1. The Uniform Crime Report is published by the:
    a. Supreme Court
    b. Federal Bureau of Investigation
    c. Bureau of Justice Statistics
    d. Census Bureau

2. Which of the following is **NOT** an element of true experiments?
    a.   a survey
    b.   random selection of subjects
    c.   a control or comparison group
    d.   an experimental condition

3. Surveys that ask crime victims about their encounters with criminals are known as the:
    a.   Uniform Crime Report
    b.   National Crime Victimization Survey
    c.   Youth Survey
    d.   Self-Report Study

4. Criminological experiments are relatively rare because:
    a.   they are prohibited in criminology
    b.   criminologists do not like to conduct them
    c.   there are no funds to conduct them
    d.   there are ethical and legal roadblocks

5. Gathering data from a number of previous studies and pooling the data together is called:
    a.   systematic review
    b.   survey research
    c.   meta-analysis
    d.   multiple study research

6. Which of the following is **NOT** a Part I crime?
    a.   arson
    b.   robbery
    c.   forcible rape
    d.   assault

7. The Uniform Crime Report does **NOT** show statistics for which of the following crimes?
    a.   traffic violations
    b.   murder
    c.   arson
    d.   motor-vehicle theft

8. The Uniform Crime Report expresses data as:
    a.   raw figures only
    b.   crime rates per 100,000
    c.   crime rates per 1,000
    d.   raw figures Part II crimes only

9. Which crime is cleared at the highest rate?
    a.   robbery
    b.   larceny
    c.   murder
    d.   motor vehicle theft

10. Most self-report studies focus on:
   a. serious crime
   b. adult crime
   c. prisoners
   d. juvenile delinquency

11. Which of the following is correct concerning the three major sources of crime data?
   a. the crime tallies are in sync
   b. the crime patterns they report are quite similar
   c. the crime trends they report are different
   d. the personal characteristics of criminals they report are different

12. Murders in this country, overall, have:
   a. declined
   b. risen
   c. stabilized
   d. none of the above

13. In recent years, the property crime rate:
   a. has dropped substantially more than the violent crime rate
   b. has dropped about the same as the violent crime rate
   c. has risen more than the violent crime rate
   d. has dropped, but not as much as the violent crime rate

14. The studies on the ecology of crime tell us that:
   a. most crimes occur in the winter
   b. crime rates are higher on pay day
   c. rural areas have high per capita rates of crime
   d. robberies occur frequently in December and January

15. The assumption that a criminal career begins early in life and that people who are deviant at a very young age are the ones most likely to persist in crime is known as:
   a. aging out
   b. aging in
   c. early onset
   d. late onset

16. The notion that female's criminality is often masked because criminal justice authorities were reluctant to take action against a woman is known as:
   a. biological view
   b. gender difference
   c. masculinity hypothesis
   d. chivalry hypothesis

17. The view that women commit crimes have biological and psychological traits similar to men is known as:
   a. biological view
   b. gender difference
   c. masculinity hypothesis
   d. chivalry hypothesis

18. Evidence of African-Americans receiving longer prison sentences than like Caucasians is an example of:
    a. institutional racism
    b. gender bias
    c. socialization
    d. masculinity hypothesis

19. According to Wolfgang, a delinquent offender who is arrested five or more times before he/she is 18 and who stands a good chance of becoming an adult criminal is known as a:
    a. compliant citizen
    b. chronic offender
    c. seasoned official
    d. none of the above

20. The view that crime begins early in life and continues throughout the life course is known as:
    a. desistance
    b. resistance
    c. continuity of crime
    d. aging out

21. The process in which crime rate declines with the perpetrator's age is known as:
    a. termination
    b. resistance
    c. continuity of crime
    d. aging out

22. Which of the following explains gender differences in crime?
    a. cognitive differences
    b. socialization differences
    c. gender schema theory
    d. all of the above

23. The perspective that America has different expectations for males and females is called:
    a. masculinity hypothesis
    b. gender schema theory
    c. chivalry hypothesis
    d. liberal feminist theory

24. The perspective that the traditionally lower crime rate for women can be explained by their "second class" economic and social position is:
    a. masculinity hypothesis
    b. gender schema theory
    c. chivalry hypothesis
    d. liberal feminist theory

25. Which of the following is **NOT** a characteristic of chronic offenders?
   a. cognitive ability problems
   b. family relations problems
   c. punishment changes their behavior
   d. lower aspirations

ESSAY QUESTIONS

1. Discuss the validity of the Uniform Crime Report.

2. Describe the National Crime Victimization Survey, explaining its purpose, its usefulness in measuring crime, and its positive and negative aspects.

3. Explain the factors that influence crime trends.

4. Explain the relationship between crime and social class.

5. List and discuss the major explanations for gender differences in crime rates.

MATCHING

1. _____ Uniform Crime Report
2. _____ Index Crimes
3. _____ Part I Crimes
4. _____ Cleared Crimes
5. _____ National Incident-Based Reporting System
6. _____ U-Shaped Curve
7. _____ Expressive Crimes
8. _____ Self-Report Survey
9. _____ Aging Out
10. _____ Early Onset

A. What the association between temperature and crime resembles.
B. The best-known and most widely cited source of official criminal statistics.
C. The eight crimes that, because of their seriousness and frequency, the FBI reports the incidence of the annual Uniform Crime Reports.
D. A new program that is attempting to provide more detailed information on individual criminal incidents by using a uniform, comprehensive program.
E. Crimes where at least one person is arrested, charged, and turned over to the court for prosecution.
F. The major analysis of the Uniform Crime Report.
G. A research approach that requires subjects to reveal their own participation in delinquent or criminal acts.
H. A term that refers to the assumption that a criminal career begins early in life and that people who are deviant at a very young age are the ones most likely to persist in crime.
I. The process by which individuals reduce the frequency of their offending behavior as they age.
J. Crimes committed that show rage, frustration, and anger against society.

CHAPTER 2 ANSWER KEY

Fill In The Blank Answers

1. surveys
2. sampling
3. cohort
4. violent crimes
5. unreported
6. healthcare
7. July, August
8. instrumental crimes
9. age
10. chivalry hypothesis

True/False Answers

1.	F	6.	T	11.	T
2.	F	7.	F	12.	F
3.	T	8.	T	13.	F
4.	T	9.	F	14.	T
5.	T	10.	F	15.	T

Multiple Choice Answers

1.	B	11.	B	21.	D
2.	A	12.	A	22.	D
3.	B	13.	D	23.	B
4.	D	14.	D	24.	D
5.	C	15.	C	25.	C
6.	D	16.	D		
7.	A	17.	C		
8.	B	18.	A		
9.	C	19.	B		
10.	D	20.	C		

Essay Questions

1. Pages 33-35
2. Pages 36-37
3. Pages 38-42
4. Pages 48-52
5. Pages 53-56

Matching Answers

1.	B	6.	A
2.	C	7.	J
3.	F	8.	G
4.	E	9.	I
5.	D	10.	H

Chapter 3

Victims and Victimization

LEARNING OBJECTIVES

1. Be familiar with the concept of victimization.

2. Know the nature of victimization.

3. Be able to discuss the problems of crime victims.

4. Be familiar with the costs of victimization.

5. Be able to discuss the relationship between victimization and antisocial behavior.

6. Recognize the age, gender, and racial patterns in victimization data.

7. Be able to discuss the association between lifestyle and victimization.

8. Be familiar with the term victim precipitation.

9. List the routine activities associated with victimization risk.

10. Be able to discuss the various victim assistance programs.

KEYWORDS AND DEFINITIONS

Victimologists: Criminologists who focus on crime victims. (page 70)

Victimization (by the justice system): While crime is still fresh in their minds, victims may find that the police interrogation following the crime is handled callously, with innuendos or insinuations that they are somehow at fault. (70)

Posttraumatic stress disorder: An emotional disturbance following exposure to stresses outside the range of normal human experience. (72)

Obsessive-compulsive disorder: An extreme preoccupation with certain thoughts and compulsive performance of certain behaviors. (72)

Cycle of violence: The idea that victims of crime, especially childhood abuse, are more likely to commit crimes themselves. (73)

Chronic victimization: Households that have experienced victimization in the past are the ones most likely to experience it again in the future; most repeat victimizations occur soon after a previous crime has occurred, suggesting repeat victims share some personal characteristic that makes them a magnet for predators. (76)

Siblicide: Sibling homicide. (76)

Victim precipitation theory: Some people may actually initiate the confrontation that eventually leads to their injury or death. (77)

Active precipitation: Occurs when victims act provocatively, use threats or fighting words, or even attack first. (77)

Passive precipitation: Occurs when the victim exhibits some personal characteristic that unknowingly threatens or encourages the attacker. (77)

Lifestyle theory: Crime is not a random occurrence but rather a function of a victim's lifestyle. (77)

Deviant place theory: Victims do not encourage crime but are victim prone because they reside in socially disorganized high-crime areas where they have the greatest risk of coming into contact with criminal offenders, irrespective of their own behavior or lifestyle. (79)

Routine activities theory: The volume and distribution of predatory crime are related to the interaction of the availability of suitable targets, the absence of capable guardians, and the presence of motivated offenders. (80

Suitable targets: A target for crime that is relatively valuable, easily transportable, and not capably guarded. (80)

Capable guardians: Effective deterrents to crime such as the police or watchful neighbors. (80)

Motivated offenders: The potential offenders in a population. (80)

Victim-witness assistance programs: Government programs that help crime victims and witnesses; may include compensation, court services, and/or crisis intervention. (84)

Victim compensation: Victim receives compensation from the state to pay for damages associated with crime. (84)

Crisis intervention: Emergency counseling for crime victims at counseling offices, victim's home, the crime scene, or a hospital. (85)

Restitution agreements: A condition of the offender's sentence in which he or she repays society or the victim of the crime for the trouble caused. (85)

Target hardening: Making one's home and business crime proof through locks, bars, alarms, or other devices. (87)

CHAPTER OUTLINE

I. Problems of crime victims
    A. Economic Loss
        1. System costs
            a. Cost of maintaining the justice system
            b. Legal costs
            c. Treatment costs
        2. Individual costs
            a. Losses in earnings and occupational attainment
            b. Psychological and physical ills
    B. System abuse: victimization by the justice system
    C. Long-term stress
        1. Among adolescents who experience abuse
        2. Post-traumatic stress disorder of spousal abuse victims
        3. Physical disability as a result of wounds
    D. Fear
        1. Victims fearful long after victimization
        2. Often victims go through a fundamental life change
    E. Antisocial behavior
        1. Crime victims likely to commit crimes themselves
        2. Cycle of violence

II. The nature of victimization
    A. The social ecology of victimization
        1. Violent crimes more likely to take place in an open, public area
        2. Neighborhood characteristics affect victimization
            a. Central cities have higher rates of theft and violence
            b. Rural areas have a victimization almost half that of city dwellers
            c. Risk of murder of both men and women is significantly higher in the disorganized inner city
    B. The victim's household
        1. Within the U.S. larger, African-American, western, and urban homes are the most vulnerable to crime
        2. Rural, white homes in the Northeast are the least likely victims
        3. Decline in household victimization rates may be due to smaller households in less populated areas
    C. Victim characteristics
        1. Gender
            a. Males are most likely to be victims

      b.   Gender differences appear to be narrowing

      c.   Females victimized by someone they know

      d.   Men more likely to be victimized by strangers

   2. Age

      a.   Young people more likely to be victimized

      b.   Elderly much safer than their grandchildren

      c.   Elderly susceptible to fraud schemes

   3. Social status

      a.   Poorest Americans are the most likely to be victims of violent and property crimes

      b.   This association holds true across all gender, age, and racial groups

      c.   Wealthy attract the attention of thieves

   4. Marital status

      a.   Never-married males and females are victimized more often than married people

      b.   Widows and widowers have the lowest victimization risk

      c.   Association between marital status and victimization probably influenced by age, gender, and lifestyle

   5. Race and ethnicity

      a.   Blacks are more likely than whites to be victims of violent crime

      b.   Income inequality influences black victimization

      c.   Rate of black victimization has been in a steep decline

   6. Repeat victimization

      a.   Prior victims are the most likely to experience it again

      b.   Characteristics that increase victimization potential

          1) Target vulnerability

          2) Target gratifiability

          3) Target antagonism

      c.   May occur when the victim does not take defensive action

D. Victims and their criminals

   1. Most crimes are committed by a single offender

   2. Victims report substance abuse in about one-third of violent crime incidents

   3. More than half of all nonfatal personal crimes are committed by persons known to the victim

III. Theories of victimization

  A. Victim precipitation theory

     1. Some people may actually initiate the confrontation that eventually leads to their injury or death

     2. Two types of victim precipitation

        a.   Active – victim provokes or threatens

        b.   Passive

           1) Victim has some personal characteristic that unknowingly threatens or encourages attacker

           2) Belongs to a group that threatens or encourages the attacker's reputation, status, or economic well-being

  B. Lifestyle theory

     1. Lifestyle increases exposure to criminal offenders

     2. High-risk lifestyles

        a.   Drinking, taking drugs, or crime involvement

      b.   Risks continue in adulthood
    3.   Victims and criminals – criminal career may lead to victimization
  C.   Deviant place theory
    1.   Victims live in socially disorganized high-crime areas
    2.   The more often a victim visits a dangerous place, the more likely they will be exposed to crime
    3.   Deviant place – poor, densely populated, highly transient neighborhoods where commercial and residential property exist side by side
  D.   Routine activities theory
    1.   Volume and distribution of predatory crime are closely related to the interaction of three variables that reflect the routine activities of American lifestyle
      a.   Availability of suitable targets
      b.   Presence of motivated offenders
      c.   Absence of capable guardians
    2.   Hot spots – congregation of motivated offenders in a particular neighborhood
    3.   Moral guardianship – peer rejection and disapproval
    4.   Lifestyle, opportunity, and routine activities are related
    5.   Empirical support

IV. Caring for the victim
  A.   The government's response
    1.   Task Force on Victims of Crime – 1982
      a.   Suggested a balance between victim's rights and the defendant's due process rights
      b.   Protecting witnesses and victims from intimidation
      c.   Requiring restitution in criminal cases
      d.   Development of guidelines for fair treatment of victims and witnesses
      e.   Expanding programs of victim compensation
    2.   Omnibus Victim and Witness Protection Act
      a.   Use of victim impact statements at sentencing in federal criminal cases
      b.   Greater protection for witnesses
      c.   More stringent bail laws
      d.   Use of restitution in criminal cases
    3.   Comprehensive Crime Control Act and the Victims of Crime Act
      a.   Federal funding for state victim compensation and assistance projects
      b.   Victim aid and assistance began with these acts
  B.   Victim service programs
    1.   Victim compensation
      a.   Victim receives compensation from the state to pay for damages from crime
      b.   No two state schemes are alike
      c.   Victim of Crime Act – grants money to state compensation boards from fines and penalties imposed on federal offenders
    2.   Court services
      a.   Help victims deal with the justice system
      b.   Many programs provide transportation to and from court and counselors
    3.   Public education – help familiarize the general public with victim services
    4.   Crisis intervention
    5.   Victim-offender reconciliation programs
      a.   Mediators facilitate face-to-face encounters between the victim and the offender

      b.   May lead to restitution agreements and possibly reconciliation
    6.   Victim impact statements – statements made before the sentencing judge
C.   Victims' rights – every state now has some form of legal rights for crime victims in its code of laws
D.   Victim advocacy
E.   Self-protection
    1.   Target hardening
    2.   Crime prevention techniques
    3.   Use of guns for self-defense
F.   Community organization

CHAPTER SUMMARY

The problems of being a victim of crime are wide and varied. There are economic losses such as the cost of the justice system, treatment costs, and the economic losses to the individual, including earnings loss, psychological pain, and physical pain and injury. Second, the crime victim often finds processing through the criminal justice system is an abusive occurrence, especially when the victim feels as if it were his or her own fault for being victimized. Among other problems are the long-term stress, long-term fear, and antisocial behavior resulting from victimization.

Victimization is not evenly distributed throughout the country. Violent crimes usually occur in open, public areas. Central cities have higher rates of theft and violence, and the disorganized inner city has the highest risk for murder of both men and women. Within the United States, larger, African-American, western, and urban homes are the most vulnerable to crime. The current decline in household victimization may be due to an increase in smaller households in less populated areas. Males are most likely to be crime victims, but gender differences appear to be narrowing. While females are victimized by someone they know, males are more likely to be the victims of strangers. Young people are more likely to be the victims of crime, as are the poor. In fact, the association between social status and crime holds true across all gender, age, and social groups. The never-married are most likely to be victimized more than married persons. Blacks are more likely than whites to be victims; however, the rate of black victimization has been in steep decline. Prior victims are the most likely to experience it again. The characteristics which increase the potential of becoming a victim are target vulnerability, target gratifiability, and target antagonism.

There are several major theories of victimization. Victim precipitation theory postulates that some people may actually initiate the confrontation that eventually leads to their injury or death. Victim precipitation may be active (they provoke or threaten) or passive (they possess a characteristic or belong to a group). Lifestyle theory argues that one's lifestyle may increase exposure to victimization by engaging in high-risk behaviors such as drinking, taking drugs, or being involved in crime. Deviant place theory proposes that victims live in socially disorganized high-crime areas or visit dangerous places. Routine activities theory argues that the volume and distribution of predatory crime are closely related to the interaction of three major variables: 1) the availability of suitable targets, 2) the presence of motivated offenders, and 3) the absence of capable guardians.

There has been a significant improvement in caring for victims over the past two decades. The Omnibus Victim and Witness Protection Act permitted the use of victim impact statements in federal criminal cases and authorized the use of restitution. The Comprehensive Crime Control Act and the Victims of Crime Act began federal funding for state victim compensation and assistance projects. No two states have victim compensation programs that are alike, but under the Victims of Crime Act all states receive federal grants to their state compensation boards from fines and penalties imposed on federal offenders. Many efforts are being taken in court services, public education, and crisis intervention. Victim-offender reconciliation programs have also worked to achieve restitution and possible reconciliation. Every state now has some form of legal rights for crime victims in its code of laws. Individuals have also begun to engage in self-protection through the use of target hardening, crime prevention techniques, and guns for self-defense.

STUDENT EXERCISES

Exercise 1

Go online to http://www.google.com and do a search using the terms "victim advocacy center." Make sure you put the three words between quotation marks. Look at several of the links in the results that deal with victim advocacy centers. Make a note of the characteristics of those advocacy centers. Summarize the results of what you found, especially noting what those victim advocacy centers have in common.

Exercise 2

Go online to http://www.ncjrs.org/pdffiles1/nij/205004.pdf and read the article, *When Violence Hits Home: How Economics and Neighborhood Play a Role* by Michael L. Benson and Greer Litton Fox. Summarize the article focusing on the relationship of socioeconomic status and neighborhood to domestic violence. How does this article's results compare to the victimization theories contained in the textbook?

CRIMINOLOGY WEB LINKS

http://www.ojp.usdoj.gov/ovc/
This is the official website of the Office for Victims of Crime sponsored by the United States Department of Justice.

http://www.cvb.state.ny.us/index.htm

This is the official website of the New York State Crime Victims Board. The material in this website concerns information on all aspects of victim support in the state of New York.

http://www.tdcj.state.tx.us/victim/victim-home.htm

This is the official website of the Victims Services Division of the Texas Department of Criminal Justice.

http://content.healthaffairs.org/cgi/reprint/12/4/186.pdf

This website contains an article entitled *Victim Costs of Violent Crime and Resulting Injuries* by Ted R. Miller, Mark A. Cohen, and Shelli B. Rossman. It addresses the total monetary costs of a wide variety of crimes.

http://www.ncjrs.org/pdffiles1/ojjdp/195737.pdf

This article entitled *Violent Victimization as a Risk Factor for Violent Offending Among Juveniles* by Jennifer N. Shaffer and R. Barry Ruback addresses the issue of the correlation between victimization and offending among juveniles.

TEST BANK

FILL-IN THE BLANKS

1.   An emotional disturbance following exposure to stresses outside the range of normal human experience is called _____ _____.

2.   The abuse-crime phenomenon is referred to as the _____

_____ _____.

3.   _____ _____ refers to some characteristics that increase risk of victimization because they arouse anger, jealousy, or destructive impulses in potential offenders.

4.   _____ _____ _____ proposes that some people may actually initiate the confrontation that eventually leads to injury or death.

5.   _____ _____ _____ states that people are victim prone because they reside in socially disorganized high-crime areas.

6.   If motivated offenders congregate in a particular neighborhood, it becomes a _____ _____ for crime and violence.

7. Peer rejection and disapproval may be a form of _____ _____ that can deter even motivated offenders from engaging in law-violating behavior.

8. Under victim compensation programs, the victim ordinarily receives compensation from the _____ to pay for damages associated with crime.

9. More than half of victim programs provide _____ _____ to victims, many of whom feel isolated, vulnerable, and in need of immediate services.

10. Making one's home and business crime proof through locks, bars, alarms, and other devices is known as _____ _____.

TRUE/FALSE QUESTIONS

1. T/F The suffering endured by crime victims ends when their attacker leaves the scene.

2. T/F the elderly, the poor, and minority group members especially fear crime.

3. T/F Victimization survey findings suggest that victimization is not random but is a function of personal and ecological factors.

4. T/F The more serious crimes, such as rape and aggravated assault, typically take place after 6:00 P.M.

5. T/F Victimization is most likely to take place in the Northeast.

6. T/F Females are more likely than males to be victimized.

7. T/F Grandparents are much safer from victimization than their grandchildren.

8. T/F Households that have experienced victimization in the past are the ones least likely to experience it in the future.

9. T/F Married people are victimized more often than single people.

10. T/F African-Americans are more likely than Whites to be victims of violent crime.

11. T/F Passive precipitation occurs when victims act provocatively, use threats or fighting words, or even attack first.

12. T/F The basis of lifestyle theory is that crime is not a random occurrence, but rather a function of the victim's lifestyle.

13. T/F One element of lifestyle that may place people at risk for victimization is ongoing involvement in a criminal career.

14. T/F Victim-offender reconciliation programs use the courts to facilitate face-to-face encounters between victims and their attackers.

15 T/F Only a few jurisdictions allow victims to make an impact statement before a sentencing judge.

MULTIPLE CHOICE QUESTIONS

1. The NCVS show that violent crimes are more likely to occur in:
    a. dark alleys
    b. secluded areas
    c. open public areas
    d. private homes

2. Neighborhood characteristics that increase the chances of victimization are:
    a. suburban area
    b. rural area
    c. high class area
    d. central city area

3. Which characteristic does **NOT** distinguish victims from non-victims?
    a. gender
    b. religion
    c. age
    d. race

4. Who is most often victimized by someone they know?
    a. whites
    b. males
    c. African-Americans
    d. females

5. To which crime are the elderly most susceptible?
    a. fraud
    b. rape
    c. assault
    d. robbery

6. A victims' physical weakness or psychological distress renders them incapable of resisting or deterring crime and makes them an easy target is:
    a. target gratifiability
    b. target vulnerability
    c. target antagonism
    d. target victims

7.   Some victims have some quality, possession, skill, or attribute that an offender wants to obtain, use, have access to, or manipulate. This is known as:
    a.   target gratifiability
    b.   target vulnerability
    c.   target antagonism
    d.   target victims

8.   What is the term for victims acting provocatively, using threats or fighting words, or even attacking first?
    a.   lifestyle
    b.   deviant place
    c.   passive precipitation
    d.   active precipitation

9.   People may become crime victims because their behaviors such as associating with young men, going out in public places late at night, or living in an urban area. This is known as:
    a.   routine activities theory
    b.   victim precipitation theory
    c.   lifestyle theory
    d.   deviant place theory

10. Victims do not encourage crime, but are victim prone because they reside in socially disorganized high-crime areas where they have the greatest risk of coming into contact with criminal offenders is known as:
    a.   victim precipitation theory
    b.   active precipitation
    c.   deviant place theory
    d.   passive precipitation

11. The volume and distribution of predatory crime is closely related to the interaction of three variables is known as:
    a.   victim precipitation theory
    b.   active precipitation theory
    c.   routine activities theory
    d.   passive precipitation theory

12. Which of the following is **NOT** a suitable target in routine activities theory?
    a.   engaging in risky behavior
    b.   guarded person
    c.   person carrying valuables
    d.   easily salable

13. Cohen and Felson argue that crime rates increased between the 1960s and 1980s because the number of adult caretakers at home during the day had decreased due to an increase in:
    a.   females in the workplace
    b.   the employment rate
    c.   automobile ownership
    d.   the number of juveniles

14. The dramatic increase in crime rates in the 1980s was due to skyrocketing drug use that created an excess of:
   a.   suitable targets
   b.   motivated offenders
   c.   weak victims
   d.   capable guardians

15. Victim compensation may be made for which of the following:
   a.   medical bills
   b.   loss of wages
   c.   loss of future earnings
   d.   all of the above

16. What is the name of the law passed in 1984 that granted money to state compensation boards derived from fines and penalties imposed on federal offenders?
   a.   Victim-Offender Act
   b.   Omnibus Crime Act
   c.   Victim of Crime Act
   d.   none of the above

17. Programs that familiarize the general public with their services to and with other agencies that assist crime victims are known as:
   a.   public education
   b.   victim-offender reconciliation programs
   c.   community service
   d.   crisis intervention

18. A local network of public and private social service agencies that can provide emergency and long-term assistance with transportation, medical care, shelter, food and clothing is known as:
   a.   victim support
   b.   crisis intervention
   c.   court services
   d.   victim education

19. When victims fight back, it may cause which of the following?
   a.   others may help
   b.   the assailant may flee
   c.   the assailant may attack in a more violent manner
   d.   all of the above

20. These programs use mediators to facilitate face-to-face encounters between victims and their attackers.
   a.   victim-offender reconciliation program
   b.   crisis intervention
   c.   community service
   d.   public education

21. Victim service programs may provide which of the following:
    a. compensation
    b. court services
    c. public education
    d. all of the above

22. The abuse-crime phenomenon is known as:
    a. deviant place hypothesis
    b. siblicide
    c. cycle of violence
    d. parricide

23. Victim advocates can be especially helpful when victims need to interact with the:
    a. courts
    b. agencies of justice
    c. police
    d. prison system

24. Using locks, bars, alarms, and other devices to make one's home or business crime proof is called:
    a. self-protection
    b. target hardening
    c. crime stopping
    d. physical security

25. Many local communities have formed:
    a. block watches
    b. neighborhood patrols
    c. both block watches and neighborhood patrols
    d. none of the above

ESSAY QUESTIONS

1. List and describe the major problems faced by crime victims.

2. Describe the characteristics of crime victims.

3. Explain victim precipitation theory.

4. Describe how American society is taking care of America's crime victims today.

5. Describe the actions citizens are taking to prevent themselves from becoming victims.

MATCHING

1. _____ Passive Precipitation
2. _____ Capable Guardians
3. _____ Chronic Victims
4. _____ Crisis Intervention
5. _____ Cycle of Violence
6. _____ Deviant Place Hypothesis
7. _____ Lifestyle Theory
8. _____ Target Vulnerability
9. _____ Motivated Offenders
10. _____ Siblicide

A. Based on the idea that crime is not a random occurrence but rather a function of one's lifestyle.
B. Victims do not encourage crime, but are victim prone because they reside in socially disorganized high-crime areas where they have the greatest risk of coming into contact with criminal offenders.
C. Victim's physical weakness or psychological distress that renders them incapable of resisting crime and makes them a target.
D. Abuse-crime phenomenon.
E. A variable of routine activities theory. An example would be a large number of teenagers.
F. A local network of public and private social service agencies that can provide emergency and long-term assistance with transportation, medical care, shelter, food and clothing.
G. Murdering one's brother or sister.
H. Individuals who are repeatedly crime victims.
I. Victim exhibits some personal characteristic that unknowingly threatens or encourages the attacker.
J. Effective deterrents to crime such as the police or watchful neighbors

CHAPTER 3 ANSWER KEY

Fill In The Blank Answers

1. posttraumatic stress syndrome
2. cycle of violence
3. target antagonism
4. victim precipitation theory
5. deviant place theory
6. hot spot
7. moral guardianship
8. state
9. crisis intervention
10. target hardening

True/False Answers

1.	F	6.	F	11.	F
2.	T	7.	T	12.	T
3.	T	8.	F	13.	T
4.	T	9.	F	14.	F
5.	F	10.	T	15.	F

Multiple Choice Answers

1.	C	11.	C	21	.D
2.	D	12.	B	22.	C
3.	B	13.	A	23.	B
4.	D	14.	B	24.	B
5.	A	15.	D	25.	C
6.	B	16.	C		
7.	A	17.	A		
8.	D	18.	B		
9.	C	19.	D		
10.	C	20.	A		

Essay Questions

1. Pages 70 – 73
2. Pages 74 – 76
3. Page 77
4. Pages 83 – 87
5. Pages 87 – 88

Matching Answers

1.	I	6.	B
2.	J	7.	A
3.	H	8.	C
4.	F	9.	E
5.	D	10.	G

Chapter 4

Choice Theory

LEARNING OBJECTIVES

1.   Be familiar with the concept of rational choice.

2.   Know the work of Beccaria.

3.   Be familiar with the concept of offense-specific crime.

4.   Be familiar with the concept of offender-specific crime.

5.   Be able to discuss why violent and drug crimes are rational.

6.   Know the various techniques of situational crime prevention.

7.   Be able to discuss the association between punishment and crime.

8.   Be familiar with the concepts of certainty, severity, and speed of punishment.

9.   Know what is meant by specific deterrence

10. Be able to discuss the issues involving the use of incapacitation.

11. Understand the concept of just desert.

KEYWORDS AND DEFINITIONS

Rational choice: the view that crime is a function of a decision-making process in which the potential offender weighs the potential costs and benefits of an illegal action. (page 98)

Marginal deterrence: the idea that if petty offenses were subject to the same punishment as more serious crimes, offenders would choose the worse crime because the resulting punishment would be the same. (98)

Reasoning criminal: the individual who, before choosing to commit a crime, evaluates the risk of apprehension, the seriousness of the expected punishment, the potential value of the criminal enterprise, and his or her immediate need for criminal gain. (100)

Offense-specific crime: offenders react selectively to the characteristics of particular offenses. (100)

Offender-specific crime: before deciding to commit crime, individuals determine whether they have the prerequisites to commit a successful criminal act, including the proper skills, motives, needs, and fears. (100)

Criminality: a personal trait of the individual as distinct from crime, which is an event. (101)

Boosters: professional shoplifters who use complex methods to avoid detection. (104)

Permeable neighborhood: neighborhood with a greater than usual number of access streets from traffic arteries into the neighborhood. (104)

Edgework: the exhilarating, momentary integration of danger, risk, and skill that motivates people to try a variety of dangerous criminal and noncriminal behaviors. (106)

Situational crime prevention: the perspective that crime prevention can be achieved by reducing opportunities people have to commit particular crimes. (107)

Defensible space: the term that signifies that crime can be prevented or displaced through the use of residential architectural designs that reduce criminal opportunity. (107)

Crime discouragers: those who manage crime, namely guardians (who monitor targets), handlers (who monitor offenders), and managers (who monitor places). (109)

Diffusion: the process whereby efforts to prevent one crime unintentionally prevent another and when control efforts in one locale reduce crime in other nontarget areas. (110)

Discouragement: the process whereby crime efforts targeting a particular locale help reduce crime in surrounding areas and populations. (111)

Crime displacement: the phenomenon in which a program that seems successful because it helps lower crime rates at specific locations or neighborhoods may simply be redistributing offenders to alternative targets; crime is not prevented but deflected or displaced. (112)

Extinction: the phenomena in which crime reduction programs may produce a short-term positive effect, but benefits dissipate as criminals adjust to new conditions. (112)

General deterrence: the concept that crime rates are influenced and controlled by the threat of criminal punishment. (112)

Deterrence theory: the view that if the probability of arrest, conviction, and sanctioning could be increased, crime rates should decline. (112)

Crackdowns: sudden changes in police activity designed to increase the communicated threat or actual certainty of punishment. (113)

Informal sanctions: occur when significant others direct their disapproval, stigma, anger, and indignation toward an offender. (115)

Specific deterrence: the perspective that criminal sanctions should be so powerful that known criminals will never repeat their criminal acts. (116)

Incapacitation effect: placing offenders behind bars during their prime crime years should lessen their lifetime opportunity to commit crime. (120)

Selective incapacitation: if a small number of people account for a relatively large percentage of the nation's crime, then an effort to incarcerate these few troublemakers might have significant payoff. (121)

Just desert: punishment is needed to preserve the social equity disturbed by crime. (122)

CHAPTER OUTLINE

I. The development of rational choice theory
    A. Roots are in the classical school of criminology
        1. Purpose of law – to produce and support the total happiness of the community it serves
        2. Punishment is harmful, so it is justified only to prevent greater evil than it creates
        3. Four objectives of punishment
            a. To prevent all criminal offenses
            b. When it cannot prevent crime, to convince the offender to commit a less serious crime
            c. To ensure that a criminal uses no more force than is necessary
            d. To prevent crime as cheaply as possible
    B. Choice theory emerges
        1. Resurgence of classical approach in the 1970s
        2. James Q. Wilson's *Thinking About Crime*
            a. Must deter would-be offenders
            b. Must incarcerate known criminals
        3. Impact on crime control
            a. Mandatory prison sentences for drug offenders
            b. Get tough attitude
            c. Rise in prison population

II. The concepts of rational choice
    A. Offense- and offender-specific crimes
        1. Offense-specific crime – offenders react selectively to the characteristics of particular offenses
        2. Offender-specific crime – offenders make a decision based on whether they have the prerequisites to commit a successful criminal act

3. Crime – an event
4. Criminality – a personal trait
B. Structuring criminality - personal factors condition people to choose crime
   1. Economic opportunity
   2. Learning and experience
      a. Learn limitations of power
      b. Know when to take chances or be cautious
   3. Knowledge of criminal techniques – to avoid detection
C. Structuring crime
   1. Choosing the type of crime
      a. Some are specialists
      b. Others are generalists
      c. Sometimes the choice of crime is based on the immediacy of the need for funds
   2. Choosing the time and place of crime
      a. Burglars like 9-11 AM and mid-afternoon
      b. Thieves avoid freestanding buildings
      c. Criminals rarely travel long distances
      d. Aware of police capabilities
   3. Choosing the target of crime
      a. Shy away from those who are armed
      b. Avoid targets if police are in the area

III. Is Crime Rational?
   A. Is theft rational?
      1. Seemingly unplanned theft-related crimes may be the product of careful risk assessment
      2. Boosters use complex methods to avoid detection
      3. Burglars use skill and knowledge when choosing targets
      4. Burglars prefer permeable neighborhoods
   B. Is drug use rational?
      1. Onset of drug use is controlled by rational decision-making
      2. Heavy drug users and dealers show signs of rationality and cunning
   C. Is violence rational?
      1. Street robbers choose vulnerable victims
      2. Robbers pick time and day to commit crimes carefully
      3. Those who carry guns and are ready to use them typically do so for rational reasons
      4. Serial murderers pick targets with care
   D. Rational rapists?
      1. Rationality in choice of victims
      2. Want to get a victim with little effort
   E. Attraction of crime
      1. Brings rewards, excitement, prestige, etc.
      2. Edgework
      3. Crime is a means to pleasure and solution to vexing personal problems

IV. Eliminating crime
   A. Situational crime prevention
      1. Originated in 1970s

2. Began with the concept of defensible space
3. Application of defensible space to nonresidential areas such as schools and factories
4. Clarke's *Situational Crime Prevention*
   a. Create an environment to reduce overall crime rate
   b. Limit access to tempting targets
5. Targeting specific crimes – situational crime prevention can also be used to reduce or eliminate a specific crime
   a. Increase effort needed to commit crime
      1) Target hardening
      2) Develop new security products
      3) Reduce opportunities for crime
   b. Reduce rewards for committing crime – target reduction strategies
   c. Increase risks of committing crime
      1) Efforts of crime discouragers
      2) Research show crime discouragers can have an impact on crime rates
      3) Use of mechanical devices
   d. Induce guilt or shame for committing crime
6. Situational crime prevention: costs and benefits
   a. Benefits
      1) Diffusion
      2) Discouragement
   b. Problems
      1) Crime displacement
      2) Extinction
B. General deterrence
   1. Inverse relationship between crime rates and the severity, certainty, and speed of legal sanctions
   2. Certainty of punishment
      a. As certainty of punishment rises, offenders will desist from crime because risks outweigh rewards
      b. Certainty is seen as the *tipping point* when the likelihood of getting caught reaches a critical level
      c. Crime persists because we have not reached the tipping point
      d. Most criminal believe
         1) There is only a small chance of arrest for crime
         2) Police are often reluctant to arrest even when they are aware of a crime
         3) Even if arrested, there is a good chance of lenient punishment
      e. Research shows experienced criminals are the ones most likely to fear the deterrent power of the law
   3. Does increasing police activity deter crime?
      a. Past – little evidence that adding officers could produce a deterrent effect
      b. Current research shows increased police levels produce substantial reductions in crime over time
      c. Crackdowns
   4. Severity of punishment and deterrence
      a. Severity of punishment is inversely proportional to the level of crime rates
      b. Little consensus that the severity of criminal sanctions alone can reduce criminal activities
      c. Not proven that just increasing punishment can reduce crime

5. Capital punishment – remains topic of debate
6. Informal sanctions
   a. Informal sanctions may have a greater crime-reducing impact than the fear of formal legal punishment
   b. Social control is influenced by the way the people perceive negative reactions from interpersonal acquaintances
7. Shame and humiliation
   a. Those who fear being rejected by family and peers are reluctant to engage in deviant behavior
   b. Anticrime campaigns have been designed to play on this fear of shame
   c. Women are more likely to fear shame and embarrassment than men
   d. Effect of informal sanctions may vary according to the cohesiveness of community
8. Critique of general deterrence
   a. Rationality – questioned
   b. Need – underclass not deterred by fear of punishment
   c. Greed – some may be immune to the deterrent effects
   d. Severity and speed – legal system is not very effective
C. Specific deterrence
   1. General deterrence focuses on future or potential criminals
   2. Specific deterrence focuses on offenders not repeating criminal acts
   3. Does not seem to work because most criminals are not deterred by punishment
   4. Punishment may bring defiance rather than deterrence
D. Incapacitation
   1. Placing offenders in prison during their prime crime years should lessen lifetime opportunity to commit crime
   2. Many criminologists believe incapacitation does not produce drops in crime rates
   3. Can incapacitation reduce crime? – research is inconclusive
   4. The logic behind incarceration
      a. Those in prison cannot commit crime
      b. Impact may be less than expected
      c. Prison experience may escalate frequency of crime on release
      d. Most crimes are committed by young teens and young adult offenders who do not go to prison for a single felony conviction
   5. Incapacitation is expensive
   6. Produces an ever expanding population
   7. Selective incapacitation
      a. Incarceration of chronic offenders
      b. Some criminologists disagree because
         1) Most three time losers are aging out
         2) Current sentences are already severe
         3) Pushes prison costs up
         4) Racial disparity in sentencing
         5) Violent offenders will resist the third arrest so police will be in danger
      c. Prison already has the high-frequency criminals
      d. More low-rate criminals will be confined

V. Public policy implications of choice theory
   A. Research on choice theory produced mixed results

62

B. Just desert
 1. Punishment needed to preserve the social equity disturbed by crime
  a. Those who violate others' rights deserve to be punished
  b. Punishment prevents more misery than it inflicts
 2. Supports the rights of the accused
 3. People deserve what they get for past deeds

CHAPTER SUMMARY

The roots of rational choice theory are contained in the classical school of criminology. According to classical theory, the purpose of the law is to produce and support the total happiness of the community it serves. Punishment is designed to prevent crime, and if punishment cannot prevent it, then it is to convince the offender to commit a less serious crime.

According to rational choice theory, crime is an event and criminality is a personal trait. Several personal factors condition people to choose crime. Among them are economic opportunity, learning and experience, and knowledge of criminal techniques. Rational choice theorists propose that offenders choose the type of crime to commit, choose the time and place of the crime, and choose the target of crime.

When criminologists study criminal behavior, they find that there is a great deal of rational decision-making in criminal behavior. Boosters use complex methods to avoid detection of their shoplifting and burglars prefer permeable neighborhoods. Heavy drug users and dealers show signs of rationality and cunning. Street robbers choose vulnerable targets, while serial murderers pick targets with care. Serial rapists look for targets that will require them to expend little effort.

Situational crime prevention originated with the concept of defensible space in an effort to raise the risks associated with crime and to reduce the rewards offenders achieve. Situational crime prevention brought programs such as target hardening and the development of new security products, both of which were designed to reduce opportunities for crime. The benefits of situational crime prevention are diffusion and discouragement, while the problems are displacement and extinction.

General deterrence argues that there is an inverse relationship between crime rates and the severity, certainty, and speed of legal sanctions. It focuses on future criminals. Specific deterrence proposes that punishment will deter offenders from repeating criminal acts. Incapacitation focuses on placing offenders in prison during their prime crime years in order to reduce their lifetime opportunity to commit crime. Research on general deterrence, specific deterrence, and incapacitation is mixed.

STUDENT EXERCISES

Exercise 1

Go online to http://www.ncjrs.org/pdffiles/cptedpkg.pdf and read the article, *Crime Prevention through Environmental Design in Parking Facilities* by Mary S. Smith. Summarize the major findings of the study concerning how to prevent crimes in parking lots.

Exercise 2

Go online and conduct a search for the words "crime displacement." Take a look at the links you retrieved and summarize your findings concerning crime displacement.

CRIMINOLOGY WEB LINKS

http://www.popcenter.org/default.htm
This is the official website of the Center for Problem-Oriented Policing of the United States Department of Justice.

http://www.crimereduction.gov.uk/
This is the official website of government of the United Kingdom. The material in this website concerns crime reduction techniques advocated by the UK government.

http://www.communitypolicing.org/publications/comlinks/cl16/cl16_kroek.htm
This is an article written for *Community Links*, a publication of the Community Policing Consortium, by the Chief of Police of Portland, Oregon on crime prevention through environmental design.

http://www.ncjrs.org/pdffiles/crimepre.pdf
This is a publication of the National Institute of Justice called *Crime Prevention Through Environmental Design and Community Policing* by Dan Fleissner and Fred Heinzelmann.

http://www.aei.org/news/newsID.18871,filter./news_detail.asp
This is an interesting article by John DiIulio, a conservative criminologist, on why deterrence is not working in the United States. DiIulio's article summarizes much of the philosophy of those criminologists who subscribe to choice theories.

TEST BANK

FILL-IN THE BLANKS

1. Rational choice theory has its roots in the _____ school of criminology.

2. Beccaria believed that crime and punishment must be _____; if not, people would be encouraged to commit more serious offenses.

3. Beccaria stated that criminals _____ to commit crime and that crime can be controlled by judicious punishment.

4. The _____ _____ evaluates the risk of apprehension, the seriousness of the expected punishment, the potential value of the criminal enterprise, and his or her immediate need for criminal gain.

5. _____ is and event; _____ is a personal trait.

6. Professional shoplifters who use complex methods to avoid detection are called _____.

7. _____ _____ refers to the use of residential architectural designs that reduce criminal opportunity.

8. Crime control efforts targeting a particular locale helping to reduce crime in the surrounding areas and populations is referred to as _____.

9. The idea that the certainty of punishment will only have a deterrent effect if the likelihood of getting caught reaches a critical level is known as _____ _____.

10. Imprisoning the small number of people who account for a relatively large percentage of the nation's crime in order to produce a significant payoff is called _____ _____.

TRUE/FALSE QUESTIONS

1. T/F Specific deterrence refers to the concept that if petty offenses were subject to the same punishment as more serious crimes, offenders would choose the worse crime.

2. T/F Jeremy Bentham helped popularize Beccaria's views in his writings on utilitarianism.

3. T/F The reasoning criminal evaluates the risk of apprehension.

4. T/F An offender-specific crime means that offenders will react selectively to the characteristics of particular offenses.

5. T/F Perceptions of economic opportunity influence the decision to commit crime.

6. T/F There is little evidence of rationality in the choosing of the type of crime to commit.

7. T/F Serial rapists show rationality in the choosing of the type of crime to commit.

8. T/F For many people, crime is attractive.

9. T/F Controlling truancy can be an element of a strategy under situational crime prevention.

10. T/F Research indicates that crime discouragers do not have much of an impact on crime.

11. T/F Research shows that experienced criminals are the ones most likely to fear the deterrent power of the law.

12. T/F The fear of informal sanctions may have a greater crime-reducing impact than the fear of formal legal punishment.

13. T/F Women fear shame and embarrassment more than men.

14. T/F Habitual offender laws that provide long or life sentences for repeat offenders reduce crime substantially.

15 T/F Desert theory is not at all concerned with the rights of the accused.

MULTIPLE CHOICE QUESTIONS

1. A prohibition against cruel and unusual punishment was incorporated into which Amendment to the U.S. Constitution?
    a. Fourth
    b. Fifth
    c. Sixth
    d. Eighth

2. The concept that if petty offenses were subject to the same punishment as more serious crimes, offenders would choose the worse crime because the punishments would be about the same is called:
    a. general deterrence
    b. specific deterrence
    c. marginal deterrence
    d. deterrence theory

3. Beccaria's writings have been credited as the basis of the elimination of:
   a. probation
   b. torture
   c. capital punishment
   d. due process

4. Which theory states that law-violating behavior occurs when an offender decides to break the law after considering both personal factors and situational factors?
   a. rational choice theory
   b. situational crime prevention
   c. classical theory
   d. deterrence theory

5. Which personal factor is one considered by someone in the decision to commit crime?
   a. economic opportunity
   b. learning and experience
   c. knowledge of criminal techniques
   d. all of the above

6. Which of the following is **NOT** a characteristic of what criminals do?
   a. travel long distances
   b. go on foot
   c. use public transportation
   d. drift toward the center of a city

7. Street robbers choose victims who have all of the following characteristics **EXCEPT**:
   a. vulnerable
   b. short
   c. low coercive power
   d. do not pose any threat

8. Robbers prefer to rob businesses that deal primarily in:
   a. credit cards
   b. checks
   c. cash
   d. convenience items

9. The rationality of a rapist is demonstrated in their desire to:
   a. find a weak victim
   b. rape an acquaintance
   c. find a victim of their own race
   d. avoid detection

10. Reducing the opportunities people have to commit crimes is known as:
    a. deterrence theory
    b. situational crime prevention
    c. defensible space
    d. environmental design

11. What are designed to reduce the value of crime to the potential criminal?
    a. target reduction strategies
    b. environmental design strategies
    c. crime discouragers
    d. diffusion strategies

12. Those who monitor targets are called:
    a. discouragers
    b. guardians
    c. handlers
    d. managers

13. Those who monitor places are called:
    a. discouragers
    b. guardians
    c. handlers
    d. managers

14. The reduction in stolen cars by using the Lojack system resulted in a decline in the sale of stolen auto parts. This is known as:
    a. crime displacement
    b. diffusion
    c. discouragement
    d. extinction

15. The effect produced by video cameras reducing shoplifting and also reducing property vandalism is known as:
    a. crime displacement
    b. diffusion
    c. discouragement
    d. extinction

16. The phenomenon in which crime reduction programs may produce a short-term positive effect, but benefits dissipate as criminals adjust to new conditions is known as:
    a. crime displacement
    b. diffusion
    c. discouragement
    d. extinction

17. The concept that crime rates are influenced and controlled by the threat of punishment is known as:
    a. general deterrence
    b. specific deterrence
    c. deterrence theory
    d. crime prevention

18. The concept that if the probability of arrest, conviction, and sanctioning could be increased, crime rates would decline is called:
    a. general deterrence
    b. specific deterrence
    c. deterrence theory
    d. crime prevention

19. The concept of tipping point is associated with:
    a. severity of punishment
    b. certainty of punishment
    c. swiftness of punishment
    d. none of the above

20. The concept that the shorter the span of opportunity, the fewer offenses they can commit during their lives is called:
    a. general deterrence
    b. incapacitation effect
    c. selective incapacitation
    d. just desert

21. What is the concept that an effort to incapacitate the few troublemakers who commit crime might have a significant payoff in crime reduction?
    a. general deterrence
    b. incapacitation effect
    c. selective incapacitation
    d. just desert

22. The utilitarian view that punishment is needed to preserve the social equity disturbed by crime is called:
    a. general deterrence
    b. incapacitation effect
    c. selective incapacitation
    d. just desert

23. Beccaria believed that to deter people from committing more serious offenses, crime and punishment must be:
    a. proportional
    b. severe
    c. certain
    d. swift

24. The idea that the rights of the person being punished should not be unduly sacrificed for the good of others is known as:
    a. deterrence theory
    b. just desert
    c. crisis intervention
    d. public education

25. Conveying a sense of normalcy and ordinariness in one's demeanor and physical appearance in order to avoid attention is:
   a. boosters
   b. selling hours
   c. projected self-image
   d. routine activities

ESSAY QUESTIONS

1. Explain the concept of rational choice.

2. Explain the differences between offense-specific crime and offender-specific crime.

3. Describe the various techniques of situational crime prevention.

4. Explain the difference between general deterrence and specific deterrence.

5. Discuss the issues involving the use of incapacitation.

MATCHING

1. _____ Crackdowns
2. _____ Crime
3. _____ Jeremy Bentham
4. _____ Offender-Specific Crime
5. _____ Offense-Specific Crime
6. _____ Permeable Neighborhood
7. _____ Diffusion
8. _____ Discouragement
9. _____ Specific Deterrence
10. _____ Incapacitation Effect

A. Offenders react selectively to the characteristics of particular offenses.
B. Efforts to prevent one crime unintentionally prevent another.
C. Criminal sanctions should be so powerful that known criminals will never repeat their criminal acts.
D. Sudden changes in police activity designed to increase the communicated threat or actual certainty of punishment.
E. The shorter the opportunity, the fewer offenses an offender can commit during his or her life, so crime is reduced.
F. Utilitarianism.
G. Criminals are not automatons who engage in random acts of antisocial behavior.
H. Crime efforts in one locale help reduce crime in surrounding areas and populations.
I. Event.
J. Greater than normal number of access streets from traffic arteries into the neighborhood.

CHAPTER 4 ANSWER KEY

Fill In The Blank Answers

1. classical
2. proportional
3. choose
4. reasoning criminal
5. crime; criminality
6. boosters
7. defensible space
8. discouragement
9. tipping point
10. selective incapacitation

True/False Answers

1.	F	6.	F	11.	T
2.	T	7.	T	12.	T
3.	T	8.	T	13.	T
4.	F	9.	T	14.	F
5.	T	10.	F	15.	F

Multiple Choice Answers

1.	D	11.	A	21.	C
2.	C	12.	B	22.	D
3.	A	13.	D	23.	A
4.	D	14.	C	24.	B
5.	B	15.	B	25.	C
6.	A	16.	D		
7.	B	17.	A		
8.	C	18.	C		
9.	D	19.	B		
10.	B	20.	B		

Essay Questions

1. Page   100
2. Pages 100 – 101
3. Pages 107 – 112
4. Pages 112 – 119
5. Pages 120 – 122

Matching Answers

1.	D	6.	J
2.	I	7.	B
3.	F	8.	H
4.	G	9.	C
5.	A	10.	E

Chapter 5

Trait Theories

LEARNING OBJECTIVES

1. Be familiar with the concept of sociobiology.

2. Know what is meant by the term equipotentiality.

3. Be able to discuss the relationship between diet and crime.

4. Be familiar with the association between hormones and crime.

5. Be able to discuss why violent offenders may suffer from neurological problems.

6. Know the factors that make up the ADHD syndrome.

7. Be able to discuss the role genetics plays in violent behavior.

8. Be familiar with the concepts of evolutionary theory.

9. Be able to discuss the psychodynamics of criminality.

10. Understand the association between media and crime.

11. Discuss the role of personality and intelligence in antisocial behaviors.

KEYWORDS AND DEFINITIONS

Inheritance school: traced the activities of several generations of families believed to have an especially large number of criminal members. (page 134)

Somatotype: criminals manifest distinct physiques that make them susceptible to particular types of delinquent behavior. (134)

Biophobia: the view that no serious consideration should be given to biological factors when attempting to understand human nature. (135)

Reciprocal altruism: even when they come to the aid of others, people are motivated by the belief that their actions will be reciprocated and that their gene survival capability will be enhanced. (135)

Trait theory: if biological (genetic) makeup controls human behavior, it follows that it should also be responsible for determining whether a person chooses law-violating or conventional behavior. (135)

Equipotentiality: not all humans are born with equal potential to learn and achieve. (135)

Wernicke-Korsakoff disease: a deadly neurological disorder to which alcoholics are susceptible because they often suffer from thiamine deficiency due to their poor diets. (137)

Hypoglycemia: occurs when glucose in the blood falls below levels necessary for normal and efficient brain functioning. (140)

Androgens: male sex hormones that produce aggressive behavior. (140)

Testosterone: the most abundant androgen, which controls secondary sex characteristics, such as facial hair and voice timbre. (140)

Neocortex: the part of the brain that controls sympathetic feelings toward others. (140)

Premenstrual syndrome (PMS): the onset of the menstrual cycle triggers excessive amounts of the female sex hormones, which affect antisocial, aggressive behavior. (141)

Cerebral allergies: allergies cause an excessive reaction in the brain. (141)

Neuroallergies: allergies that affect the nervous system. (141)

Neurophysiology: the study of brain activity. (142)

Electroencephalograph (EEG): records the electrical impulses given off by the brain. (142)

Attention deficit hyperactivity disorder (ADHD): a condition in which a child shows a developmentally inappropriate lack of attention, impulsivity, and hyperactivity. (143)

Conduct disorder (CD): behaviors such as fighting that are early signs that the child is among the most at risk for persistent antisocial behaviors continuing into adulthood. (143)

Chemical restraints or chemical straitjackets: antipsychotic drugs such as Haldol, Stelazine, Prolixin, and Risperdal, which help control levels of neurotransmitters (such as serotonin/dopamine). (144)

Arousal theory: for a variety of genetic and environmental reasons, some people's brains function differently in response to environmental stimuli. (145)

Contagion effect: it is possible that what appears to be a genetic effect picked up by the twin research is actually the effect of sibling influence on criminality. (147)

Defective intelligence: Charles Goring uncovered a significant relationship between crime and traits as feeblemindedness, epilepsy, insanity, and defective social instinct, which he called defective intelligence. (151)

Psychoanalytic or psychodynamic perspective: focus is on early childhood experience and its effect on personality. (151)

Behaviorism: stresses social learning and behavior modeling as the keys to criminality. (151)

Cognitive theory: analyzes human perception and how it affects behavior. (151)

Id: the primitive part of an individual's mental makeup present at birth; it represents unconscious biological drives for sex, food, and other life-sustaining necessities. (151)

Pleasure principle: the id requires instant gratification without concern for the rights of others. (151)

Ego: that part of the personality that compensates for the demands of the id by helping the individual guide his or her actions to remain within the boundaries of social convention. (151)

Reality principle: ego takes into account what is practical and conventional by societal standards. (151)

Superego: develops as a result of incorporating within the personality the moral standards and values of parents, community, and significant others. It is the moral aspect of an individual's personality; it passes judgments on behavior. (151)

Conscience: tells what is right and wrong. (151)

Ego ideal: directs the individual into morally acceptable and responsible behaviors, which may not be pleasurable. (151)

Eros: the instinct to preserve and create life. (151)

Thanatos: the death instinct, which is expressed as aggression. (151)

Oral stage: named by Freud, it is the first year of life in which a child attains pleasure by sucking and biting. (152)

Anal stage: the second and third years of life in which the focus of sexual attention is on the elimination of bodily wastes. (152)

Phallic stage: occurs during the third year when children focus their attention on their genitals. (152)

Oedipus complex: a stage of development when males begin to have sexual feelings for their mothers. (152)

Electra complex: a stage of development when females begin to have sexual feelings for their fathers. (152)

Latency: begins at age 6; during this period, feelings of sexuality are repressed until the genital stage begins at puberty. (152)

Fixated: an adult who exhibits behavior traits characteristic of those encountered during infantile sexual development. (152)

Inferiority complex: coined by Alfred Adler, it describes people who have feelings of inferiority and compensate for them with a drive for superiority. (152)

Identity crisis: a period of serious personal questioning people undertake in an effort to determine their own values and sense of direction. (152)

Latent delinquency: a predisposition that psychologically prepares youths for antisocial acts. (152)

Bipolar disorder: a condition in which a person's moods alternate between periods of wild elation and deep depression. (152)

Psychosis: includes severe mental disorders, such as depression, bipolar disorder (manic depression), and schizophrenia. (153)

Disorders: the condition in which a person exhibits illogical and incoherent thought processes and a lack of insight into their behavior. (153)

Schizophrenia: the conditions in which a person may hear nonexistent voices, hallucinate, and make inappropriate behavioral responses. (153)

Paranoid schizophrenic: suffers complex behavior delusions involving wrongdoing or persecution; they think everyone is out to get them. (153)

Social learning: the branch of behavior theory that proposes that people are not actually born with the ability to act violently but that they learn to be aggressive through their life experiences. (154)

Behavior modeling: process of learning behavior (notably aggression) by observing others; the models may be parents, criminals in the neighborhood, or characters on television or in the movies. (154)

Moral development: concerned with the way people morally represent and reason about the world. (155)

Humanistic psychology: stresses self-awareness and "getting in touch with feelings." (155)

Information processing: focuses on the way people process, store, encode, retrieve, and manipulate information to make decisions and solve problems. (155)

Personality: the reasonably stable patterns of behavior, including thoughts and emotions that distinguish one person from another. (159)

Minnesota Multiphasic Personality Inventory (MMPI): the test that has subscales designed to measure many different personality traits, including psychopathic deviation (Pd scale), schizophrenia (Sc), and hypomania (Ma). (161)

California Personality Inventory (CPI): has been used to distinguish deviants from nondeviant groups. (161)

Multidimensional Personality Questionnaire (MPQ): allows researchers to assess such personality traits as control, aggression, alienation, and well-being. (161)

Nature theory: argues that intelligence is largely determined genetically, that ancestry determines IQ, and that low intelligence, as demonstrated by low IQ, is linked to criminal behavior. (161)

Nurture theory: states that intelligence must be viewed as partly biological but primarily sociological. (161)

Wechsler Adult Intelligence Scale: one of the standard IQ tests. (164)

Primary prevention programs: programs that seek to treat personal problems before they manifest themselves as crime. (165)

Secondary prevention programs: provide treatment such as psychological counseling to youths and adults after they have violated the law. (165)

CHAPTER OUTLINE

I. Foundations of trait theory
    A. General
        1. Lombroso and biological theory
        2. Inheritance school
        3. Body types
            a. Mesomorphs
            b. Endomorphs
            c. Ectomporphs
    B. Impact of sociobiology
        1. Biophobia
        2. Sociobiology stresses that biological and genetic conditioning affect how social behaviors are learned and perceived
        3. Gene is the ultimate unit of life that controls all human destiny

4. Since biology controls human behavior, it is responsible for a person's choice to violate the law

C. Modern trait theories
   1. Trait theories are not overly concerned with the legal definitions of crime
   2. Trait theorists focus on human behavior and drives
   3. Traits do not produce criminality
   4. Crime involves both personal traits and environmental factors
   5. Equipotentiality
   6. Chronic offenders suffer some biological/psychological condition or trait that renders them incapable of resisting social pressures and problems
   7. Two major subdivisions of trait theories
      a. One that stresses psychological functioning
      b. One that stresses biological functioning

II. Biosocial trait theories
   A. Biochemical conditions and crime
      1. Chemical and mineral influences
         a. Minimal levels of minerals and chemicals are needed for normal brain functioning
         b. Oversupply or undersupply of certain chemicals and minerals can lead to depression, mania, cognitive, and other problems
         c. What people eat and take into their bodies may influence their behavior
         d. Vitamin deficiency or dependency can manifest many physical, mental, and behavioral problems
      2. Diet and crime
         a. Excessive amounts of harmful substances such as food dyes and artificial colors/flavors seem to provoke hostile, impulsive, and antisocial behaviors
         b. Recent research supports the link
      3. Sugar and crime
         a. High sugar content in diets is linked to violence and aggression
         b. Other research does not support the link
      4. Glucose metabolism/hypoglycemia
         a. Abnormality in the brain's metabolizing glucose has been linked to antisocial behaviors
         b. Hypoglycemia is linked to outbursts of antisocial behavior and violence
      5. Hormonal influences
         a. Wilson argues that hormones, enzymes, and neurotransmitters may be the key to understanding human behavior
         b. Androgens
         c. Testosterone
      6. How hormones may influence behavior
         a. Hormones cause areas of the brain to become less sensitive to environmental stimuli
         b. Hormones influence the neocortex
         c. Physical effects of excessive hormones promotes violence
      7. Premenstrual syndrome (PMS)
         a. Menstrual cycle triggers excessive amounts of female hormones which affect antisocial, aggressive behavior
         b. Fishbein concludes that there is an association between female aggression and menstruation

8. Allergies
   a. Cerebral allergies cause excessive reaction in the brain
   b. Neuroallergies affect the nervous system
   c. Cerebral allergies and neuroallergies have been linked to hyperactivity in children
9. Environmental contaminants are found in the environment
10. Lead levels
   a. Research studies suggest that lead ingestion is linked to aggressive behaviors at both a macro- and micro-level
   b. Areas of the U.S. with high lead levels had the highest levels of homicide
   c. High lead ingestion is related to lower IQ

B. Neurophysiological conditions and crime
   1. General
      a. Some researchers believe that neurological and physical abnormalities are acquired as early as in the fetal or prenatal stage or through birth delivery trauma
      b. Research indicates that this relationship can be detected quite early
   2. Neurological impairments and crime
      a. Neurological tests have been found to distinguish criminal offenders from noncriminal control groups
      b. Chronic violent offenders have far higher levels of brain dysfunction than the general population
   3. Minimal brain dysfunction
      a. Linked to serious antisocial acts
      b. Criminals have been characterized as having dysfunction of the dominant hemisphere of the brain
   4. Attention deficit hyperactivity disorder (ADHD)
      a. Most common reason children are referred to mental health clinics
      b. ADHD linked to the onset and sustenance of a delinquent career
      c. Many ADHD suffer from conduct disorder and engage in aggressive and antisocial behavior in early childhood
      d. Relationship between chronic delinquency and attention disorders may be mediated by school performance
      e. Early school-based intervention programs may be of special benefit to ADHD children
   5. Tumors, lesions, injury, and disease
      a. Brain tumors and lesions have been linked to a wide variety of psychological problems
      b. People with tumors are prone to depression, irritability, temper outbursts, and even homicide attacks
   6. Brain chemistry
      a. Abnormal levels of neurotransmitters are associated with aggression
      b. Individuals with low monamine oxidase (MAO) engage in behaviors linked with violence and property crime
      c. Violence prone people are commonly treated with antipsychotic drugs

C. Arousal theory
   1. Obtaining thrills is a crime motivator
   2. Crime can satisfy the personal needs for thrills and excitement

D. Genetics and crime
   1. Parental deviance

      a.   If criminal tendencies are inherited, then children of criminal parents should be more likely to be criminal than children of non-criminal parents

      b.   Schoolyard aggression or bullying may be both inter- and intragenerational

      c.   Quality of family life may be a key in determining children's behavior

      d.   Parental conflict and authoritarian parenting were related to early childhood conduct problems in two successive generations

2.   Sibling similarities

      a.   Research shows if one sibling engages in antisocial behavior, so do the siblings

      b.   Effect is greatest among same sex siblings

      c.   Effect can be explained by genetics, but also by other factors such as environment

3.   Twin behavior

      a.   Monozygotic (MZ) twins share the same genetic makeup

      b.   Dizygotic (DZ) twins share only 50% of their genetic combinations

      c.   Research shows a greater probability of shared criminal behavior in MZ twins than in DZ twins

      d.   Research shows similarities between twins is due to genes, not environment

4.   Evaluating genetic research

      a.   Not all criminologists support the idea that crime is genetically predetermined

      b.   Opponents point to inadequate research designs and weak methodologies

      c.   Also point to contagion effect

5.   Adoption studies

      a.   Avoids the pitfalls of twin studies

      b.   Relationship exists between biological parents' behavior and the behavior of children even when contact has been nonexistent

      c.   Gene-crime relationship controversial

          1)   Implies propensity to crime cannot be altered

          2)   Raises moral dilemmas

E.   Evolutionary theory

1.   Violence and evolution – violent offenses driven by evolutionary and reproductive factors

2.   Gender and evolution

      a.   Aggressive males have had the highest impact on the gene pool

      b.   Descendants of aggressive males now account for the disproportionate amount of male aggression and violence

3.   Theories of evolutionary criminology

      a.   Rushton's theory of race and evolution

          1)   Evolutionary changes are responsible for present-day crime rate differences between the races

          2)   Harshly received and condemned

      b.   R/K selection theory

          1)   R-people are cunning and deceptive

          2)   K-people are cooperative and sensitive

      c.   Cheater theory

          1)   Subpopulation of men with genes that incline them toward low parental involvement

          2)   Prey on young, less intelligent women who have children at very early ages

           3)   Producing an ever expanding supply of cheaters who are antisocial and sexually aggressive

    F.   Evaluation of the biosocial branch of trait theory
        1.   Critics find the theories racist and dysfunctional
        2.   Cannot explain geographic social and temporal patterns in crime rates
        3.   Biggest complaint is the lack of empirical testing
        4.   Biosocial theorists argue that they maintain only that some people carry the potential for violence and antisocial behavior
        5.   They argue that the environment triggers antisocial responses
        6.   Biosocial theorists have the view that behavior is the product of biology and environment

III. Psychological trait theories
    A.   Psychodynamic perspective – developed by Freud
        1.   Elements of psychodynamic theory
            a.   Id – pleasure principle
            b.   Ego – reality principle
            c.   Superego – conscience and ego ideal
        2.   Psychosexual stages of human development
            a.   Oral stage
            b.   Anal stage
            c.   Phallic stage
                1)   Oedipus complex
                2)   Electra complex
        3.   The psychodynamics of antisocial behavior
            a.   Inferiority complex
            b.   Identity crisis
            c.   Latent delinquency
            d.   Psychodynamic model depicts an aggressive, frustrated, person dominated by early childhood events
            e.   Crime is a manifestation of oppression and the inability to develop proper psychological defenses
        4.   Mood disorders and crime
            a.   Disruptive behavior disorder
                1)   Oppositional defiant disorder
                2)   Conduct disorder
            b.   Causes – biosocial and psychological factors
        5.   Crime and mental illness
            a.   Psychosis – includes several mental disorders
            b.   Depression often found in serious, violent offenders
            c.   Diagnosed mentally ill appear in court at a rate disproportionate to their presence in the population
        6.   Is the link valid?
            a.   Questions exist about whether there is a mental illness link to crime and violence
            b.   Link between crime and mental illness may be spurious
    B.   Behavioral theories
        1.   Human actions are developed through learning experiences
        2.   People alter their behavior according to reactions they receive from others

3. Behavior
    a. Supported by rewards
    b. Extinguished by negative reactions or punishments
C. Social learning theory
    1. Bandura – people learn to be aggressive through their life experiences
    2. Experiences include
        a. Observing others act aggressively to achieve some goal
        b. Watching people rewarded for violent acts
    3. Social learning and violence
        a. Violence learned through behavior modeling
        b. Modeled after three sources
            1) Family interaction
            2) Environmental experiences
            3) Mass media
        c. Four factors contribute to violent/aggressive behavior
            1) Event that heightens arousal
            2) Aggressive skills
            3) Expected incomes
            4) Consistency of behavior with values
D. Cognitive theory
    1. Moral and intellectual development theory
        a. Most important for criminological theory
        b. Piaget – people's reasoning develops in an orderly process
        c. Kohlberg – applied moral development to issues in criminology
        d. Decision not to commit crimes may be influenced by one's stage of moral development
    2. Information processing
        a. People who use information properly are best able to avoid antisocial behavior
        b. Crime-prone people may have cognitive deficits
    3. Shaping perceptions
        a. Hostile children may have learned improper scripts by observing how others react to events
        b. May have had early and prolonged exposure to violence
E. Personality and crime
    1. Personality reflects a characteristic way of adapting to life's demands and problems
    2. Criminal personality traits
        a. Impulsivity
        b. Hostility
        c. Aggressiveness
    3. Antisocial personality/psychopathy/sociopathy
        a. Disturbed personality that makes them incapable of developing enduring relationships
        b. Came from dysfunctional homes
        c. Uncertain of causes
    4. Research on personality
        a. Wide variety of personality tests
        b. Crime control efforts might be better focused on helping families raise children

F. Intelligence and crime
    1. Nature theory
        a. Intelligence determined genetically
        b. Low intelligence linked to crime
    2. Nurture theory
        a. IQ is partly biological, but primarily sociological
        b. Low IQs result from an environment that also encourages delinquent and criminal behavior
    3. Rediscovering IQ and criminality
        a. Hirschi and Hindelang – IQ is more important than race and socioeconomic class in predicting crime and delinquency
        b. Their research has been supported by other research
    4. Cross-national studies – supported by research in other countries
    5. IQ and crime reconsidered
        a. Recent studies find IQ has negligible effect on crime
        b. Herrnstein and Murray conclude there is a link

IV. Public policy implications of trait theory
    A. Primary prevention programs to treat personal problems before they manifest themselves as crime
    B. Secondary prevention programs provide support after crime has occurred

CHAPTER SUMMARY

The foundations of trait theory are found in Cesare Lombroso and biological theory. Many criminologists reacted harshly to the crime-biology link, and this reaction was called biophobia. Sociobiology developed later, stressing that biological and genetic conditioning affect how social behaviors are learned and perceived. They argued that the gene is the ultimate unit of life that controls human destiny. Under this argument, since biology controls human behavior, it is responsible for a person's choice to violate the law.

Modern trait theories are not overly concerned with the legal definitions of crime. Trait theorists focus on human behavior and drives and argue that traits do not produce criminality. Rather, crime involves both personal traits and environmental factors. Chronic offenders suffer some biological/psychological condition or trait that renders them incapable of resisting social pressures and problems.

There are two major subdivisions of trait theories, one that stresses biological functioning and one that stresses psychological functioning. Biosocial trait theories look at the relationship between a wide variety of variables and crime. Among those variables are biochemical conditions, neuropsychological conditions, arousal, genetics, and evolution. Biochemical conditions include chemicals, diet, hormones, allergies, and environmental contaminants. Neurophysical conditions include impairments, minimal brain dysfunction, ADHD, tumors, and brain chemistry. Arousal deals with the thrills some offenders obtain from crime, so the motivation for crime becomes the obtaining of thrills. Research on the relationship between genetics and crime has focused on the criminal behavior of offenders and their parents, the criminal behavior of twins (both identical and fraternal), and adoption studies. Evolutionary theory addresses the idea that violent offenses are driven by evolutionary and reproductive factors.

Psychological trait theories include a wide range of theories. Among them are the psychodynamic perspective developed by Sigmund Freud, behavioral theories, social learning theory, cognitive theory, personality and crime, and intelligence and crime.

Trait theories have two major implications for public policy on crime prevention. First, primary prevention programs are those crime prevention programs that focus on the treatment of personal problems before they manifest themselves as crime. The next policy involves secondary prevention programs that provide treatment and support after crime has occurred.

STUDENT EXERCISES

Exercise 1

Go online to http://www.google.com and search the internet using the words "diet" and "crime". Check out the various links that you receive and make a short summary of your search results. How does the search results compare with the material presented in the textbook?

Exercise 2

Go online to http://www.vathek.com/ijpsm/pdf/jpsm.4.4.344.pdf and read the article, *The Relationship of Attention Deficit Hyperactivity Disorder to Crime and Delinquency: a Meta-Analysis* by Travis C. Pratt, Francis T. Cullen, Kristie R. Blevins, Leah Daigle and James D. Unnever. Summarize the major findings of the study concerning the relationship between ADHD and crime.

CRIMINOLOGY WEB LINKS

http://www.ncjrs.org/pdffiles1/ojjdp/fs200120.pdf
This is a fact sheet from the Office of Juvenile Justice and Delinquency Prevention concerning ADHD and the delinquency. It relates to a study from the National Institute of Health.

http://www.psychology.iastate.edu/faculty/caa/abstracts/1995-1999/95ADD.pdf
This is an article entitled *Hot Temperatures, Hostile Affect, Hostile Cognition, and Arousal: Tests of a General Model of Affective Aggression* by Craig A. Anderson, William E. Deuser, and Kristina M. Deneve.

http://www.psychology.iastate.edu/faculty/caa/abstracts/2000-2004/03CA.pdf
This is an article entitled *Theory in the Study of Media Violence: The General Aggression Model* by Nicholas L. Carnagey and Craig A. Anderson.

http://cms.psychologytoday.com/articles/pto-20030514-000001.html
This an article from *Psychology Today* on crime and nutrition.

http://www.schizophrenia.com/poverty.htm
This is the official website of schizophrenia.com and contains information pertaining to the relationship between schizophrenia and crime.

TEST BANK

FILL-IN THE BLANKS

1. The _____ school held that criminals manifest distinct physiques that make them susceptible to particular types of delinquent behavior.

2. The concept that not all humans are born with equal potential to learn and achieve is called _____.

3. Diets high in sugar and carbohydrates have been linked to _____ and _____.

4. Many people with attention deficit hyperactivity disorder (ADHD) also suffer from _____ _____ and continually engage in aggressive and antisocial behavior in early childhood.

5. _____ _____ have identical genetic make up and are significantly close in personal characteristics, such as intelligence.

6. _____ _____ suggests that a subpopulation of men has evolved with genes that incline them toward extremely low parental involvement.

7. _____ _____ analyzes human perception and how it affects behavior.

8. In _____ _____, moods alternate between periods of wild elation and deep depression.

9. Social learning theorists view violence as something learned through a process known as _____ _____.

10. _____ can be defined as the reasonably stable patterns of behavior, including thoughts and emotions, that distinguish one person from another.

TRUE/FALSE QUESTIONS

1.   T/F The inheritance school traced the activities of several generations of families believed to have an especially large number of criminal members.

2.   T/F Some trait theorists believe biochemical conditions, including both those that are genetically predetermined and those acquired through diet and the environment, control and influence antisocial behavior.

3.   T/F Some recent research efforts have failed to find a link between sugar consumption and violence.

4.   T/F An association between hormonal activity and antisocial behavior is suggested because rates of both factors peak in adulthood.

5.   T/F Neuroallergies cause excessive reaction in the brain, whereas cerebral allergies affect the nervous system.

6.   T/F Neurophysiology is the study of brain activity.

7.   T/F According to Jack Katz, there are immediate gratifications from criminality.

8.   T/F Although there is a significant correspondence of twin behavior in many activities, crime is not one of them.

9.   T/F Sibling influence on criminality is referred to as the contagion effect.

10. T/F According to evolutionary theory, crime rate differences between the genders may be a matter of socialization.

11. T/F The biosocial view is that behavior is a product of interacting biological and environmental events.

12. T/F Behaviorism focuses on early childhood experience and its effect on personality.

13. T/F The ego follows the pleasure principle.

14. T/F The superego is divided into two parts: conscience and ego ideal.

15 T/F Humanistic psychology stresses self-awareness and "getting in touch with feelings."

MULTIPLE CHOICE QUESTIONS

1. According to the somatotype school, the person with well-developed muscles and an athletic appearance is a(n):
    a. mesomorph
    b. ectomorph
    c. endomorph
    d. mesclomorph

2. According to the somatotype school, the person with a heavy build and who is slow moving is a(n):
    a. mesomorph
    b. ectomorph
    c. endomorph
    d. mesclomorph

3. The concept that not all humans are born with equal potential to learn and achieve is known as:
    a. trait theory
    b. equpotentiality
    c. reciprocal altruism
    d. sociobiology

4. Unusual or excessive reaction of the body to foreign substances are:
    a. allergies
    b. environmental contaminants
    c. normal
    d. contaminants

5. Allergies which cause an excessive reaction to the brain are:
    a. neuroallergies
    b. environmental contaminants
    c. cerebral allergies
    d. neurological impairments

6. Dangerous amounts of copper, cadmium, mercury and inorganic gases found in the ecosystem are known as:
    a. environmental contaminants
    b. neuroallergies
    c. cerebral allergies
    d. hyperactivity

7. The study of brain activity is called:
   a. arousal theory
   b. neurophysiology
   c. minimal brain dysfunction
   d. genetics

8. An abruptly appearing maladaptive behavior that interrupts an individual's lifestyle and life flow is called:
   a. minimal brain dysfunction (MBD)
   b. attention deficit hyperactive disorder (ADHD)
   c. conduct disorder (CD)
   d. hypoglycemia

9. Which theory holds that all organisms can be located along a continuum based upon their reproductive drives?
   a. R/K selection theory
   b. arousal theory
   c. cheater theory
   d. evolutionary theory

10. Which theory suggests that a subpopulation of men has evolved with genes that incline them toward extremely low parental involvement?
    a. R/K selection theory
    b. arousal theory
    c. cheater theory
    d. evolutionary theory

11. According to Goring, traits such as feeblemindedness, epilepsy, insanity and defective social instinct are referred to as:
    a. defective intelligence
    b. genius
    c. criminal mind
    d. paranoid schizophrenic

12. Which perspective analyzes human perception and how it affects behavior?
    a. psychosexual theory
    b. psychodynamic perspective
    c. behaviorism
    d. cognitive theory

13. Instant gratification without concern for the rights of others is called the:
    a. reality principle
    b. conscience
    c. superego
    d. pleasure principle

14. The concept that takes into account what is practical and conventional by societal standards is called:
    a. reality principle
    b. conscience
    c. superego
    d. pleasure principle

15. The part of the superego that tells us what is right or wrong is called:
    a. conscience
    b. reality principle
    c. id
    d. ego ideal

16. The most basic human drive present at birth is the instinct to preserve and create life, and this concept is called:
    a. thantos
    b. eros
    c. oedipus
    d. latency

17. During the phallic stage, girls begin to have sexual feelings for their fathers, and this concept is called:
    a. identity crisis
    b. fixation
    c. Oedipus complex
    d. Electra complex

18. Seeking immediate gratification, satisfying one's own needs being more important than relating to others, and satisfying urges without considering right or wrong is a mental state known as:
    a. superiority complex
    b. identity crisis
    c. latent delinquency
    d. bipolar disorder

19. When an individual's moods alternate between periods of wild elation and deep depression, it is referred to as:
    a. disruptive behavior disorder (DBD)
    b. bipolar disorder
    c. latent delinquency
    d. inferiority complex

20. Disruptive behavior disorder (DBD) can take on two distinct forms; the more mild condition of uncooperative, defiant, and hostile behavior toward authority figures that seriously interferes with the youngster's day-to-day functioning is called:
    a. oppositional defiant disorder (ODD)
    b. conduct disorder (CD)
    c. psychosis
    d. schizophrenia

21. The branch of behavior theory most relevant to criminology is:
    a. moral development branch
    b. social learning theory
    c. humanistic psychology
    d. information theory

22. According to social learning theorists, violence is something learned through a process called:
    a. behavior modeling
    b. environmental processes
    c. disinhibition
    d. information processing

23. What branch of cognitive theory stresses self-awareness and "getting in touch with feelings?"
    a. nurture theory
    b. nature theory
    c. humanist theory
    d. moral development theory

24. Reasonably stable patterns of behavior, including thoughts and emotions that distinguish one person from another is:
    a. normal
    b. personality
    c. adolescence
    d. adulthood

25. Which theory argues that intelligence is largely determined genetically, that ancestry determines IQ, and that low intelligence, as demonstrated by low IQ, is linked to criminal behavior?
    a. humanist theory
    b. nature theory
    c. latency theory
    d. nurture theory

ESSAY QUESTIONS

1. Discuss the correlation between diet and crime.

2. Discuss the association between hormones and crime.

3. Describe the role genetics plays in crime.

4. Discuss the psychodynamics of criminality.

5. Discuss the role personality and intelligence in antisocial behaviors.

MATCHING

1. _____ Hypoglycemia
2. _____ Attention Deficit Hyperactive Disorder (ADHD)
3. _____ Arousal Theory
4. _____ Fixated
5. _____ Oedipus Complex
6. _____ Identity Crisis
7. _____ Albert Bandura
8. _____ Lawrence Kohlberg
9. _____ Antisocial Personality
10. _____ The Bell Curve

A. A period of serious personal questioning people undertake in an effort to determine their own values and sense of direction.
B. IQ-crime link.
C. Social learning theory.
D. Disturbed character structure.
E. Lack of attention, impulsivity, and hyperactivity.
F. Person exhibits behavior traits characteristic of those encountered during infantile sexual development.
G. Applied the concept of moral development to crime.
H. Below normal levels of glucose in the blood.
I. Some peoples' brains function differently in response to environmental stimuli.
J. Males have sexual feelings for their mothers.

CHAPTER 5 ANSWER KEY

Fill In The Blank Answers

1. somatotype
2. equipotentiality
3. violence; aggression
4. conduct disorder
5. monozygotic (or identical) twins
6. cheater theory
7. cognitive theory
8. bipolar disorder
9. behavior modeling
10. personality

True/False Answers

1.	T	6.	T	11.	T
2.	T	7.	T	12.	F
3.	T	8.	F	13.	F
4.	F	9.	T	14.	T
5.	F	10.	F	15.	T

Multiple Choice Answers

1.	A	11.	A	21.	B
2.	C	12.	D	22.	A
3.	B	13.	D	23.	C
4.	A	14.	A	24.	B
5.	C	15.	A	25.	D
6.	A	16.	B		
7.	B	17.	D		
8.	A	18.	C		
9.	A	19.	B		
10.	C	20.	A		

Essay Questions

1. Page 138
2. Pages 140 – 141
3. Pages 145 – 148
4. Pages 151 – 154
5. Pages 159 – 161

Matching Answers

1.	H	6.	A
2.	E	7.	C
3.	I	8.	G
4.	F	9.	D
5.	J	10.	B

Chapter 6

Social Structure Theories

LEARNING OBJECTIVES

1. Be familiar with the concept of social structure.

2. Have knowledge of the socioeconomic structure of American society.

3. Be able to discuss the concept of social disorganization.

4. Be familiar with the works of Shaw and McKay.

5. Know the various elements of ecological theory.

6. Be able to discuss the association between collective efficacy and crime.

7. Know what is meant by the term anomie.

8. Be familiar with the concept of strain.

9. Understand the concept of cultural deviance.

KEYWORDS AND DEFINITIONS

Stratified society: a society in which social strata are created by the unequal distribution of wealth, power, and prestige. (page 178)

Culture of poverty: a culture marked by apathy, cynicism, helplessness, and mistrust of social institutions such as schools, government agencies. (180)

At risk: neighborhoods that contain large numbers of single-parent families and unrelated people living together, have gone from having owner-occupied to renter-occupied units, and have an economic base that has lost semiskilled and unskilled jobs (indicating a growing residue of discouraged workers who are no longer seeking employment). (180)

Underclass: a group of people that is cut off from society, its members lacking the education and skills needed to be effectively in demand in modern society. (180)

Social structure theory: the theory that social and economic forces operating in deteriorated lower-class areas push many of their residents into criminal behavior patterns. (181)

Social disorganization theory: focuses on the conditions within the urban environment that affect crime rates. (182)

Strain theory: holds that crime is a function of the conflict between the goals people have and the means they can use to legally obtain them. (182)

Strain: feelings of anger, frustration, and resentment. (183)

Cultural deviance theory: combines elements of both strain and social disorganization; according to this view, because of strain and social isolation, a unique lower-class culture develops in disorganized neighborhoods. (183)

Subcultures: groups that maintain a unique set of values and beliefs that are in conflict with conventional social norms. (183)

Cultural transmission: subcultural values are handed down from one generation to the next. (183)

Transitional neighborhoods: poverty-ridden neighborhoods that suffer high rates of population turnover and are incapable of inducing residents to remain and defend the neighborhoods against criminal groups. (185)

Concentration effect: working- and middle-class families flee inner-city poverty areas resulting in the most disadvantaged population being consolidated in urban ghettos. (187)

Incivilities: rowdy youth, trash and litter, graffiti, abandoned storefronts, burned-out buildings, littered lots, strangers, drunks, vagabonds, loiterers, prostitutes, noise, congestion, angry words, dirt, and stench. (189)

Siege mentality: the idea that the outside world is considered the enemy out to destroy the neighborhood. (190)

Gentrification: that part of the life cycle that includes changing racial or ethnic makeup, population thinning, and finally, a renewal stage in which obsolete housing is replaced and upgraded. (190)

Collective efficacy: mutual trust, a willingness to intervene in the supervision of children, and the maintenance of public order. (190)

Social altruism: voluntary mutual support systems, such as neighborhood associations and self-help groups that reinforce moral and social obligations. (192)

Strain theorists: criminologists who view crime as a direct result of lower-class frustration and anger. (193)

Mechanical solidarity: characteristic of a preindustrial society, which is held together by traditions, shared values, and unquestioned beliefs. (194)

Organic solidarity: in postindustrial social systems, which are highly developed and dependent upon the division of labor, people are connected by their interdependent needs for one another's services and production. (194)

Theory of anomie: two elements of culture interact to produce potentially anomic conditions: culturally defined goals and socially approved means for obtaining them. (194)

Truly disadvantaged: the group that is socially isolated; where people dwell in urban inner cities, occupy the bottom rung of the social ladder, and are the victims of discrimination. (195)

Institutional anomie theory: the view that anomie pervades U.S. culture because the drive for material wealth dominates and undermines social and community values. (195)

American Dream: the success goal is pervasive in American culture. (196)

Relative deprivation: a collective sense of social injustice directly related to income inequality tends to develop in communities or nations in which the poor and wealthy live in close proximity to each other. (197)

General strain theory (GST): the view that multiple sources of strain interact with an individual's emotional traits and responses to produce criminality. (197)

Negative affective states: the anger, frustration, and adverse emotions that emerge in the wake of negative and destructive social relationships. (197)

Conduct norms: the concept that the lower class develops a unique culture in response to strain. (202)

Culture conflict: occurs when the rules expressed in the criminal law clash with the demands of group conduct norms. (202)

Focal concerns: the unique value system that defines lower-class culture. (202)

Status frustration: a form of culture conflict that lower-class youths experience because social conditions make them incapable of achieving success legitimately. (203)

Middle-class measuring rods: the standards set by authority figures such as teachers, employers, or supervisors. (203)

Corner boy: the most common response to middle-class rejection; he is not a chronic delinquent but may be a truant who engages in petty or status offenses, such as precocious sex and recreational drug abuse. (203)

College boy: embraces the cultural and social values of the middle class; rather than scorning middle-class measuring rods, he actively strives to be successful by those standards. This type of youth is embarking on an almost hopeless path, since he is ill-equipped academically, socially, and linguistically to achieve the rewards of middle-class life. (203)

Delinquent boy: adopts a set of norms and principles in direct opposition to middle-class values; he engages in short-run hedonism, living for today and letting "tomorrow take care of itself." Reaction formation: frustrated by their inability to succeed, these boys resort to overly intense responses that seem disproportionate to the stimuli that trigger them. (205)

Differential opportunity: people in all strata of society share the same success goals but that those in the lower class have limited means of achieving them; those who conclude that there is little hope for advancement by legitimate means may join with like-minded peers to form a gang. (205)

CHAPTER OUTLINE

I. Socioeconomic structure and crime
    A. General
        1. People in the U.S. live in a stratified society
        2. Created by the unequal distribution of wealth, power, and prestige
        3. Lower class members have inadequate housing and health care, disrupted family lives, underemployment, and despair
    B. Child poverty
        1. Children of low-income homes are less likely to achieve in school
        2. Poor children more likely to suffer health problems
    C. The underclass
        1. Culture of poverty passed from one generation to the next
        2. Underclass is cut off from society
        3. Lack of educational success and lack of success in the workplace lead to crime and drug use
    D. Minority group poverty
        1. Burdens of underclass are most often felt by minorities
        2. Rates of child poverty vary by race and ethnicity
        3. Significant portion of all minority males are under the control of the criminal justice system

II. Social structure theories
    A. General
        1. Disadvantaged economic class is the primary cause of crime
        2. Lower-class crime is often violent, committed by gang members or marginally employed young adults

3. Social structure theorists argue that people living in equivalent circumstances behave in similar, predictable ways
   B. Three branches of social structure theories
      1. Social disorganization theories
      2. Strain theories
      3. Cultural deviance theories

III. Social disorganization theories
   A. The work of Shaw and McKay
      1. Heavily influenced by the work of Burgess and Park
      2. Studied Chicago, a city fairly typical of the transition taking place in many other urban areas
      3. City was deteriorating
      4. Transitional neighborhoods
         a. Suffered high population turnovers
         b. Low rents attracted groups with different racial and ethnic backgrounds
         c. Immigrants congregated in these transitional neighborhoods
         d. These neighborhoods had dissolution of the neighborhood culture and organization caused by
            1) Successive changes in the population composition
            2) Disintegration of traditional cultures
            3) Diffusion of divergent cultural standards
            4) Gradual industrialization
      5. Concentric zones
         a. Shaw and McKay identified the areas in Chicago that had excessive crime rates
         b. These were the transitional inner-city zones
         c. Zones farthest from the city center had the lowest crime rates
         d. This pattern was stable over a period of 65 years
         e. Even though crime rates changed, the highest crime rates were always in the central city
         f. The areas with the highest crime rates retained high crime rates even when the ethnic composition changed
      6. The legacy of Shaw and McKay
         a. Social disorganization concepts have remained prominent for more than 75 years
         b. Most important finding – crime rates correspond to neighborhood structure – still holds up
         c. Crime is the result of destructive ecological conditions in lower-class neighborhoods
         d. Crime is a normal response to adverse social conditions
   B. The social ecology school
      1. Community deterioration
         a. Crime rates associated with deterioration, disorder, poverty, alienation, disassociation, and fear of crime
         b. Slum areas have the highest violence rates and gun crime
      2. Poverty concentration
         a. Concentration effect – elements of the most disadvantaged population are concentrated in ghetto areas
         b. Businesses are disinclined to locate in poverty areas

   c. Concentration effect contradicts Shaw and McKay's assumption that crime rates increase in transitional neighborhoods

  3. Chronic unemployment
   a. Relationship between unemployment and crime is unsettled
   b. Unemployment destabilizes households

  4. Community fear
   a. Those in disorganized neighborhoods suffer social and physical incivilities
   b. Fear is contagious
   c. Fear is associated with other community-level factors
    1) Race and fear
    2) Gangs and fear
    3) Mistrust and fear

  5. Community change
   a. Change, not stability, is the hallmark of inner-city areas
   b. As areas decline, residents flee to more stable areas

  6. Cycles of community change

  7. Change and decline
   a. Neighborhoods most at risk for crime rate increases contain large numbers of single-parent families
   b. Changing lifestyles (declining economic status, increasing population, and racial shifts) are associated with increased neighborhood crime rates

  8. Collective efficacy – three forms
   a. Informed social control
   b. Institutional social control
   c. Public social control

  9. Social support/altruism
   a. Neighborhoods with strong social supports can help the young deal with life's stressors
   b. Areas with caring for fellow citizens are less crime prone than those that stress self-reliance

IV. Strain theories
 A. The definition of anomie
  1. Without norms
  2. Rules of behavior (norms) have broken down or become inoperative during periods of rapid social change or social crisis
  3. Anomie most likely to occur in a society moving from mechanical to organic solidarity
  4. Anomie undermines the social control function

 B. Theory of anomie – Robert Merton
  1. Modified the concept of anomie for the modern U.S. society
  2. Two elements of culture interact to produce potentially anomic conditions
   a. Culturally defined goals
   b. Socially approved means to obtain them
  3. Legitimate means are stratified across class and status lines
  4. Those with little education and few economic resources find they are denied the ability to acquire wealth
  5. Social adaptations
   a. Conformity
   b. Innovation

  c. Ritualism

  d. Retreatism

  e. Rebellion

 6. Evaluation of anomie theory

  a. Merton's view is one of the most enduring and influential sociological theories of crime

  b. Theory explains high-crime areas and predominance of crime among the lower-class

  c. Why people choose certain types of crime not explained

  d. Theory assumes we all share the same goals and values

 7. Anomie reconsidered

  a. Strain fell out of favor

  b. Resurgence of interest in strain and anomie

  c. Newer versions of Merton's concepts

C. Institutional anomie theory

 1. Messner and Rosenfeld

 2. Antisocial behavior is a function of cultural and institutional influences

 3. Refer to the American Dream as a

  a. Goal – means accumulating material goods and wealth by competition

  b. Process – being socialized to pursue material successes and believing prosperity is an achievable goal

 4. Impact of anomie

  a. American institutions that might control exaggerated emphasis on financial success have been rendered powerless or obsolete

   1) Noneconomic functions and roles have been devalued

   2) Noneconomic roles became subordinate to and must accommodate economic roles

   3) Economic language, standards, and norms penetrate into the noneconomic realms

  b. High crime rates are explained by the interrelationship between culture and institutions

 5. Supporting research

  a. Number of research efforts support institutional anomie theory

  b. May be a blueprint for crime reduction strategies

D. Relative deprivation theory

 1. Neighborhood-level income inequality is a significant predictor of neighborhood crime rates

 2. Sharp divisions between rich and poor create an atmosphere of envy and mistrust that leads to violence and aggression

 3. Lower-class may feel deprived and embittered

 4. Relative deprivation is truly relative

E. General strain theory – Robert Agnew

 1. Identifies micro-level or individual influences of strain

 2. Multiple sources of stress

 3. Negative affective states

 4. Elements of general strain theory

  a. Failure to achieve positively valued goals

  b. Disjunction of expectations and achievements

  c. Removal of positively valued stimuli

  d. Presentation of negative stimuli

5. The greater the intensity and frequency of strain experiences, the greater their impact and the greater the likelihood of crime

F. Sources of strain
   1. Social sources of strain
   2. Community sources of strain

G. Coping with strain
   1. May be a function of both individual traits and personal experiences over the life course
   2. Some defenses are cognitive
   3. Strain and criminal careers

H. Evaluating general strain theory
   1. Clarifies the concept of strain
   2. Directs future research agendas
   3. Empirical support for general strain theory
   4. Evidence that the presence of negative stimuli provokes strain
   5. Gender issues
      a. One of the biggest question marks about general strain theory
      b. Females experience as much or more strain, but their crime rate is much lower

V. Cultural deviance theories
   A. Conduct norms
      1. Lower class develops a unique culture
      2. Group maintains their own set of conduct norms
      3. Conflict norms exist when more or less divergent rules of life govern the specific life situation of a person
      4. Culture conflict – rules expressed in criminal law clash with the demands of group conduct norms
   B. Focal Concerns – Miller
      1. Trouble
      2. Toughness
      3. Smartness
      4. Excitement
      5. Fate
      6. Autonomy
   C. Theory of delinquent subcultures – Cohen
      1. Behavior of lower-class youths is a protest against the norms and values of middle-class culture
      2. Status frustration
      3. Delinquent gang is a separate subculture
      4. Delinquent subculture results from socialization practices of ghettos and slums
      5. Middle-class measuring rods
         a. Inability to impress authority figures
         b. Failure to meet the standards of the middle-class measuring rod is the primary cause of delinquency
      6. Formation of deviant subcultures
         a. Corner boy
         b. College boy

  c. Delinquent boy
   1) Adopts a set of norms and principles in direct opposition to the middle-class
   2) Resorts to a process of reaction formation
 D. Theory of differential opportunity – Cloward and Ohlin
  1. Differential opportunities
   a. All people share the same success goals, but the lower class has limited means of achieving them
   b. Those that cannot advance by legitimate means join with like-minded peers to form a gang
   c. Opportunity for successful conventional and criminal careers is limited
    1) Stable areas have professional criminals
    2) Unstable areas do not have criminal opportunities
   d. Opportunities for success, both illegal and legal, are closed for the "truly disadvantaged" youth
   e. Kids join one of 3 gangs
    1) Criminal gangs
    2) Conflict gangs
    3) Retreatist gangs
  2. Analysis of differential opportunity
   a. Integrates cultural deviance and social disorganization concepts
   b. Relates to treatment and rehabilitation of delinquents
   c. Shows delinquency can be prevented by providing opportunities
 E. Evaluating social structure theories
  1. They have influenced both criminological theory and crime prevention strategies
  2. Core concepts seem to be valid
  3. Each branch seems to support and amplify others
  4. Critics charge
   a. Cannot be sure lower class culture promotes crime
   b. Residence in an urban area alone does not cause violations of the law
   c. Questionable whether a lower-class culture exists

VI. Public policy implications of social structure theory
 A. Provide opportunities to share rewards of conventional society
 B. Improve community structure in high crime areas to reduce crime
 C. War on Poverty used concepts from differential opportunity
 D. Weed and Seed

CHAPTER SUMMARY

  Social structure theories propose that being in the disadvantaged economic class is the primary cause of crime, and as a result, lower-class crime is often violent, committed by gang members, or marginally employed young adults. Social structure theorists argue that people living in equivalent circumstances behave in similar, predictable ways. The three branches of social structure theories are social disorganization theories, strain theories, and cultural deviance theories.

Social disorganization theories were heavily influenced by the work of Burgess and Park. Shaw and McKay studied Chicago, a city fairly typical of the transition taking place in many other urban areas. Shaw and McKay found what they call transitional neighborhoods, the neighborhoods that had excessive crime rates. At the opposite end, those zones farthest from the city center had the lowest crime rates. This pattern was stable over a period of 65 years; even though crime rates changed, the highest crime rates were always in the central city. The areas with the highest crime rates retained high crime rates even when the ethnic composition changed.

Emile Durkheim coined the term anomie, the condition in which the rules of behavior (norms) have broken down or become inoperative during periods of rapid social change or social crisis. Durkheim noted that anomie undermines the social control function. Robert Merton modified the concept of anomie for the modern U.S. society. According to Merton, two elements of culture interact to produce potentially anomic conditions: culturally defined goals and socially approved means to obtain them. He noted that legitimate means of achieving success are stratified across class and status lines, so those with little education and few economic resources find they are denied the ability to acquire wealth. It is this inability to succeed that leads to crime.

Messner and Rosenfeld developed institutional anomie theory that states that antisocial behavior is a function of cultural and institutional influences. He described the American Dream as a goal, the accumulation of material goods and wealth by competition, and as a process, being socialized to pursue material successes and believing prosperity is an achievable goal. American institutions that might control exaggerated emphasis on financial success have been rendered powerless or obsolete because noneconomic functions and roles have been devalued, noneconomic roles became subordinate to and must accommodate economic roles, and economic language, standards, and norms penetrate into the noneconomic realms.

Robert Agnew developed general strain theory which identifies micro-level or individual influences of strain. According to the theory, crime arises from failure to achieve positively valued goals, a disjunction of expectations and achievements, the removal of positively valued stimuli, or the presentation of negative stimuli. The greater the intensity and frequency of strain experiences, the greater their impact and the greater the likelihood of crime.

Cohen developed the theory of delinquent subcultures which state that the behavior of lower-class youths is a protest against the norms and values of the middle-class culture. The delinquent gang is a separate subculture that results from socialization practices of ghettos and slums. Cohen identified the middle-class measuring rods that arise from the inability to impress authority figures and the failure to meet the standards of the middle-class measuring rod is the primary cause of delinquency. As a result, three possible types of gangs develop: corner boy, college boy, or delinquent boy. The delinquent boy adopts a set of norms and principles in direct opposition to the middle-class and resorts to a process of reaction formation.

Cloward and Ohlin's theory of differential opportunity states that all people share the same success goals, but the lower class has limited means of achieving them. Those that cannot advance by legitimate means join with like-minded peers to form a gang. Opportunities for success, both illegal and legal, are closed for the "truly disadvantaged" youth. These young people join one of three gangs: criminal gangs, conflict gangs, retreatist gangs.

STUDENT EXERCISES

Exercise 1

Go online to http://www.aei.org/publications/pubID.14891/pub_detail.asp and read the article, "The Underclass Revisited" by Charles Murray. This provides you with a conservative view of the issue of the underclass. After reading the article, write a one to two page essay that contrasts Murray's view with that contained in the textbook.

Exercise 2

Take a ride in your city or a nearby city. Make sure you drive from the center of the city out to the boundaries of the city. Make a note of what each neighborhood looks like as far as types of buildings, environment, what the land is used for, types of residences, etc. How do the neighborhoods change as one moves out from the center of town, and how dramatic are the changes? Do the changes in your city support the social structure theories?

CRIMINOLOGY WEB LINKS

http://www.iejs.com/Criminology/anomie_and_strain_theory.htm
This website provides a summary of anomie from the viewpoint of both Durkheim and Merton. It also gives a little background information on the two authors.

http://www.ncjrs.org/pdffiles1/nij/186049.pdf
This website provides a six page article on the relationship between urban disorder and crime from two of America's leading criminologists.

http://www.crimereduction.gov.uk/
This website shows how the United Kingdom is using social structure theories as the foundations for its crime prevention programs.

http://faculty.ncwc.edu/toconnor/301/301lect08.htm
This website provides and excellent summary of the Chicago School, social disorganization theory, gang theory, and other references to social structure theory.

http://www.news.wisc.edu/6148.html
This website provides and excellent example of using social structure theory to drive policy decisions. The article provides a review of the results of a study on providing early intervention to at risk children in the Chicago area.

TEST BANK

FILL-IN THE BLANKS

1. _____ _____ are created by the unequal distribution of wealth, power, and prestige.

2. Economic disparity will continually haunt members of the _____ and their children over the course of their life span.

3. Social structure theory views the disadvantaged _____ class position as a primary cause of crime.

4. Subcultural values are handed down from one generation to the next in a process called _____ _____.

5. Aggregate crime rates and aggregate unemployment rates seem _____ related.

6. _____ _____ is mutual trust, a willingness to intervene in the supervision of children, and the maintenance of public order.

7. _____ _____ is a characteristic of a preindustrial society, which is held together by traditions, shared values, and unquestioned beliefs.

8. According to the _____ _____ view, lower-class people might feel both deprived and embittered when they compare their life circumstances to those of the more affluent.

9. Agnew suggests that criminality is the direct result of _____ _____ _____ — the anger, frustration, and adverse emotions that emerge in the wake of negative and destructive social relationships.

10. _____ _____ are the unique value system that defines lower class culture.

TRUE/FALSE QUESTIONS

1. T/F Findings suggest that poverty during early childhood may have a more severe impact than poverty during adolescence and adulthood.

2. T/F The underclass lacks an education and the skills necessary to be effectively in demand in modern society.

3. T/F The rates of child poverty in the United States vary by race and ethnicity, but not significantly.

4. T/F William Julius Wilson provided a description of the plight of the lowest levels of the underclass, which he labeled the truly disadvantaged.

5. T/F Although members of the middle and upper classes also engage in crime, social structure theorists view middle-class, or white-collar, crime as being of relatively lower frequency, seriousness, and danger to the general public.

6. T/F Transitional neighborhoods are those that have low crime rates.

7. T/F Modern-day social ecologists developed a "purer" form of structural theory that emphasizes the association of community deterioration and economic decline to criminality but places more emphasis on value conflict.

8. T/F Siege mentality refers to the rich considering the poor as their enemy out to destroy the neighborhood.

9. T/F Public social control is not an element of collective efficacy.

10. T/F Social altruism has been found to be inversely related to crime rates both in the United States and abroad.

11. T/F Merton used a modified version of the concept of anomie to fit social, economic, and cultural conditions found in modern U.S. society.

12. T/F Retreatists reject the goals and accept the means of society.

13. T/F Because social conditions make them incapable of achieving success legitimately, lower-class youths experience a form of culture conflict that Cohen labels status frustration.

14. T/F Differential opportunity states that people in all strata of society share the same success goals but that those in the lower class do not take advantage of the opportunities given to them.

15 T/F Retreatist gang members are double failures, unable to gain success through legitimate means and unwilling to do so through illegal ones.

MULTIPLE CHOICE QUESTIONS

1. What is produced by the crushing lifestyle of slum areas and passed from one generation to the next?
    a. underclass
    b. at-risk adults
    c. culture of poverty
    d. ritualism

2. The lowest levels of the underclass are called:
    a. truly disadvantaged
    b. at-risk
    c. poor
    d. transitional neighborhoods

3. Subcultural values are handed down from one generation to the next in a process called:
    a. cultural mutation
    b. cultural transmission
    c. subcultural transmission
    d. subcultural mutation

4. Poverty-ridden areas that suffer high rates of population turnover and are incapable of inducing residents to remain and defend the area against criminal groups are called:
    a. at-risk neighborhoods
    b. transitional neighborhoods
    c. concentric zones
    d. anomic areas

5. In some neighborhoods, neighbors are willing to practice informal social control through:
    a. staying indoors
    b. arresting criminals
    c. being auxiliary police
    d. surveillance

6. Substitution of an alternative set of goals and means for conventional ones is called:
    a. innovation
    b. ritualism
    c. rebellion
    d. retreatism

7. Agnew suggests that criminality is the direct result of:
    a. negative affective states
    b. poverty
    c. underclass
    d. neighborhood

8. The elements of general strain theory include all of the following **EXCEPT**:
   a. introduction into a life of poverty
   b. failure to achieve positively valued goals
   c. disjunction of expectations and achievements
   d. removal of positively valued stimuli

9. According to general strain theory, why is it that some people who experience strain do **NOT** fall into a life of crime and eventually resort to criminality?
   a. they do not really experience strain.
   b. they have coping skills.
   c. people help them out.
   d. they live in good communities.

10. One of the biggest question marks about GST is its ability to adequately explain what concerning the crime rate?
    a. age differences
    b. racial differences
    c. economic status differences
    d. gender differences

11. What occurs when the rules expressed in the criminal law clash with the demands of group conduct norms?
    a. focal concerns
    b. strain
    c. culture conflict
    d. concentration effect

12. Who wrote Culture Conflict and Crime, a theoretical attempt to link cultural adaptation to criminality?
    a. Cloward
    b. Miller
    c. Sellin
    d. Ohlin

13. Which of the following is one of Miller's lower class focal concerns?
    a. trouble
    b. toughness
    c. smartness
    d. criminality

14. Being independent of authority figures, such as the police, teachers, and parents is an example of:
    a. trouble
    b. autonomy
    c. toughness
    d. smartness

15. The author of the classic book, *Delinquent Boys*, was:
    a. Freud
    b. Martin
    c. Sutherland
    d. Cohen

16. A truant who engages in petty or status offenses is a:
    a. corner boy
    b. college boy
    c. delinquent boy
    d. conflict boy

17. One who embraces the cultural and social values of the middle class is a:
    a. corner boy
    b. college boy
    c. delinquent boy
    d. conflict boy

18. One who adopts a set on norms and principles in direct opposition to middle-class values is a:
    a. corner boy
    b. college boy
    c. delinquent boy
    d. conflict boy

19. Overly intense responses that seem disproportionate to the stimuli that trigger them are called:
    a. reaction formation
    b. reality principle
    c. cultural deviance
    d. group autonomy

20. Who wrote the classic Delinquency and Opportunity?
    a. Winfree and Mays
    b. Martin and Gordon
    c. Brown and Dennis
    d. Cloward and Ohlin

21. The concept that people in all strata of society share the same success goals, but those in the lower class have limited means of achieving them is known as:
    a. differential opportunity
    b. differential association
    c. differential reinforcement
    d. differential timing

22. Those who are double failures and unable to gain success through legitimate means and unwilling to do so through illegal ones are likely to join which of the following gangs?
    a. criminal
    b. conflict
    c. retreatist
    d. corner boy gang

23. Gangs which exist in stable slum area in which close connections among adolescent, young adult and adult offenders create an environment for successful enterprise are known as:
    a. criminal
    b. conflict
    c. retreatist
    d. corner boy gang

24. Gangs which develop in communities unable to provide either legitimate or illegitimate opportunities are known as:
    a. criminal
    b. conflict
    c. retreatist
    d. corner boy gang

25. The foremost structural theory based crime reduction strategy today is known as:
    a. War on Poverty
    b. Operation Weed and Seed
    c. VISTA (the urban Peace Corps)
    d. Head Start

ESSAY QUESTIONS

1. Describe three major issues concerning poverty in America.

2. Discuss the concept of social disorganization.

3. Describe the association between collective efficacy and crime.

4. Discuss the term anomie, including the points of view of both Durkheim and Merton.

5. Discuss the concept of cultural deviance.

MATCHING

1. Siege Mentality
2. Stratified Society
3. Concentration Effect
4. Incivilities
5. Collective Efficacy
6. Social Altruism
7. Anomie
8. American Dream
9. Status Frustration
10. Reaction Formation

A. Mutual trust, a willingness to intervene in the supervision of children, and the maintenance of public order.
B. Outside world is considered the enemy out to destroy the neighborhood.
C. Rowdy youth, trash and litter, graffiti, abandoned storefronts, burned-out buildings, littered lots, strangers.
D. Accumulating material goods and wealth via open individual competition.
E. Created by the unequal distribution of wealth, power, and prestige.
F. Overly intense responses that seem disproportionate to the stimuli that trigger them.
G. Lower-class youths experience a form of culture conflict because social conditions make them incapable of achieving success legitimately.
H. Rules of behavior have broken down or become inoperative.
I. working- and middle-class families flee inner-city poverty areas in which elements of the most disadvantaged population are consolidated in urban ghettos.
J. People are generous and caring.

CHAPTER 6 ANSWER KEY

Fill In The Blank Answers

1. social strata
2. underclass
3. economic
4. cultural transmission
5. weakly
6. collective efficacy
7. mechanical solidarity
8. relative deprivation
9. negative affective states
10. focal concerns

True/False Answers

1.	T	6.	F	11.	T
2.	T	7.	F	12.	F
3.	F	8.	F	13.	T
4.	T	9.	F	14.	F
5.	T	10.	T	15.	T

Multiple Choice Answers

1.	C	11.	C	21.	D
2.	A	12.	C	22.	C
3.	B	13.	D	23.	A
4.	B	14.	B	24.	B
5.	D	15.	D	25.	B
6.	C	16.	A		
7.	A	17.	B		
8.	A	18.	C		
9.	B	19.	A		
10.	D	20.	D		

Essay Questions

1. Pages 178 – 181
2. Pages 184 – 186
3. Pages 190 – 192
4. Pages 193 – 195
5. Pages 201 – 204

Matching Answers

1.	B	6.	J
2.	E	7.	H
3.	I	8.	D
4.	C	9.	G
5.	A	10.	F

Chapter 7

Social Process Theories

LEARNING OBJECTIVES

1. Be familiar with the concept of socialization.

2. Discuss the effect of schools, family, and friends on crime.

3. Be able to discuss the differences of learning, control, and reaction.

4. Be familiar with the concept of differential association.

5. Be able to discuss what is meant by a definition toward criminality.

6. Understand the concept of neutralization.

7. Be able to discuss the relationship between self-concept and crime.

8. Know the elements of the social bond.

9. Describe the labeling process and how it leads to criminal careers.

10. Be familiar with the concepts of primary and secondary deviance.

KEYWORDS AND DEFINITIONS

Social process theory: the view that if relationships are positive and supportive, people can succeed within the rules of society; if these relationships are dysfunctional and destructive, conventional success may be impossible, and criminal solutions may become a feasible alternative. (page 218)

Social control theory: maintains that everyone has the potential to become a criminal but that most people are controlled by their bonds to society. (225)

Social reaction theory (labeling theory): holds that people become criminals when significant members of society label them as such, and they accept those labels as a personal identity. (225)

Differential association theory: criminality stemmed neither from individual traits nor from socioeconomic position; instead, he believed it to be a function of a learning process that could affect any individual in any culture. (226)

Differential reinforcement theory: attempts to explain crime as a type of learned behavior; first proposed by Ronald Akers in collaboration with Robert Burgess in 1966, it is a version of the social learning view that employs both differential association concepts along with elements of psychological learning theory. (229)

Direct conditioning (or differential reinforcement): occurs when behavior is reinforced by being either rewarded or punished while interacting with others. (229)

Negative reinforcement: when behavior is punished. (229)

Neutralization theory: views the process of becoming a criminal as a learning experience in which potential delinquents and criminals master techniques that enable them to counterbalance or neutralize conventional values and drift back and forth between illegitimate and conventional behavior. (230)

Subterranean values: morally tinged influences that have become entrenched in the culture but are publicly condemned. (230)

Drift: refers to the movement from one extreme of behavior to another, resulting in behavior that is sometimes unconventional, free, or deviant and at other times constrained and sober. (230)

Self-control: a strong moral sense, which renders people incapable of hurting others and violating social norms. (232)

Commitment to conformity: conformity is adhered to because there is a real, present, and logical reason to obey the rules of society. (232)

Containment theory: a strong self-image insulates a youth from the pressures and pulls of crimogenic influences in the environment. (233)

Normative groups: groups, such as the high school in-crowd, that conform to the social rules of society. (233)

Social bond: the ties that bind people to society; according to Hirschi, it has four main elements: attachment, commitment, involvement, and belief. (234)

Symbolic interaction theory: holds that people communicate via symbols – gestures, signs, words, or images – that stand for or represent something else. (236)

Stigma: an enduring label that taints a person's identity and changes him or her in the eyes of others. (239)

Differential social control: the process of labeling may produce a re-evaluation of the self, which reflects actual or perceived appraisals made by others. (239)

Reflective role taking: when youths believe that others view them as antisocial or troublemakers, they take on attitudes and roles that reflect this assumption; they expect to become suspects and then to be rejected. (239)

Retrospective reading: people begin to react to the label description and what it signifies instead of reacting to the actual behavior of the person who bears it. (239)

Dramatization of evil: as the negative feedback of law enforcement agencies, parents, friends, teachers, and other figures amplifies the force of the original label, stigmatized offenders may begin to re-evaluate their own identities. The person becomes the thing he or she is described as being. (240)

Primary deviance: norm violations or crimes that have very little influence on the actor and can be quickly forgotten. (240)

Secondary deviance: occurs when a deviant event comes to the attention of significant others or social control agents who apply a negative label. (240)

Contextual discrimination: refers to judges' practices in some jurisdictions of imposing harsher sentences on African Americans only in some instances, such as when they victimize whites and not other African Americans. (241)

Diversion programs: designed to remove both juvenile and adult offenders from the normal channels of the criminal justice process by placing them in programs designed for rehabilitation. (245)

CHAPTER OUTLINE

I.   Socialization and crime
    A.   Family relations
        1.   Children from households characterized by conflict and tension are susceptible to the crime-promoting forces in the environment
        2.   Living in a disadvantaged neighborhood places terrific strain on family functioning
        3.   Relationship between family structure and crime is critical when the high rates of divorce and single parents are considered
        4.   Family conflict and discord are more important determinants of behavior than family structure
        5.   Children living with a stepparent exhibit
            a.   As many problems as youth in single-parent families
            b.   Considerably more problems than those who are living with both biological parents

B. Child abuse and crime
1. There is also a suspected link between child abuse, neglect, sexual abuse, and crime
2. The effect of the family on delinquency has also been observed in other cultures
C. Educational experience
1. Educational process and adolescent achievement in school have been linked to criminality
2. Schools contribute to criminality in that when they label problem youths they set them apart from conventional society
3. Many school dropouts, especially those who have been expelled, face a significant chance of entering a criminal career
4. Schools can also be the scene of crime and violence
5. School level and size have a significant impact on the likelihood of experiencing theft and violence
6. Presence of weapons and violence
D. Peer relations
1. General
a. Peer influence may be a universal norm
b. Peer relations are a vital aspect of maturation
c. Adolescents feel a persistent pressure to conform to group values
d. When the peer group is not among friends who are positive influences, adolescent criminal activity can begin to be initiated as a group process
2. Peer rejection/peer acceptance
a. Peers may abandon or snub those who are unpopular, out of control, or unruly
b. Peer rejection may help increase and sustain antisocial behaviors
c. Having prosocial friends who are committed to conventional success may help shield kids from crime
3. Peers and criminality
a. Paths to the onset and continuation of criminality
1) Delinquent friends cause law-abiding youth to "get in trouble"
2) Antisocial youths seek out and join up with like-minded friends
3) Antisocial friends help youths maintain delinquent careers and obstruct the aging-out process
4) Troubled kids choose delinquent peers out of necessity rather than desire
b. Criminal peers may exert tremendous influence on behavior, attitudes, and beliefs
c. Some children join more than one deviant group
1) Leadership role in one
2) Follower in another
E. Institutional involvement and belief
1. Those who regularly attend religious services should also eschew crime and other antisocial behaviors
2. Association between religious attendance and belief and delinquent behavior patterns is negligible and insignificant
3. Participation seems to be a more significant inhibitor of crime than merely having religious beliefs and values
F. The effects of socialization on crime
1. Socialization, not the social structure, which determines life chances
2. The more social problems encountered during the socialization process, the greater the likelihood that youths will encounter difficulties and obstacles

II. Social learning theory
  A. Differential association theory
    1. General
      a. Contained in Edwin H. Sutherland's Principles of Criminology
      b. One of the most enduring explanations of criminal behavior
      c. Crime is a function of a learning process that could affect any individual in any culture
    2. Principles of differential association
      a. Criminal behavior is learned
      b. Learning is a by-product of interaction
      c. Learning occurs within intimate groups
      d. Criminal techniques are learned
      e. Perceptions of legal code influence motives and drives
      f. A person becomes a criminal when he or she perceives more favorable than unfavorable consequences to violating the law
      g. Differential associations may vary in frequency, duration, priority, and intensity
      h. The process of learning criminal behavior by association with criminal and anticriminal patterns involves all of the mechanisms involved in any other learning process
      i. Criminal behavior is an expression of general needs and values, but it is not excused by those general needs and values because noncriminal behavior is also an expression of those same needs and values
    3. Testing differential association theory
      a. Relatively sparse research
      b. Difficult to conceptualize the principles of the theory
      c. Notable research efforts have shown a correlation between
        1) Having deviant friends
        2) Holding deviant attitudes
        3) Committing deviant acts
      d. Relevant in trying to explain
        1) Onset of substance abuse
        2) Career in the drug trade
    4. Analysis of differential association theory
      a. Some oppose the idea that criminals are people "properly" socialized into a deviant subculture
      b. Fails to explain why one youth who is exposed to delinquent definitions eventually succumbs to them, while another does not
      c. Important place in the study of criminal behavior
  B. Differential reinforcement theory
    1. Akers and Burgess
    2. Employs both differential association concepts and elements of psychological learning theory
    3. Same processes used in learning both deviant and conventional behavior
    4. Several learning processes shape behavior
      a. Direct conditioning or differential reinforcement
      b. Negative reinforcement
    5. People evaluate their behavior through interactions with significant others and groups in their lives

6. Principal influence on behavior comes from those who
   a. Control reinforcement and punishment
   b. Expose them to behavioral models and normative definitions
7. Testing differential reinforcement
   a. Strong association between drug and alcohol abuse and social learning variables
   b. Learning-deviant behavior link is not static

C. Neutralization theory
   1. Sykes and Matza
   2. Delinquents learn to counterbalance or neutralize conventional values so they can drift back and forth between legitimate and illegitimate behavior
   3. Subterranean values
   4. Drift – move from legal to illegal behavior
   5. Bases of the theory
      a. Criminals voice guilt over illegal acts
      b. Offenders respect and admire honest, law-abiding people
      c. Criminals draw a line between whom they can victimize and whom they cannot
      d. Criminals are not immune to the demands of conformity
   6. Techniques of neutralization
      a. Deny responsibility
      b. Deny injury
      c. Deny victim
      d. Condemn the condemners
      e. Appeal to higher loyalties
   7. Testing neutralization theory
      a. Results have been inconclusive
      b. Weight of evidence is that
         1) Most delinquents disapprove of violence
         2) Neutralizations enable youth to engage in delinquency
      c. Major contribution to crime and delinquency literature

D. Are learning theories valid?
   1. Explain the onset of criminal behavior
   2. Subject to criticism
   3. Who was the first teacher?
   4. Fail to explain spontaneous and wanton acts of violence
   5. Maintain an important place in the study of crime and delinquency

III. Social control theory
   A. Self-concept and crime
      1. Early control theories speculated that low self-control was a product of weak self-concept and poor self-esteem
      2. Reckless' containment theory argued that strong self-image insulates one from the pressures and pulls of criminogenic influences in society
      3. Kaplan argued that
         a. Youths with poor self-concepts are the ones most likely to engage in delinquent behavior
         b. Successful participation in criminality actually helps raise their self-esteem
   B. Hirschi's social bond theory (also called social control theory)
      1. Onset of criminality is linked to the weakening of the bonds to society
      2. All individuals are potential law violators

3. Without these social ties or bonds, a person is free to commit criminal acts
4. Elements of the bond
   a. Attachment
   b. Commitment
   c. Involvement
   d. Belief
5. Testing social bond theory
   a. Hirschi found considerable evidence to support social bond theory
   b. Corroborated by numerous research studies that show delinquents detached from society
   c. Cross-national surveys have also supported the general findings of Hirschi's control theory
6. Opposing views
   a. Research efforts do show that delinquents maintain relationships with deviant peers and are influenced by members of their deviant peer group
   b. Not all elements of the bond are equal
   c. Rather than deter delinquency, attachment to deviant peers may support and nurture antisocial behavior
   d. Some question as to whether the theory can explain all modes of criminality
   e. Social bonds seem to change over time
   f. Agnew claims that Hirschi miscalculated the direction of the relationship between criminality and a weakened social bond

IV. Social reaction theory
   A. General
      1. Roots are found in the symbolic interaction theory
      2. People communicate via symbols that stand for or represent something else
      3. Both positive and negative labels involve subjective interpretation of behavior
      4. If a devalued status is conferred by a significant other, the negative label may cause permanent harm
      5. Depending on the visibility of the label and the manner and severity with which it is applied, a person may have an increasing commitment to a deviant career
   B. Crime and labeling theory
      1. Crime and deviance are defined
         a. By the social audience's reaction to people and their behavior and the subsequent effects of that reaction
         b. Not by the moral content of the illegal act itself
      2. Social reaction theory argues that such crimes as murder, rape, and assault are only bad or evil because people label them as such
      3. People who create rules are moral entrepreneurs
      4. Crime is a subjective concept whose definition is totally dependent on the viewing audience
   C. Differential enforcement
      1. Important principle of social reaction theory is that the law is differentially applied
      2. Social reaction theorists also argue that the content of the law reflects power relationships in society
      3. The law
         a. Favors the powerful members of society who direct its content
         b. Penalizes people whose actions represent a threat to those in control

121

D. Becoming labeled
   1. Social reaction theory is not especially concerned with why people originally engage in acts that result in their being labeled
   2. Not all labeled people have chosen to engage in label-producing activities

E. Consequences of labeling
   1. Social reaction theorists are most concerned with two effects of labeling
      a. The creation of stigma
      b. The effect on self-image
   2. Public condemnation an important part of the label-producing process
   3. Differential social control
      a. Process of labeling may produce a re-evaluation of the self, which reflects actual or perceived appraisals made by others
      b. When they believe that others view them as antisocial or troublemakers
         1) They take on attitudes and roles that reflect this assumption
         2) They expect to become suspects and then to be rejected
   4. Joining deviant cliques
      a. Those labeled as deviant, they may join up with similarly outcast delinquent peers who facilitate their behavior
      b. Antisocial behavior becomes habitual and automatic
      c. May acquire motives to deviate from social norms
   5. Retrospective reading
      a. Labels tend to redefine the whole person
      b. People begin to react to the label description and what it signifies instead of reacting to the actual behavior of the person who bears it
      c. Past of the labeled person is reviewed and re-evaluated to fit his or her current status
      d. We can now understand what prompted his current behavior
      e. The label must be accurate
   6. Dramatization of evil
      a. Labels become the basis of personal identity
      b. Stigmatized offenders may begin to re-evaluate their own identities
      c. The person becomes what he is described as
      d. Process is called the dramatization of evil

F. Primary and secondary deviance
   1. Primary deviance – norm violations or crimes that have very little influence on the actor and can be quickly forgotten
   2. Secondary
      a. Deviant event comes to the attention of significant others or social control agents who apply a negative label
      b. Involves resocialization into a deviant role
      c. Produces a deviance amplification effect

G. Research on social reaction theory
   1. Who gets labeled?
      a. The poor and powerless people are victimized by the law and justice system
      b. Reviews indicate that race bias adversely influences decision making in many critical areas of the justice system
      c. Little definitive evidence exists that the justice system is inherently unfair and biased

2. Effects of labeling
   a. Empirical evidence that negative labels actually have a dramatic influence on self-image and subsequent behavior
   b. Family interaction can influence the labeling process
3. Labeling and criminal careers
   a. Empirical evidence supports the fact that labeling plays an important role in persistent offending
   b. Official intervention actually increases the probability that a labeled person will get involved in subsequent involvement in antisocial behavior
H. Is labeling theory valid?
   1. Its inability to specify the conditions that must exist before an act or individual is labeled deviant
   2. Fails to explain differences in crime rates
   3. Ignores the onset of deviant behavior
   4. Tittle claims that many criminal careers occur without labeling
   5. Labeling reexamined
      a. Important contributions to the study of criminality
         1) The labeling perspective identifies the role played by social control agents in the process of crime causation
         2) Labeling theory recognizes that criminality is not a disease or pathological behavior
         3) Shows that the concepts of primary and secondary deviance must be interpreted and treated differently
      b. Focus on interaction as well as the situations surrounding the crime

V. Evaluating social process theories
   A. Social process theories suggest that criminal behavior is part of the socialization process
   B. Theories do not always account for the patterns and fluctuations in the crime rate

VI. Public policy implications of social process theory
   A. Social process theories have had a major influence on policymaking since the 1950s
   B. Learning theories have greatly influenced the way criminal offenders are dealt with and treated
   C. Control theories have also influenced criminal justice and other public policy
   D. Labeling theorists caution against too much intervention
   E. The influence of labeling theory can be viewed in the development of diversion and restitution programs
   F. Despite their good intentions, stigma-reducing programs have not met with great success

CHAPTER SUMMARY

This chapter deals with the association between socialization and crime. Social process theories argue that socialization, not the social structure, determines life chances. The more social problems encountered during the socialization process, the greater the likelihood that youths will encounter difficulties and obstacles. The relationship between family structure and crime is critical when the high rates of divorce and single parents are considered, but family conflict and discord are more important determinants of behavior than are family structure. The effect of the family on delinquency has also been observed in other cultures. Educational process and adolescent achievement in school have been linked to criminality. Schools contribute to criminality in that when they label problem youths they set them apart from conventional society. Many school dropouts, especially those who have been expelled, face a significant chance of entering a criminal career. Peer influence may be a universal norm. Peer relations are a vital aspect of maturation and adolescents feel a persistent pressure to conform to group values. Those who regularly attend religious services should also eschew crime and other antisocial behaviors. The association between religious attendance and belief and delinquent behavior patterns is negligible and insignificant; participation seems to be a more significant inhibitor of crime than merely having religious beliefs and values.

Differential association theory, contained in Edwin H. Sutherland's Principles of Criminology, is one of the most enduring explanations of criminal behavior. The principles of differential association include 1) criminal behavior is learned; 2) learning is a by-product of interaction; 3) learning occurs within intimate groups; 4) criminal techniques are learned; 5) perceptions of legal code influence motives and drives; 6) a person becomes a criminal when he or she perceives more favorable than unfavorable consequences to violating the law; 7) differential associations may vary in frequency, duration, priority, and intensity; 8) The process of learning criminal behavior by association with criminal and anticriminal patterns involves all of the mechanisms involved in any other learning process; 9) criminal behavior is an expression of general needs and values, but it is not excused by those general needs and values because noncriminal behavior is also an expression of those same needs and values. Differential reinforcement theory by Akers and Burgess employs both differential association concepts and elements of psychological learning theory. The same processes used in learning both deviant and conventional behavior. Several learning processes shape behavior, including direct conditioning or differential reinforcement and negative reinforcement.

Sykes and Matza's neutralization theory argues that delinquents learn to counterbalance or neutralize conventional values so they can drift back and forth between legitimate and illegitimate behavior. The techniques of neutralization include the denial of responsibility, the denial of injury, the denial of a victim, the condemning of the condemners, and an appeal to higher loyalties. Early control theories speculated that low self-control was a product of weak self-concept and poor self-esteem. The major social control theory is Hirschi's social bond theory (also called social control theory) which states that the onset of criminality is linked to the weakening of the bonds to society. It also argues that all individuals are potential law violators and without these social ties or bonds, a person is free to commit criminal acts. The four elements of the bond are attachment, commitment, involvement, and belief.

The roots of social reaction theory are found in the symbolic interaction theory which postulates that people communicate via symbols that stand for or represent something else. One of the most prominent social reaction theories is labeling theory. Under this approach, crime and deviance are defined by the social audience's reaction to people and their behavior and the subsequent effects of that reaction, not by the moral content of the illegal act itself. Crime, therefore, is a subjective concept whose definition is totally dependent on the viewing audience. An important principle of social reaction theory is that the law is differentially applied because the law favors the powerful members of society who direct its content and it penalizes people whose actions represent a threat to those in control.

Social reaction theory is not especially concerned with why people originally engage in acts that result in their being labeled; they are most concerned with two effects of labeling: the creation of stigma and the effect on self-image. One key component of labeling theory is retrospective reading. Labels tend to redefine the whole person and people begin to react to the label description and what it signifies instead of reacting to the actual behavior of the person who bears it. The past of the labeled person is reviewed and re-evaluated to fit his or her current status. Society can now understand what prompted his or her current behavior. Labels become the basis of personal identity and stigmatized offenders may begin to re-evaluate their own identities. The person becomes what he is described as in a process is called the dramatization of evil. Two other major concepts are primary and secondary deviance. Primary deviance means norm violations or crimes that have very little influence on the actor and can be quickly forgotten. Secondary deviance refers to the deviant event that comes to the attention of significant others or social control agents who apply a negative label. It involves resocialization into a deviant role and produces a deviance amplification effect.

STUDENT EXERCISES

Exercise 1

Go online to http://www.ncjrs.org/pdffiles1/ojjdp/173423.pdf and read the article, "Families and Schools Together: Building Relationships" by Lynn McDonald and Heather E. Frey. After reading the article, write a one to two page essay that compares and contrasts McDonald and Frey's view with that of Hirschi's social bond theory contained in the textbook.

Exercise 2

Social control theories rather than explain the causes of crime explain why most people do not commit crime. Hirschi's social bond theory explains this through the four bonds of attachment, commitment, involvement, and belief. Think back to your younger years and make a listing for each of those bonds describing your life and what was happened in each of the bonds as your life progressed. For example, under involvement – I played high school baseball; under attachment – I strongly identified with my family. How does your list compare with those of two of your other classmates?

CRIMINOLOGY WEB LINKS

http://www.allaboutkids.umn.edu/WingfortheWeb/42189%20AmSch_Libbey.pdf
The article by Heather P. Libbey at this website provides an interesting look at the relationship between attachment to school and the impact on students' lives.

http://www.pineforge.com/isw4/overviews/pdfs/Svensson.pdf
The article by Robert Svensson at this website provides the results of an investigation into gender differences in adolescent drug use in terms of parental monitoring and peer deviance.

http://www.findarticles.com/p/articles/mi_m0825/is_4_61/ai_61522787
This website contains the article, "Hirschi's Social Control Theory: A Sociological Perspective on Drug Abuse Among Persons with Disabilities" by Reginald J. Alston, Debra Harley, and Karen Lenhoff. The study the authors completed looks at social control theory as an explanation for drug abuse among the disabled.

http://www.shsu.edu/~piic/summer2002/Hanser.htm
This article provides an excellent discussion of the labeling theory paradigm as an explanation for the complex developments that lead from an inmate's first rape victimization to the eventual acceptance of their new label.

http://www.findarticles.com/p/articles/mi_m2248/is_n125_v32/ai_19417313
This article looks at social control theory, labeling theory, and the delivery of services for drug abuse to adolescents under the supervision of the juvenile justice system. This will provide you with an understanding of how two theories can explain the same phenomenon.

TEST BANK

FILL-IN THE BLANKS

1. For some time, family relationships have been considered a major determinant of

    _____.

2. The educational process and adolescent achievement in school have been linked to

    _____.

3. _____ rejection helps lock these already aggressive kids into a cycle of persistent violence that is likely to continue into early adulthood.

4. _____ seems to be a more significant inhibitor of crime than merely having religious beliefs and values.

5. _____ _____ occurs when behavior is reinforced by being either rewarded or punished while interacting with others.

6. _____ _____ are morally tinged influences that have become entrenched in the culture but are publicly condemned.

7. _____ refers to the movement from one extreme of behavior to another, resulting in behavior that is sometimes unconventional, free, or deviant and at other times constrained and sober.

8. _____ _____ argues that a strong self-image insulates a youth from the pressures and pulls of crimogenic influences in the environment.

9. _____ _____ _____ that people communicate via symbols – gestures, signs, words, or images – that stand for or represent something else.

10. _____ _____ is a process in which the past of the labeled person is reviewed and re-evaluated to fit his or her current status.

TRUE/FALSE QUESTIONS

1. T/F Many criminologists agree that a person's place in the social structure alone can control or predict the onset of criminality.

2. T/F The relationship between family structure and crime is critical when the high rates of divorce and single parents are considered.

3. T/F Schools contribute to criminality in that when they label problem youths they set them apart from conventional society.

4. T/F School level and size have little impact on the likelihood of experiencing theft and violence.

5. T/F As children move through the life course, antisocial friends help youths maintain delinquent careers and obstruct the aging-out process.

6. T/F Social learning theory assumes people are born good and learn to be bad.

7. T/F According to differential association theory, criminal behavior is an expression of general needs and values and is excused by those general needs and values.

8. T/F Negative reinforcement occurs when behavior is punished.

9. T/F Sykes and Matza suggest that people develop a distinct set of justifications for their law-violating behavior.

10. T/F Self-control is manifested through a strong moral sense, which renders people incapable of hurting others and violating social norms.

11. T/F Hirschi's version of social control theory has not been corroborated by other research studies.

12. T/F People interpret symbolic gestures from others and incorporate them in their self-image.

13. T/F Social reaction theory is especially concerned with why people originally engage in acts that result in their being labeled.

14. T/F Secondary deviance involves resocialization into a deviant role.

15 T/F In an in-depth analysis of research on the crime-producing effects of labels, criminologist Charles Tittle found little evidence that stigma produces crime.

MULTIPLE CHOICE QUESTIONS

1. The social process theories include all of the following **EXCEPT**:
    a. social learning theory
    b. social control theory
    c. labeling theory
    d. theory of anomie

2. Which is **NOT** one of Sutherland's principles of differential association?
    a. criminal behavior is learned.
    b. learning criminal behavior is different from other learning.
    c. learning is a by-product of interaction.
    d. criminal techniques are learned.

3. Punishing behavior is referred to as:
    a. differential reinforcement
    b. direct conditioning
    c. negative reinforcement
    d. differential association

4. Morally tinged influences that have become entrenched in the culture but are publicly condemned are called:
   a. techniques
   b. drift
   c. neutralizations
   d. subterranean values

5. The movement from one extreme of behavior to another, resulting in behavior that is sometimes unconventional, free, or deviant and at other times constrained and sober is called:
   a. drift
   b. schizophrenia
   c. neutralizations
   d. subterranean values

6. Which of the following is **NOT** one of Sykes and Matza's techniques of neutralization?
   a. deny a victim
   b. deny responsibility
   c. deny the crime
   d. condemn the condemners

7. The theory that argued that a strong self-image insulates a youth from the pressures and pulls of crimogenic influences in the environment is called:
   a. social bond theory
   b. containment theory
   c. neutralization theory
   d. normative theory

8. A person's sensitivity to and interest in others is known as:
   a. involvement
   b. attachment
   c. commitment
   d. belief

9. According to Hirschi, which social institution is the most important attachment an individual should have?
   a. parents
   b. schools
   c. peers
   d. police

10. Time, energy, and effort expended in conventional lines of action such as getting an education and saving money for the future is known as:
    a. attachment
    b. belief
    c. involvement
    d. commitment

11. When people who live in the same social setting often share values, sensitivity to the rights of others and admiration for the legal code, it is known as:
    a. attachment
    b. involvement
    c. belief
    d. commitment

12. Labeling theory is also known as:
    a. social control theory
    b. social learning theory
    c. social reaction theory
    d. neutralization theory

13. The important principle of social reaction theory that the law is applied in a manner benefiting those who hold economic and social power and penalizing the powerless is called:
    a. differential association
    b. differential enforcement
    c. retrospective interpretation
    d. deviance amplification

14. What is **NOT** one of the concerns of labeling theory?
    a. why people are labeled
    b. why people originally engage in criminal acts
    c. the effects of labeling
    d. how the label is applied

15. What is an enduring label that taints a person's identity and changes him or her in the eyes of others called?
    a. primary deviance
    b. reflective role taking
    c. differential social control
    d. stigma

16. The process of labeling produces a re-evaluation of the self, which reflects actual or perceived appraisals made by others. This concept is called:
    a. reflective role taking
    b. stigma
    c. differential social control
    d. secondary deviance

17. When youths believe that others view them as antisocial or troublemakers, they take on attitudes and roles that reflect this assumption; they expect to become suspects and then to be rejected. This process is called:
    a. reflective role taking
    b. stigma
    c. differential social control
    d. secondary deviance

18. The process in which the past of the labeled person is reviewed and re-evaluated to fit his or her current status is called:
    a. deviance amplification
    b. dramatization of evil
    c. reflective role taking
    d. retrospective reading

19. As the negative feedback of law enforcement agencies, parents, friends, teachers, and other figures amplifies the force of the original label, stigmatized offenders may begin to re-evaluate their own identities in a process called:
    a. deviance amplification
    b. dramatization of evil
    c. reflective role taking
    d. retrospective reading

20. Norm violations or crimes that have very little influence on the actor and can be quickly forgotten are called:
    a. contextual discrimination
    b. deviance amplification
    c. primary deviance
    d. secondary deviance

21. The concept of what occurs when a deviant event comes to the attention of significant others or social control agents who apply a negative label?
    a. contextual discrimination
    b. deviance amplification
    c. primary deviance
    d. secondary deviance

22. The term that refers to judges' practices in some jurisdictions of imposing harsher sentences on African Americans only in some instances, such as when they victimize whites and not other African Americans is called:
    a. contextual discrimination
    b. deviance amplification
    c. primary deviance
    d. secondary deviance

23. A person who has been arrested and therefore labeled multiple times over the course of his or her offending career is called a:
    a. labeled person
    b. chronic offender
    c. deviant
    d. stigmatist

24. What is designed to remove both juvenile and adult offenders from the normal channels of the criminal justice process by placing them in programs designed for rehabilitation?
    a. restitution
    b. diversion program
    c. probation
    d. parole

25. When an offender is asked to either pay back the victim of the crime for any loss incurred, or do some useful work in the community in lieu of receiving a court-ordered sentence, it is known as:
    a. restitution
    b. diversion programs
    c. probation
    d. parole

ESSAY QUESTIONS

1. Discuss socialization and the effect of schools, family, and friends on crime.

2. Discuss what is meant by a definition toward criminality.

3. List the techniques of neutralization and describe the concept of neutralization.

4. Describe the elements of the social bond as contained in social bond theory.

5. Describe the labeling process and how it leads to criminal careers.

MATCHING

1. Self-Control
2. Commitment to Conformity
3. Normative Groups
4. Symbolic Interaction Theory
5. Travis Hirschi
6. Primary Deviance
7. Drift
8. Stigma
9. Sykes and Matza
10. Secondary Deviance

A. Social bond theory.
B. Norm violations or crimes that have very little influence on the actor.
C. A strong moral sense.
D. An enduring label that taints a person's identity and changes him or her in the eyes of others.
E. Techniques of neutralization.
F. There is a real, present, and logical reason to obey the rules of society.
G. Occurs when a deviant event comes to the attention of significant others or social control agents who apply a negative label.
H. People communicate via gestures, signs, words, or images that represent something else.
I. The movement from one extreme of behavior to another, resulting in behavior that is sometimes unconventional, free, or deviant and at other times constrained and sober.
J. The high school "in-crowd."

CHAPTER 7 ANSWER KEY

Fill In The Blank Answers

1. behavior
2. criminality
3. peer
4. participation
5. differential reinforcement (or direct conditioning)
6. subterranean values
7. drift
8. containment theory
9. symbolic interaction theory
10. retrospective reading

True/False Answers

1.	F	6.	T	11.	F
2.	T	7.	F	12.	T
3.	T	8.	T	13.	F
4.	F	9.	T	14.	T
5.	T	10.	T	15.	T

Multiple Choice Answers

1.	D	11.	D	21.	D
2.	B	12.	A	22.	A
3.	C	13.	B	23.	B
4.	D	14.	B	24.	B
5.	A	15.	D	25.	A
6.	C	16.	C		
7.	B	17.	A		
8.	B	18.	D		
9.	A	19.	B		
10.	D	20.	C		

Essay Questions

1. Pages 218 – 225
2. Pages 226 – 229
3. Pages 230 – 232
4. Page 234
5. Pages 236 – 238

Matching Answers

1.	C	6.	B
2.	F	7.	I
3.	J	8.	D
4.	H	9.	E
5.	A	10.	G

Chapter 8

Social Conflict Theories: Critical Criminology and Restorative Justice

LEARNING OBJECTIVES

1. Be familiar with the concept of social conflict and how it shapes behavior.

2. Be able to discuss elements of conflict in the justice system.

3. Be familiar with the idea of critical criminology.

4. Be able to discuss the difference between structural and instrumental Marxism.

5. Know the various techniques of critical research.

6. Be able to discuss the term left realism.

7. Understand the concept of patriarchy.

8. Know what is meant by feminist criminology.

9. Be able to discuss peacemaking.

10. Understand the concept of restorative justice.

KEYWORDS AND DEFINITIONS

Marxist criminologists (or radical criminologists): conflict theorists who stress the role that the capitalist economic system has on crime rates. (page 256)

Social conflict theory: criminological theories that allege that criminal behavior is a function of social conflict, a reaction to the unfair distribution of wealth and power in society. (256)

Communist manifesto: Marx focused his attention on the economic conditions perpetuated by the capitalist system. He stated that its development had turned workers into a dehumanized mass who lived an existence that was at the mercy of their capitalist employers. (256)

Productive forces: include such things as technology, energy sources, and material resources. (257)

Productive relations: the relationships that exist among the people producing goods and services. (257)

Capitalist bourgeoisie: the owners of the means of production. (257)

Lumpen proletariat: at the bottom, the fringe members who produce nothing and live, parasitically, off the work of others. (257)

Surplus value: the laboring class produces goods that exceed wages in value. (258)

Dialectic method: based on the analysis developed by the philosopher Georg Hegel (1770–1831). Hegel argued that for every idea, or thesis, there exists an opposing argument, or antithesis. Since neither position can ever be truly accepted, the result is a merger of the two ideas, a synthesis. Marx adapted this analytic method for his study of class struggle. (259)

Thesis: an idea. (259)

Antithesis: an opposing argument to a thesis. (259)

Synthesis: since neither a thesis nor an antithesis can ever be truly accepted, the result is a merger of the two ideas. (259)

Imperatively coordinated associations: these associations comprise two groups: those who possess authority and use it for social domination and those who lack authority and are dominated. (260)

Social reality of crime: criminal definitions (law) represent the interests of those who hold power in society. Where there is conflict between social groups—for example, the wealthy and the poor—those who hold power will be the ones to create the laws that benefit themselves and hold rivals in check. (261)

Power: refers to the ability of persons and groups to determine and control the behavior of others and to shape public opinion to meet their personal interests. (262)

Marginalization: displacement of workers, pushing them outside the economic and social mainstream. (262)

Critical criminologists: view crime as a function of the capitalist mode of production and not the social conflict which might occur in any society regardless of its economic system. (264)

Critical criminology: capitalism produces haves and have-nots, each engaging in a particular branch of criminality. The mode of production shapes social life. Because economic competitiveness is the essence of capitalism, conflict increases and eventually destabilizes social institutions and the individuals within them. (264)

Globalization: usually refers to the process of creating transnational markets, politics, and legal systems—that is, creating a global economy. (264)

Instrumental critical theory: criminal law and the criminal justice system act solely as instruments for controlling the poor, have-not members of society. (265)

Demystify: to unmask the true purpose of law and justice. (265)

Structural critical theory: the relationship between law and capitalism is unidirectional, not always working for the rich and against the poor. (265)

Left realism: a branch of conflict theory that holds that crime is a "real" social problem experienced by the lower classes and that lower-class concerns about crime must be addressed by radical scholars. (268)

Preemptive deterrence: an approach in which community organization efforts eliminate or reduce crime before police involvement becomes necessary. (268)

Critical feminist: view gender inequality as stemming from the unequal power of men and women in a capitalist society, which leads to the exploitation of women by fathers and husbands. Under this system, women are considered a commodity worth possessing, like land or money. (268)

Patriarchy: a system in which men dominate public, social, economic, and political affairs. (269)

Paternalistic families: fathers assume the traditional role of breadwinners, while mothers tend to have menial jobs or remain at home to supervise domestic matters. Within the paternalistic home, mothers are expected to control the behavior of their daughters while granting greater freedom to sons. (270)

Role exit behaviors: without legitimate behavioral outlets, girls who are unhappy or dissatisfied with their status are forced to seek out risky behaviors, including such desperate measures as running away and contemplating suicide. (270)

Egalitarian families: those in which the husband and wife share similar positions of power at home and in the workplace—daughters gain a kind of freedom that reflects reduced parental control. (270)

Power–control theory: encourages a new approach to the study of criminality, one that includes gender differences, class position, and the structure of the family. (272)

Postmodernists (or deconstructionists): have embraced semiotics as a method of understanding all human relations, including criminal behavior. (272)

Semiotics: the use of language elements as signs or symbols beyond their literal meaning. (272)

Peacemaking: the main purpose of criminology is to promote a peaceful, just society. (272)

Restorative justice: using humanistic, nonpunitive strategies to right wrongs and restore social harmony. (273)

Reintegrative shaming: disapproval is extended to the offenders' evil deeds, while at the same time they are cast as respected people who can be reaccepted by society. (274)

Sentencing circle: In some Native American communities, people accused of breaking the law will meet with community members, victims (if any), village elders, and agents of the justice system in a sentencing circle. Members of the circle express their feelings about the act that was committed and raise questions or concerns. (276)

CHAPTER OUTLINE

I. Marxist thought
   A. Productive forces and productive relations
      1. Marx issues the communist manifesto in 1848
      2. Marx identified the economic structures in society that control all human relations
      3. Production has two components
         a. Productive forces
         b. Productive relations
      4. Social classes
         a. Class does not refer to an attribute or characteristic of a person or a group
         b. It denotes position in relation to others
         c. Capitalist bourgeoisie
         d. Proletariat
         e. Lumpen proletariat
   B. Surplus value
      1. The theory of surplus value
      2. Marx believed the ebb and flow of the capitalist business cycle contained the seeds of its own destruction
      3. He used the dialectic method
         a. Thesis
         b. Antithesis
         c. Synthesis
         d. In the end, the capitalist system will destroy itself
   C. Marx on crime
      1. Did not write on crime, but mentioned it
      2. Saw a connection between criminality and the inequities found in the capitalist system
      3. Engels portrayed crime as a function of social demoralization
      4. Workers, demoralized by capitalist society, are caught up in a process that leads to crime and violence
      5. Working people committed crime because their choice is a slow death of starvation or a speedy one at the hands of the law

II. Developing a conflict-based theory of crime
   A. The contribution of Willem Bonger
      1. Famous for his Marxist socialist concepts of crime causation
      2. Crime lies within the boundaries of normal human behavior
      3. Society is divided into haves and have-nots because of capitalism, not ability
      4. Criminal law punishes only the acts that do not injure the interests of the dominant ruling class
      5. Attempts to control law violations through force are a sign of a weak society
      6. Both the proletariat and bourgeoisie are crime-prone
      7. But only the proletariat is officially recognized criminals
         a. The legal system discriminates against the poor by defending the actions of the wealthy
         b. The proletariat is deprived of the materials that are monopolized by the bourgeoisie
      8. Upper-class individuals will commit crime if
         a. They sense a good opportunity to make a financial gain
         b. Their lack of moral sense enables them to violate social rules
      9. Bonger believed that redistribution of property according to one's needs would be the demise of crime
   B. The contribution of Ralf Dahrendorf
      1. Modern society is organized into imperatively coordinated associations
         a. Those that possess authority and use it for social domination
         b. Those that lack authority and are dominated
      2. Proposed a unified conflict theory human behavior
         a. Every society is at every point subject to processes of change as social change is everywhere
         b. Every society displays at every point dissent and conflict as social conflict is everywhere.
         c. Every element in a society contributes to its disintegration and change
         d. Every society is based on the coercion of some of its members by others
   C. The contribution of George Vold
      1. Conflict theory was actually adapted to criminology by George Vold
      2. Crime can also be explained by social conflict
      3. Criminal acts are a consequence of direct contact between forces struggling to control society
      4. Does not explain all types of crime – limited to those involving intergroup clashes

III. Social conflict theory
   A. Social Conflict Research
      1. Comparing the crime rates of members of powerless groups with those of members of the elite classes
      2. Criminologists routinely have found evidence that measures of social inequality are highly associated with crime rates
      3. Economic marginalization produces an inevitable upswing in the murder rate
      4. Racial profiling
      5. Criminal courts are more likely to dole out harsh punishments to the powerless and disenfranchised

IV. Critical criminology
  A. Fundamentals of critical criminology
    1. Critical criminologists view crime as
      a. A function of the capitalist mode of production
      b. Not the social conflict which might occur in any society regardless of its economic system
    2. Capitalism produces haves and have-nots
    3. Each engages in a particular branch of criminality
    4. The mode of production shapes social life
    5. In a capitalist society, those with economic and political power control
      a. The definition of crime
      b. The manner in which the criminal justice system enforces the law
    6. The only crimes available to the poor, or proletariat, are the severely sanctioned "street crimes"
    7. The rich are insulated from street crimes because they live in areas far removed from crime
    8. Globalization
      a. Has replaced imperialism and colonization as a new form of economic domination and oppression
      b. Many critical criminologists blame globalization for the recent upswing in international crime rates
  B. Instrumental versus structural theory
    1. Instrumental view
      a. Criminal law and the criminal justice system act solely as instruments for controlling the poor, have-not members of society
      b. Capitalist justice
        1) Serves the powerful and rich
        2) Enables them to impose their morality and standards of behavior on the entire society
      c. Those who wield economic power define illegal or criminal behavior
      d. They impose the law on those who might threaten the status quo or interfere with their quest for ever-increasing profits
      e. The poor
        1) May or may not commit more crimes than the rich
        2) Certainly are arrested and punished more often
      f. The poor are driven to crime out of frustration because affluence is well publicized but unattainable
      g. Goal of instrumental theorists – demystify law and justice
    2. Structural view
      a. The relationship between law and capitalism
        1) Is unidirectional
        2) Is not always working for the rich and against the poor
      b. Law
        1) Is not the exclusive domain of the rich
        2) Is used to maintain the long-term interests of the capitalist system
        3) Controls members of any class who threaten its existence
        4) Is designed to keep the capitalist system operating efficiently
      c. Anyone, capitalist or proletarian who rocks the boat is targeted for sanction

141

C. Research on critical criminology
  1. Critical criminologists rarely use standard social science methodologies to test their views
  2. Many believe the traditional approach of measuring research subjects is antihuman and insensitive
  3. There have been some important efforts to test its assumptions quantitatively
  4. Critical research tends to be
     a. Historical and analytical
     b. Not quantitative and empirical
  5. Crime, the individual, and the state
     a. Two common themes emerge
        1) Crime and its control are a function of capitalism
        2) The justice system is biased against the working class and favors upper-class interests
     b. Research efforts have yielded evidence linking operations of the justice system to class bias
     c. This type of research
        1) Does not set out to prove statistically that capitalism causes crime
        2) Shows that capitalism creates an environment where crime is inevitable
     d. Must rethink the criminal justice system
  6. Historical analysis – goals
     a. To show how changes in criminal law correspond to the development of the capitalist economy
     b. To investigate the development of modern police agencies
D. Critique of critical criminology
  1. Some charge that its contribution has been "hot air, heat, but no real light"
  2. Some argue that critical theory rehashes the old tradition of helping the underdog
  3. Others suggest that critical theory fails to show attempts at self-regulation by the capitalist system
  4. Some argue critical criminologists refuse to address the problems and conflicts that exist in socialist countries

V. Contemporary forms of critical theory
A. Left realism
  1. Connected to the writings of British scholars John Lea and Jock Young
  2. Reject the utopian views of "idealistic" critical criminologists who portray street criminals as revolutionaries
  3. Their approach is that street criminals prey on the poor and disenfranchised
  4. The poor doubly abused
     a. First by the capitalist system
     b. Then by members of their own class
  5. Approach closely resembles the relative deprivation approach
  6. Crime protection
     a. They argue that crime victims in all classes need and deserve protection
     b. Crime control reflects community needs
     c. Advocate preemptive deterrence
     d. Something must be done to control crime under the existing capitalist system
     e. Left realism has been criticized by radical thinkers as legitimizing the existing power structure

B. Critical feminist theory
   1. Views gender inequality as stemming from the unequal power of men and women in a capitalist society
   2. The origin of gender differences can be traced to
      a. The development of private property
      b. Male domination of the laws of inheritance
   3. This led to male control over property and power
   4. Capitalism lends itself to male supremacy
   5. Capitalist societies are built around patriarchy
   6. Patriarchy and crime
      a. Criminal behavior patterns linked to the gender conflict created by the economic and social struggles common in postindustrial societies
      b. Women are also denied access to male-dominated street crimes
      c. Powerlessness increases the targeting of women in violent acts
      d. Feminists argue that men achieve masculinity at the expense of women
      e. Men need to defend themselves from being contaminated with femininity
      f. Female victimization should decline as women's place in society is elevated
   7. Exploitation and criminality
      a. Sexual victimization of females is a function of male socialization
      b. Exploitation triggers the onset of female delinquent and deviant behavior
   8. How the justice system penalizes women
      a. The justice system and its patriarchal hierarchy contribute to the onset of female delinquency
      b. The juvenile justice system has viewed most female delinquents as sexually precocious girls who have to be brought under control
C. Power–control theory
   1. Hagan's view is that crime and delinquency rates are a function of two factors
      a. Class position (power)
      b. Family functions (control)
   2. Parents reproduce the power relationships they hold in the workplace
   3. A position of dominance at work is equated with control in the household
   4. Parents' work experiences and class position influence the criminality of children.
   5. Paternalistic families
      a. Fathers assume the traditional role as breadwinners
      b. Mothers tend to have menial jobs or serve as homemakers
      c. Mothers are expected to control the behavior of their daughters
      d. Grant greater freedom to sons
      e. Unhappy or dissatisfied girls seek out risky role exit behaviors
   6. Egalitarian families
      a. Husbands and wives share similar positions of power at home and at work
      b. Daughters gain a kind of freedom that reflects reduced parental control
      c. Daughters law-violating behavior mirrors their brothers' behavior
      d. These relationships occur in female-headed households with absent fathers
   7. Evaluating power-control
      a. It encourages a new approach to the study of criminality
      b. It looks at gender differences, class position, and the structure of the family
      c. Not all research is as supportive
D. Postmodern theory
   1. Embrace semiotics as a method of understanding all human relations, including criminal behavior

2. Analyze communication and language in legal codes to determine whether they contain language and content that institutionalize racism or sexism
3. Postmodernists rely on semiotics to conduct their research efforts
4. Postmodernists assert that there are different languages and ways of knowing
5. Those in power can use their own language to define crime and law

E. Peacemaking theory
1. The main purpose of criminology is to promote a peaceful, just society
2. View the efforts of the state to punish and control as crime-encouraging rather than crime-discouraging
3. Advocate such policies as mediation and conflict resolution

VI. Public policy implications of social conflict theory: restorative justice
A. Reintegrative shaming
1. Shame is a powerful tool of informal social control
2. Braithwaite divides the concept of shame into two distinct types
a. The most common form of shaming typically involves stigmatization
1) Stigma is doomed to failure
2) Those who suffer humiliation at the hands of the justice system "reject their rejecters" by joining a deviant subculture of like-minded people
b. The second is reintegrative shaming
1) Disapproval is extended to the offenders' evil deeds
2) Begin to understand and recognize their wrongdoing and shame themselves
3. To be reintegrative, shaming must be brief and controlled and then followed by ceremonies of
a. Forgiveness
b. Apology
c. Repentance
4. To prevent crime, society must encourage reintegrative shaming

B. The concept of restorative justice
1. Often hard to define because it encompasses a variety of programs and practices
2. Its core value can be put into one word: respect
3. Respect insists that we balance concern for all parties
4. What is needed instead is a justice policy that
a. Repairs the harm caused by crime
b. Includes all parties who have suffered from that harm, including
1) Victim
2) Community
3) Offender
5. Offenders must accept
a. Accountability for their actions
b. Responsibility for the harm their actions caused

C. The process of restoration
1. Most conflicts are better settled in the community than in a court
2. Restoration programs typically involve all the parties caught in the complex web of a criminal act in a mutual healing process
3. Elements of the program
a. Offender is asked to recognize that he or she caused injury to personal and social relations and a determination and acceptance of responsibility
b. A commitment to both material restitution and symbolic reparation

      c.   Determination of community support and assistance for both victim and offender
4.   Restoration programs
5.   Balanced and restorative justice
      a.   Restorative justice should be centered on the principle of balance
      b.   Should give equal weight to
            1)   Holding offenders accountable to victims
            2)   Providing competency development for offenders in the system so they can pursue legitimate endeavors after release
            3)   Ensuring community safety

D.   The challenge of restorative justice
1.   While restorative justice holds great promise, there are also some concerns
2.   Fairness cannot be sacrificed for the sake of restoration
3.   Must be wary of the cultural and social differences that can be found throughout our heterogeneous society
4.   The greatest challenge to restorative justice is the difficult task of balancing the needs of offenders with those of their victims
5.   Criminologists are now conducting numerous demonstration projects to find the most effective means of returning the ownership of justice to the people and the community

CHAPTER SUMMARY

In 1848, Karl Marx issued the communist manifesto identifying the economic structures in society that control all human relations. According to Marx, class does not refer to an attribute or characteristic of a person or a group; rather, it denotes position in relation to others. One of his key concepts is that of surplus value, the laboring class produces goods that exceed wages in value. Marx did not write on crime, but he mentioned it, seeing a connection between criminality and the inequities found in the capitalist system. Engels portrayed crime as a function of social demoralization in which workers, demoralized by capitalist society, are caught up in a process that leads to crime and violence.

Conflict-based theories of crime are founded on the works of Bonger, Dahrendorf, and Vold. Bonger argues that criminal law punishes only the acts that do not injure the interests of the dominant ruling class. The legal system discriminates against the poor by defending the actions of the wealthy. The contribution of Ralf Dahrendorf is based on his idea that modern society is organized into imperatively coordinated associations: 1) those that possess authority and use it for social domination and 2) those that lack authority and are dominated. Vold stated that crime can be explained by social conflict because criminal acts are a consequence of direct contact between forces struggling to control society.

Critical criminologists view crime as a function of the capitalist mode of production and not the social conflict which might occur in any society regardless of its economic system. Capitalism produces haves and have-nots and each engages in a particular branch of criminality.

In a capitalist society, those with economic and political power control the definition of crime and the manner in which the criminal justice system enforces the law. Critical criminology has two components: instrumental theory and structural theory. In the instrumental view, criminal law and the criminal justice system act solely as instruments for controlling the poor, have-not members of society and those who wield economic power define illegal or criminal behavior. The goal of instrumental theorists is to demystify law and justice. The structural view argues that the relationship between law and capitalism is unidirectional and is not always working for the rich and against the poor. The law is not the exclusive domain of the rich, but it is used to maintain the long-term interests of the capitalist system.

Some contemporary forms of critical theory are left realism which rejects the utopian views of "idealistic" critical criminologists who portray street criminals as revolutionaries. Their approach is that street criminals prey on the poor and disenfranchised, so the poor are doubly abused: first by the capitalist system and then by members of their own class. This approach closely resembles the relative deprivation approach. Critical feminist theory views gender inequality as stemming from the unequal power of men and women in a capitalist society. Capitalist societies are built around patriarchy. The justice system and its patriarchal hierarchy contribute to the onset of female delinquency. The juvenile justice system has viewed most female delinquents as sexually precocious girls who have to be brought under control. Power–control theory states that crime and delinquency rates are a function of two factors: class position (power) and family functions (control). Parents' work experiences and class position influence the criminality of children. In paternalistic families, mothers are expected to control the behavior of their daughters and grant greater freedom to sons. Unhappy or dissatisfied girls seek out risky role exit behaviors. On the other hand, egalitarian families are ones in which husbands and wives share similar positions of power at home and at work. Daughters gain a kind of freedom that reflects reduced parental control, so the law-violating behavior of daughters mirrors their brothers' behavior.

Postmodern theory analyzes communication and language in legal codes to determine whether they contain language and content that institutionalize racism or sexism. Peacemaking theory promotes a peaceful, just society. Advocates support such policies as mediation and conflict resolution. Reintegrative shaming theory argues that shame is a powerful tool of informal social control. In reintegrative shaming, disapproval is extended to the offenders' evil deeds and offenders begin to understand and recognize their wrongdoing and shame themselves. The concept of restorative justice is often hard to define because it encompasses a variety of programs and practices. Its core value can be put into one word – respect. Respect insists that we balance concern for all parties – victim, community, and offender. Most conflicts are better settled in the community than in a court.

STUDENT EXERCISES

Exercise 1

Go online to http://www.doc.state.mn.us/aboutdoc/restorativejustice/default.htm and evaluate in one or two pages, the restorative justice program that the Minnesota Department of Corrections is using. In your answer address the following questions: does this program serve the interests of the offender? The interests of the victim? The interests of the community? Justify your answers.

Exercise 2

Go to http://www.critcrim.org/redfeather/journal-pomocrim/vol-1-intro/001overview.html and read the article that provides an excellent overview of the postmodernist school of criminology. Then prepare a one to two page paper that provides five major key points contained in the article.

CRIMINOLOGY WEB LINKS

http://www.critcrim.org/
This is the official website of the American Society of Criminology - Division on Critical Criminology and the Academy of Criminal Justice Sciences - Section on Critical Criminology.

http://www.arasite.org/critcrim.html
The website provides a wealth of information about critical criminology. Make sure you check out the various links contained in the homepage.

http://barjproject.org/index.htm
This website contains information on the Community Justice Institute of Florida Atlantic University. It contains links to a substantial number of websites on balanced and restorative justice.

http://www.findarticles.com/p/articles/mi_m2294/is_n5-6_v28/ai_14154682
This article looks at sexual assault and stranger aggression on a Canadian university campus. The main purpose of the paper is to present exploratory Canadian incidence data collected from a sample of eastern Ontario female university students.

http://www.malcolmread.co.uk/JockYoung/
This website contains a number of articles written by Professor Jock Young on left realism.

TEST BANK

FILL-IN THE BLANKS

1. According to Marxist theory, the people who do the actual labor in society are called the
_____.

2. In his analysis, Marx used the _____ _____, based on
the analysis developed by the philosopher Georg Hegel.

3. Bonger believed crime lies within the boundaries of _____ human
behavior.

4. According to Travis Pratt and Christopher Lowenkamp, with economic
_____, people turn to violent crime for survival.

5. According to instrumental critical theory, criminal law and the criminal justice system act
solely as instruments for controlling the _____.

6. _____ deterrence is an approach in which community organization efforts
eliminate or reduce crime before police involvement becomes necessary.

7. _____ is a system in which men dominate public, social, economic, and
political affairs.

8. In _____ families, husband and wife share similar positions of power at
home and in the workplace.

9. Shame is a powerful tool of _____ social control.

10. According to restorative justice, crime is an offense against human
_____.

TRUE/FALSE QUESTIONS

1. T/F Marx wrote a great deal on the subject of crime.

2. T/F Bonger believed society is divided into groups, on the basis of people's innate ability.

3. T/F According to Quinney, criminal definitions (law) represent the interests of all those in
society.

4.   T/F Critical criminologists view crime as a function of the capitalist mode of production and not the social conflict which might occur in any society regardless of its economic system.

5.   T/F An important goal of instrumental theorists is to demystify law and justice.

6.   T/F Left realists state that the poor doubly are abused, first by the capitalist system and then by members of their own class.

7.   T/F Within the paternalistic home, mothers are expected to control the behavior of their sons while granting greater freedom to daughters.

8.   T/F The second priority of restorative justice is to restore the community, to the degree that it is possible to do.

9.   T/F In reintegrative shaming disapproval is extended to the offenders' evil deeds, while at the same time the offenders are cast as respected people who can be reaccepted by society.

10. T/F At the core of all the varying branches of critical criminology is the fact that social structure causes crime.

11. T/F The strength of feminist theory is that it explains how gender differences in the crime rate are a function of capitalist competition and the exploitation of women.

12. T/F The strength of the critical criminology is that it accounts for the associations between economic structure and crime rates.

13. T/F Peacemakers view the efforts of the state to punish and control as promoting a peaceful, just society.

14. T/F Semiotics refers to the use of language elements as signs or symbols beyond their literal meaning.

15 T/F Role exit behaviors include such desperate measures as running away and contemplating suicide.

MULTIPLE CHOICE QUESTIONS

1.   An approach in which community organization efforts eliminate or reduce crime before it becomes necessary to employ police forces is:
   a.   preemptive deterrence
   b.   relative deprivation
   c.   left realism
   d.   specific deterrence

2. Youth who feel that they are not part of society and have nothing to lose by committing crime are known as:
   a. successful
   b. college-bound
   c. graduates
   d. marginalized

3. The theory that experiencing poverty in the midst of plenty creates discontent is known as:
   a. preemptive deterrence
   b. relative deprivation
   c. marginalization
   d. left realism

4. A system where men's work is valued and women's work is devalued is known as:
   a. patriarchal
   b. matriarchal
   c. feminism
   d. status-quo

5. This concept explains why females in a capitalist society commit fewer crimes than males:
   a. patriarchy
   b. capitalism
   c. elite deviance
   d. double marginality

6. White-collar and economic crimes are known as:
   a. patriarchy
   b. capitalism
   c. elite deviance
   d. double marginality

7. Men who struggle to dominate women in order to prove their manliness are:
   a. being gender
   b. having gender
   c. doing gender
   d. have no gender

8. Which group indicts the justice system and its patriarchal hierarchy as contributing to the onset of female delinquency?
   a. female victims
   b. radical feminists
   c. radical Marxists
   d. macho males

9. Women began to be exploited because they provided what type of labor in their homes?
   a. skilled
   b. paid
   c. unskilled
   d. free reproductive

10. Which of the following have been intertwined in an effort to sustain the subordination of women?
    a. capitalism and patriarchy
    b. patriarchy and industrialization
    c. capitalism and industrialization
    d. patriarchy and egalitarianism

11. Who wrote Structural Criminology?
    a. Chesney-Lind
    b. Karl Marx
    c. George Vold
    d. John Hagan

12. Using language as signs or symbols beyond their literal meaning is:
    a. semiotics
    b. phonics
    c. symphonics
    d. acoustics

13. Which theory views the efforts of the state to punish and control as crime-encouraging rather crime-discouraging?
    a. postmodern theory
    b. peacemaking criminology
    c. left realism
    d. feminist theory

14. Restorative justice relies on what type of strategies for crime prevention and control?
    a. punitive
    b. prison
    c. non-punitive
    d. pretrial detention

15. Which of the following is a powerful tool of informal social control?
    a. shame
    b. restitution
    c. diversion programs
    d. probation

16. The most common form of shaming involves:
    a. prison
    b. restitution
    c. stigmatization
    d. compensation

17. When disapproval is extended to the offenders' evil deeds, while at the same time they are cast as respected people who can be reaccepted by society this is known as:
    a. forgiving
    b. reintegrative shaming
    c. stigmatized
    d. punitive

18. Turning the justice system into a "healing" process rather than being a distributor of retribution and revenge is known as:
   a.   restoration
   b.   justice
   c.   restitution
   d.   reintegration

19. Which of the following principles does **NOT** guide restorative justice?
   a.   community ownership of conflict
   b.   material and symbolic reparation for victims and community
   c.   social reintegration of the offender
   d.   ceremonies of forgiveness

20. The core value of restorative justice is:
   a.   honesty
   b.   respect
   c.   truth
   d.   restoration

21. The second priority of restorative justice is:
   a.   to assist victims
   b.   to improve human relationships
   c.   to restore the community
   d.   to restore the offender

22. The major strength of what theory is that it explains the existence of white-collar crime and business control laws?
   a.   structural critical theory
   b.   instrumental critical theory
   c.   left realism
   d.   feminist theory

23. Which theory holds that criminals are revolutionaries?
   a.   structural critical theory
   b.   instrumental critical theory
   c.   left realism
   d.   feminist theory

24. Which theory holds that crime is a rebellion of the lower class?
   a.   structural critical theory
   b.   instrumental critical theory
   c.   left realism
   d.   critical criminology

25. The strengths of which theory are that it accounts for class differentials in the crime rate and shows how class conflict influences behavior?
    a. structural critical theory
    b. instrumental critical theory
    c. social conflict theory
    d. critical criminology

ESSAY QUESTIONS

1. Discuss the concept of social conflict and how it shapes behavior.

2. Discuss the difference between structural and instrumental critical theory.

3. Discuss the concept of patriarchy.

4. Describe feminist criminology.

5. Describe the concept of restorative justice.

MATCHING

1. _____ Demystify
2. _____ Marginalization
3. _____ Paternalistic
4. _____ Karl Marx
5. _____ Bourgeoisie
6. _____ Surplus Value
7. _____ Conflict Theory
8. _____ Antithesis
9. _____ Role Exit Behaviors
10. _____ Left Realism

A. A branch of conflict theory that holds that crime is a "real" social problem experienced by the lower-classes and radical scholars must address those lower-class concerns about crime.
B. People who are thrust outside of the economic mainstream.
C. Communist manifesto.
D. Marx held that the laboring class produces goods that exceed wages in value.
E. The view that the inter-group conflicts and rivalry that exists in every society causes crime.
F. Desperate measures.
G. Leaders are seen as father figures and others are treated as children.
H. People who do the actual labor.
I. An opposing argument.
J. To unmask the true purpose of law and justice.

CHAPTER 8 ANSWER KEY

Fill In The Blank Answers

1. proletariat
2. dialectic method
3. normal
4. marginalization
5. poor
6. preemptive
7. patriarchy
8. egalitarian
9. informal
10. relationships

True/False Answers

1.	F	6.	T	11.	T
2.	F	7.	F	12.	T
3.	F	8.	T	13.	F
4.	T	9.	T	14.	T
5.	T	10.	F	15.	T

Multiple Choice Answers

1.	A	11.	D	21.	C
2.	D	12.	A	22.	A
3.	B	13.	B	23.	B
4.	A	14.	C	24.	C
5.	D	15.	A	25.	D
6.	C	16.	C		
7.	C	17.	B		
8.	B	18.	A		
9.	D	19.	D		
10.	A	20.	B		

Essay Questions

1. Pages 261 – 263
2. Page 265
3. Pages 268 – 270
4. Pages 268 – 272
5. Pages 274 – 275

Matching Answers

1.	J	6.	D
2.	B	7.	E
3.	G	8.	I
4.	C	9.	F
5.	H	10.	A

Chapter 9

Developmental Theories: Life Course and Latent Trait

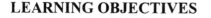

LEARNING OBJECTIVES

1. Be familiar with the concept of developmental theory.

2. Know the factors that influence the life course.

3. Recognize that there are different pathways to crime.

4. Be able to discuss the social development model.

5. Describe what is meant by interactional theory.

6. Be familiar with the "turning points in crime."

7. Be able to discuss the influence of social capital on crime.

8. Know what is meant by a latent trait.

9. Be able to discuss Gottfredson and Hirschi's General Theory of Crime.

10. Be familiar with the concepts of impulsivity and self-control.

KEYWORDS AND DEFINITIONS

Desist: age out of crime as one matures. (page 288)

Developmental theories: seek to identify, describe, and understand the developmental factors that explain the onset and continuation of a criminal career. (288)

Integrated theories: do not focus on the relatively simple question: Why do people commit crime, but on more complex issues: Why do some offenders persist in criminal careers while others desist from or alter their criminal activity as they mature? Why do some people continually escalate their criminal involvement while others slow down and turn their lives around? Are all criminals similar in their offending patterns, or are there different types of offenders and paths to offending? (288)

Life course theories: view criminality as a dynamic process, influenced by a multitude of individual characteristics, traits, and social experiences. As people travel through the life course, they are constantly bombarded by changing perceptions and experiences, and as a result their behavior will change directions, sometimes for the better and sometimes for the worse. (288)

Latent trait theories: hold that human development is controlled by a "master trait," present at birth or soon after. Some criminologists believe that this master trait remains stable and unchanging throughout a person's lifetime, whereas others suggest that it can be altered, influenced, or changed by subsequent experience. (288)

Problem behavior syndrome (PBS): crime is one among a group of antisocial behaviors that cluster together and typically involve family dysfunction, sexual and physical abuse, substance abuse, smoking, precocious sexuality and early pregnancy, educational underachievement, suicide attempts, sensation seeking, and unemployment. (291)

Authority conflict pathway: begins at an early age with stubborn behavior. This leads to defiance (doing things one's own way, disobedience) and then to authority avoidance (staying out late, truancy, running away). (292)

Covert pathway: begins with minor, underhanded behavior (lying, shoplifting) that leads to property damage (setting nuisance fires, damaging property). This behavior eventually escalates to more serious forms of criminality, ranging from joyriding, pocket picking, larceny, and fencing to passing bad checks, using stolen credit cards, stealing cars, dealing drugs, and breaking and entering. (292)

Overt pathway: escalates to aggressive acts beginning with aggression (annoying others, bullying), leading to physical (and gang) fighting, and then to violence (attacking someone, forced theft). (293)

Adolescent-limited offenders: These kids may be considered "typical teenagers" who get into minor scrapes and engage in what might be considered rebellious teenage behavior with their friends. (296)

Life course persisters: begin their offending career at a very early age and continue to offend well into adulthood; they combine family dysfunction with severe neurological problems that predispose them to antisocial behavior patterns. (296)

Social development model (SDM): attempts to integrate social control, social learning, and structural models. (296)

Prosocial bonds: are developed within the context of family life, which not only provides prosocial opportunities but reinforces them by consistent, positive feedback; socialized attachment to conventional institutions, activities, and beliefs. (297)

Interactional theory: an age-graded view of crime that believes that the onset of crime can be traced to a deterioration of the social bond during adolescence, marked by weakened attachment to parents, commitment to school, and belief in conventional values. (301)

Life domains: the way an individual reacts to constraints and motivations are shaped by five key elements of human development: self, family, school, peers, and work. (303)

Turning points: the life events that enable adult offenders to desist from crime. Two critical turning points are marriage and career. (303)

Social capital: positive relations with individuals and institutions that are life sustaining. (305)

Latent trait: a number of people in the population have a personal attribute or characteristic that controls their inclination or propensity to commit crimes. This disposition may be either present at birth or established early in life, and it can remain stable over time. (307)

Human nature theory: personal traits (such as genetic makeup, intelligence, and body build) may outweigh the importance of social variables as predictors of criminal activity. (307)

General Theory of Crime (GTC): modified and redefined some of the principles articulated in Hirschi's social control theory by integrating the concepts of control with those of biosocial, psychological, routine activities, and rational choice theories. (309)

Self-control theory: attributes the tendency to commit crimes to a person's level of self-control. People with limited self-control tend to be impulsive; they are insensitive to other people's feelings, physical (rather than mental), risk-takers, shortsighted, and nonverbal. (310)

Interpersonal coercion: direct, involving the use or threat of force and intimidation from parents, peers, and significant others. (314)

Impersonal coercion: involves pressures beyond individual control, such as economic and social pressure caused by unemployment, poverty, or competition among businesses or other groups. (314)

Coercive ideation: the world is conceived as full of coercive forces that can only be overcome through the application of equal or even greater coercive responses. (314)

Differential Social Support and Coercion Theory (DSSCT): consistently applied social support may eventually negate or counterbalance the crime-producing influence of coercion. Social support comes in two forms: (1) expressive, which includes the sharing of emotions and the affirmation of self-worth and dignity, and (2) instrumental, which includes material and financial assistance and the giving of advice, guidance, and connections for positive social advancement in legitimate society. (315)

Control Balance Theory: expands on the concept of personal control as a predisposing element for criminality. The concept of control has two distinct elements: the amount of control one is subject to by others and the amount of control one can exercise over others. Conformity results when these two elements are in balance; control imbalances produce deviant and criminal behaviors. (315)

Predation: direct forms of physical violence, such as robbery, sexual assault, or other forms of physical violence. (315)

Defiance: challenges control mechanisms but stops short of physical harm: for example, vandalism, curfew violations, and unconventional sex. (315)

Submission: passive obedience to the demands of others, such as submitting to physical or sexual abuse without response. (315)

Exploitation: involves using others to commit crimes: for example, as contract killers or drug runners. (315)

Plunder: involves using power without regard for others, such as committing a hate crime or polluting the environment. (315)

Decadence: involves spur of the moment, irrational acts such as child molesting. (315)

CHAPTER OUTLINE

I.   The life course view
    A.   The Glueck research
        1.   One of the cornerstones of recent life course theories
        2.   Followed the careers of known delinquents to determine the factors that predicted persistent offending
        3.   Focused on early onset of delinquency as a harbinger of a criminal career
        4.   Noted the stability of offending careers
        5.   Children who are antisocial early in life are most likely to continue offending careers into adulthood
        6.   Personal and social factors related to persistent offending
            a.   The most important factor related to persistent offending – family relations
           b.   Physical and mental factors played a role in determining persistent offenders
               1)   Low intelligence
               2)   Background of mental disease
               3)   Powerful (mesomorph) physique
    B.   Life course concepts
        1.   Sampson and Laub
           a.   Rediscovered the Glueck legacy
           b.   Reanalyzed the Glueck data
        2.   Loeber and LeBlanc – criminologists must pay attention to how a criminal career unfolds
        3.   The factors that produce crime and delinquency at one point in the life cycle may not be relevant at another
        4.   As people mature, the social, physical, and environmental influences on their behavior are transformed
    C.   Problem behavior syndrome
        1.   Crime is one among a group of antisocial behaviors that cluster together

2. All forms of antisocial behavior have similar developmental patterns
3. PBS sufferers are prone to more difficulties than the general population
4. PBS has been linked to
    a. Individual-level personality problems
    b. Family problems
    c. Educational failure
D. Pathways to crime
    1. Career criminals may travel more than a single road
    2. Loeber has identified three distinct paths to a criminal career
        a. Authority conflict pathway
        b. Covert pathway
        c. Overt pathway
    3. Each of these paths may lead to a sustained deviant career
    4. Some research support
E. Age of onset/continuity of crime
    1. Age of onset
        a. Most life course theories assume that
            1) The seeds of a criminal career are planted early in life
            2) Early onset of deviance strongly predicts later and more serious criminality
        b. Research supports this
        c. But not all persistent offenders begin at an early age
    2. Continuity and desistance
        a. Age of onset is associated with the continuity of crime
        b. Patterson and his colleagues conclude
            1) Onset of a criminal career is a function of poor parenting skills
            2) Maintenance and support of a criminal career are connected to social relations that emerge later in life
    3. Gender similarities and differences
        a. Males and females – age of onset related to continuity of crime
        b. Some distinct gender differences
            1) For males, the path runs from early onset to problems at work and substance abuse
            2) For females – early onset leads to relationship problems, depression, tendency to commit suicide, and poor health in adulthood
    4. Adolescent-limiteds and life course persisters
        a. Adolescent-limiteds – typical kids
        b. Life course persisters – small group
    5. Supporting research
        a. Recent research has found support for Moffitt's views
        b. Early-onset delinquents are both more prevalent and more generalized in their delinquent activity
        c. Life course persisters manifest significantly more mental health problems
        d. Late-onset adolescent delinquents are more strongly influenced by their delinquent peers and by conflict with parents
        e. Early-onset delinquents also appear to be more violent than their older peers

II. Theories of the criminal life course
A. The social development model
    1. Integrates social control, social learning, and structural models

2. A number of community-level risk factors make some people susceptible to developing antisocial behaviors
3. Children are socialized and develop bonds to their families through four distinct interactions and processes
    a. Perceived opportunities for involvement in activities and interactions with others
    b. The degree of involvement and interaction with parents
    c. The children's ability to participate in these interactions
    d. The reinforcement (such as feedback) children perceive for their participation
4. To control the risk of antisocial behavior, a child must maintain prosocial bonds
5. Antisocial behavior also depends on the quality of their attachments to parents and other influential relations
6. The social development model of antisocial behaviors
    a. Commitment and attachment to conventional institutions, activities, and beliefs insulate youths from criminogenic influences
    b. The most likely to engage in criminal behaviors
        1) Kids who learn deviant attitudes and behaviors
        2) Kids who also have weak ties to conventional institutions
B. Farrington's Integrated Cognitive Antisocial Potential (ICAP) theory
    1. One of the most serious attempts to isolate the factors that predict lifelong continuity of criminal behavior
    2. Many of the same patterns found in the United States
        a. Existence of chronic offenders
        b. Continuity of offending
        c. Early onset of criminal activity
    3. The chronic criminal
        a. Typically a male
        b. Begins as a property offender
        c. Born into a low-income, large family
        d. Family headed by parents who have criminal records
        e. Has delinquent older siblings
    4. Chronic offender tends to associate with friends who are also future criminals
    5. Nonoffenders and desisters
        a. The factors that protected high-risk youths from beginning criminal careers
            1) Having a somewhat shy personality
            2) Having few friends (at age 8)
            3) Having nondeviant families
            4) Being highly regarded by their mothers
        b. What caused offenders to desist?
            1) Holding a relatively good job
            2) Getting married
            3) Employment, marriage, and relocation – but not all succeeded
    6. The ICAP theory
        a. key element – antisocial potential (AP), the potential for antisocial acts
        b. People can be ordered on their antisocial potential along a continuum ranging from low to high AP
            1) High levels of AP are at risk for offending over the life course
            2) Low AP levels live more conventional lives
        c. Short-term AP – a person is influenced by situational inducements to crime
        d. It reflects criminal opportunities and the availability of victims

162

        e.   Crime depends on the interaction between the individual and the environment

C. Interactional theory
   1.   An age-graded view of crime
   2.   The onset of crime can be traced to
      a.   A deterioration of the social bond during adolescence
      b.   Weakened attachment to parents
      c.   Weakened commitment to school
      d.   Weakened belief in conventional values
   3.   Seriously delinquent youth form belief systems consistent with their deviant lifestyle
   4.   Causal influences are bidirectional
      a.   Weak bonds lead kids to develop friendships with deviant peers and get involved in delinquency
      b.   Frequent delinquency involvement further weakens bonds
   5.   Criminality
      a.   Is a developmental process
      b.   Takes on different meaning and form as a person matures
   6.   Testing interactional theory
      a.   Research supports how peer groups influence delinquency
      b.   Research supports the idea that
         a.   Weakened bonds causes delinquency
         b.   Delinquency causes weakened bonds
      c.   Life events can make even high-risk youth resilient to delinquency
      d.   Criminality is part of a dynamic social process and not just an outcome of that process

D. Agnew's General theory of crime and delinquency (GTCD)
   1.   The way an individual reacts to constraints and motivations are shaped by five key elements of human development
      a.   Self
      b.   Family
      c.   School
      d.   Peers
      e.   Work
   2.   Developmental theory because the structure and impact of each life domain continuously evolves
   3.   Each life domain influences the others
   4.   The life domains have largely contemporaneous effects on one another and on crime

E. Sampson and Laub: age-graded theory
   1.   Identify the turning points in a criminal career
   2.   Turning points
      a.   Marriage
      b.   Career
   3.   Social capital influences the trajectory of a criminal career
   4.   Testing age-graded theory
      a.   Criminality appears to be dynamic and is affected by behaviors occurring over the life course
      b.   Of critical importance is early labeling by the justice system
      c.   Career trajectories can be reversed if life conditions improve

      d.   A number of research efforts have supported the idea that social capital reduces crime rates

      e.   High-risk adults who obtain high-quality jobs reduce their criminal activities

      f.   People who maintain a successful marriage and become parents are the most likely to mature out of crime

      g.   The marriage benefit may also be intergenerational

III. Latent trait view

    A. General

       1. Latent traits to explain the flow of crime over the life cycle

       2. People have a personal attribute or characteristic that controls their inclination or propensity to commit crimes

       3. Latent traits are stable

       4. The opportunity to commit crime fluctuates over time

       5. As people mature, they lose the strength and vigor to commit crimes

    B. Crime and human nature

       1. Personal traits outweigh the importance of social variables as predictors of criminal activity

       2. All human behavior, including criminality, is determined by its perceived consequences

       3. A criminal incident occurs when an individual chooses criminal over conventional behavior after weighing the potential gains and losses of each

IV. Latent trait theories

    A. General theory of crime

       1. The act and the offender

          a.   The criminal offender and the criminal act are separate concepts

             1) Criminal acts are illegal events or deeds that offenders engage in when they perceive them to be advantageous

             2) Criminal offenders are predisposed to commit crimes

          b.   Crime is rational and predictable

          c.   If targets are well guarded, crime rates diminish

       2. The theory

          a.   The propensity to commit crimes remains stable throughout a person's life

          b.   What makes people crime-prone?

             1) A person's level of self-control

             2) People with limited self-control tend to be impulsive

             3) They are insensitive to other people's feelings

             4) They are physical (rather than mental)

             5) Risk-takers, shortsighted, and nonverbal

          c.   Those with low self-control enjoy risky, exciting, or thrilling behaviors with immediate gratification

          d.   Root cause of poor self-control is inadequate childrearing practices

          e.   Low self-control develops early in life

          f.   It remains stable into and through adulthood

       3. Self-control and crime

          a.   Explains all varieties of criminal behavior

          b.   Explains all the social and behavioral correlates of crime

          c.   Self-control applies equally to all crimes

       4. There is research support for the general theory of crime

5. Analyzing the general theory of crime
   a. Theory explains
      1) Why some people who lack self-control can escape criminality
      2) Why some people who have self-control might not escape criminality
   b. Criticisms
      1) Tautological – involves circular reasoning
      2) Other research shows different classes of criminals
      3) Fails to address biological/individual differences
      4) Racial and gender differences
B. Differential coercion theory
   1. Identifies another master trait that may guide behavioral choices – coercion
   2. There are two sources of coercion
      a. Interpersonal
      b. Impersonal
   3. A person's ability to maintain self-control is a function of the amount, type, and consistency of coercion experienced as he or she goes through the life course
   4. Prosocial behavior – when the amount of coercion is minimal
   5. Even more debilitating – inconsistent or erratic episodes of coercive behavior
   6. Coercion and criminal careers
      a. Chronic offenders grew up in homes where parents used
         1) Erratic control
         2) Applied it in an inconsistent fashion
      b. Coercive ideation
   7. Differential Social Support and Coercion Theory (DSSCT)
      a. Consistently applied social support may eventually negate or counterbalance the crime-producing influence of coercion
      b. Social support comes in two forms
         1) Expressive
         2) Instrumental
      c. To reduce crime rates, societies must
         1) Enhance the legitimate sources of social support
         2) Reduce the forces of coercion
C. Control balance theory
   1. The concept of personal control as a predisposing element for criminality
   2. The concept of control has two distinct elements
      a. The amount of control one is subject to by others
      b. The amount of control one can exercise over others
   3. Conformity results when these two elements are in balance
   4. Control imbalances produce deviant and criminal behaviors
   5. Those people who sense a deficit of control turn to three types of behavior to restore balance
      a. Predation
      b. Defiance
      c. Submission
   6. An excess of control can also lead to deviance and crime
   7. Those who have an excess of control engage in
      a. Exploitation
      b. Plunder
      c. Decadence

165

V. Evaluating developmental theories
    A. The theories in this chapter share some common ground
        1. Criminal career must be understood as a passage along which people travel
        2. The factors that affect a criminal career may include
            a. Structural factors
            b. Socialization factors
            c. Biological factors
            d. Psychological factors
            e. Opportunity factors
    B. These perspectives differ in their view of human development

VI. Public policy implications of developmental theory

CHAPTER SUMMARY

Problem behavior syndrome (PBS) states that crime is one among a group of antisocial behaviors that cluster together and that all forms of antisocial behavior have similar developmental patterns. PBS has been linked to individual-level personality problems, family problems, and educational failure. Pathways to crime argues that career criminals may travel more than a single road. In fact, Loeber has identified three distinct paths to a criminal career: authority conflict pathway, covert pathway, overt pathway. Each of these paths may lead to a sustained deviant career.

The social development model integrates social control, social learning, and structural models into one new theory. Children are socialized and develop bonds to their families through four distinct interactions and processes. They are 1) perceived opportunities for involvement in activities and interactions with others, 2) the degree of involvement and interaction with parents, 3) the children's ability to participate in these interactions, and 4) the reinforcement (such as feedback) children perceive for their participation. To control the risk of antisocial behavior, a child must maintain prosocial bonds.

The key element in Farrington's Integrated Cognitive Antisocial Potential (ICAP) theory is antisocial potential (AP), the potential for antisocial acts. People can be ordered on their antisocial potential along a continuum ranging from low to high AP. High levels of AP are at risk for offending over the life course while low AP levels live more conventional lives. Interactional theory proposes that the onset of crime can be traced to a deterioration of the social bond during adolescence, weakened attachment to parents, weakened commitment to school, and weakened belief in conventional values. The theory also argues that causal influences are bidirectional. Agnew's General theory of crime and delinquency (GTCD) proposes that the way an individual reacts to constraints and motivations are shaped by five key elements of human development: self, family, school, peers, and work, which continuously evolve and each life domain influences the others. Sampson and Laub's age-graded theory identifies the turning points in a criminal career, marriage and career. Social capital influences the trajectory of a criminal career.

Crime and human nature argues that all human behavior, including criminality, is determined by its perceived consequences. A criminal incident occurs when an individual chooses criminal over conventional behavior after weighing the potential gains and losses of each. General theory of crime states that the propensity to commit crimes remains stable throughout a person's life. What makes people crime-prone is a person's level of self-control. People with limited self control tend to be impulsive, are insensitive to other people's feelings, are physical (rather than mental), risk-takers, shortsighted, and nonverbal. Those with low self-control enjoy risky, exciting, or thrilling behaviors with immediate gratification. The root cause of poor self-control is inadequate childrearing practices. Low self-control develops early in life and it remains stable into and through adulthood.

Differential coercion theory identifies another master trait that may guide behavioral choices – coercion. There are two sources of coercion, interpersonal and impersonal. A person's ability to maintain self-control is a function of the amount, type, and consistency of coercion experienced as he or she goes through the life course. Prosocial behavior occurs when the amount of coercion is minimal. Chronic offenders grew up in homes where parents used erratic control or applied it in an inconsistent fashion. A variation of this theory is differential social support and coercion theory (DSSCT). This theory states that consistently applied social support may eventually negate or counterbalance the crime-producing influence of coercion. Social support comes in two forms, expressive and instrumental. To reduce crime rates, societies must enhance the legitimate sources of social support and reduce the forces of coercion. Control balance theory postulates the concept of personal control as a predisposing element for criminality. The concept of control has two distinct elements: 1) the amount of control one is subjected to by others and 2 the amount of control one can exercise over others. Conformity results when these two elements are in balance. Control imbalances produce deviant and criminal behaviors. Those who sense a deficit of control turn to three types of behavior to restore balance. Those behaviors are predation, defiance, and submission. An excess of control can also lead to deviance and crime and those who have an excess of control engage in exploitation, plunder, and decadence.

The theories in this chapter share some common ground. First, criminal career must be understood as a passage along which people travel. Second, the factors that affect a criminal career may include structural factors, socialization factors, biological factors, psychological factors, and opportunity factors.

STUDENT EXERCISES

Exercise 1

Go online to http://www.wjh.harvard.edu/soc/faculty/sampson/2004.2.pdf and read the article, "A General Age-Graded Theory of Crime: Lessons Learned and the Future of Life-Course Criminology." After reading the article, write a two to three page paper comparing Sampson and Laub's age-graded theory to Hirschi's social bond theory.

Exercise 2

Go to http://wcr.sonoma.edu/v4n1/Manuscripts/katzarticle.pdf and read the article by Rebecca S. Katz. Then prepare a listing of five major key points contained in the article. Next, compare your results with those of one of your classmates, and then two of you are to come up with an agreement on the five most important points in the article.

CRIMINOLOGY WEB LINKS

http://www.lse.ac.uk/collections/methodologyInstitute/pdf/SKanazawa/JCCJ2002.pdf
This is website provides an interesting article on social capital, crime, and human nature. The authors state that their article demonstrates how evolutionary psychology ". . . can bridge theories on the proximate causes of crime with the "ultimate" causes of human nature and human behavior."

http://www.roxbury.net/clcwebch1.pdf
The website provides chapter 1 of *Crime and the Life Course: An Introduction* by Michael L. Benson. It provides a good insight into the book and a basic review of what life course theory is.

http://www.ncjrs.org/pdffiles1/nij/grants/184551.pdf
This website contains a research article titled "Influence of Neighborhood, Peer, and Family Context: Trajectories of Delinquent/Criminal Offending Across the Life Course" by Kenneth C. Land.

http://www.findarticles.com/p/articles/mi_m2294/is_n5-6_v28/ai_14154682
This article looks at sexual assault and stranger aggression on a Canadian university campus. The main purpose of the paper is to present exploratory Canadian incidence data collected from a sample of eastern Ontario female university students.

http://www.malcolmread.co.uk/JockYoung/
This website contains a number of articles written by Professor Jock Young on left realism.

TEST BANK

FILL-IN THE BLANKS

1. _____ _____ _____ view criminality as a dynamic process, influenced by a multitude of individual characteristics, traits, and social experiences.

2. The view that criminality may best be understood as one of many social problems faced by at-risk youth is called _____ _____ _____.

3. Most life course theories assume that the seeds of a _____ _____ are planted early in life and that early onset of deviance strongly predicts later and more serious criminality.

4. Age of onset is associated with another key life course concept, the _____ _____ _____.

5. Moffitt finds that there is a small group of _____ _____ _____ who begin their offending career at a very early age and continue to offend well into adulthood.

6. According to the social development model, a child must maintain _____ _____ to control the risk of antisocial behavior.

7. _____ _____ states that the onset of crime can be traced to a deterioration of the social bond during adolescence, marked by weakened attachment to parents, commitment to school, and belief in conventional values.

8. Sampson and Laub's age-graded theory states that marriage and career are _____ _____ in one's life.

9. _____ _____ involves pressures beyond individual control, such as economic and social pressure caused by unemployment, poverty, or competition among businesses or other groups.

10. _____ involves using power without regard for others, such as committing a hate crime or polluting the environment.

TRUE/FALSE QUESTIONS

1.   T/F According to life course theory, even as toddlers, people begin relationships and behaviors that will determine their adult life course.

2.   T/F The covert pathway escalates to aggressive acts beginning with aggression (annoying others, bullying), leading to physical (and gang) fighting, and then to violence (attacking someone, forced theft).

3.   T/F Not all persistent offenders begin at an early age.

4.   T/F Males, but not females, who have early experiences with antisocial behavior are the ones most likely to be continually involved in this type of behavior throughout the life course.

5.   T/F Early-onset delinquents appear to be more violent than their older peers, who are likely to be involved in nonviolent crimes such as theft.

6.   T/F Unlike Hirschi's version of control theory, which assumes that all attachments are beneficial, the social development model suggests that interaction with antisocial peers and adults promotes participation in delinquency and substance abuse.

7.   T/F According to Farrington's integrated cognitive antisocial potential (ICAP) theory, there are no biological elements to high antisocial potential.

8.   T/F The key idea in interactional theory is that causal influences are bidirectional.

9.   T/F Agnew's General Theory of Crime and Delinquency is essentially an age-graded theory because the structure and impact of each of the life domains are continuously evolving.

10.   T/F According to Sampson and Laub, when adolescents achieve adulthood, those who had significant problems with the law are able to desist from crime if they become attached to a spouse who supports and sustains them, even when the spouse knows they had gotten in trouble when they were young.

11.   T/F Wilson and Richard Herrnstein's human nature theory argues that personal traits—such as genetic makeup, intelligence, and body build—may outweigh the importance of social variables as predictors of criminal activity.

12.   T/F Gottfredson and Hirschi attribute the tendency to commit crimes to a person's level of self-esteem.

13.   T/F Colvin's differential coercion theory suggests that a person's ability to maintain self-control is a function of the amount, type, and consistency of coercion experienced as he or she goes through the life course.

14.   T/F Differential social support and coercion theory posits that consistently applied social support may eventually negate or counterbalance the crime-producing influence of coercion.

15   T/F Plunder involves spur of the moment, irrational acts such as child molesting.

MULTIPLE CHOICE QUESTIONS

1. Which theories seek to identify, describe, and understand the developmental factors that explain the onset and continuation of a criminal career?
   a. latent trait theories
   b. developmental theories
   c. integrated theories
   d. life course theories

2. Which theories view criminality as a dynamic process, influenced by a multitude of individual characteristics, traits, and social experiences?
   a. latent trait theories
   b. developmental theories
   c. integrated theories
   d. life course theories

3. Those who suffer what find themselves with a range of personal dilemmas ranging from drug abuse to being accident prone, to requiring more healthcare and hospitalization, to becoming teenage parents, to having mental health problems?
   a. problem behavior syndrome
   b. latent trait
   c. antisocial potential
   d. criminal onset

4. What begins at an early age with stubborn behavior that leads to defiance (doing things one's own way, disobedience) and then to authority avoidance (staying out late, truancy, running away)?
   a. covert pathway
   b. overt pathway
   c. authority conflict pathway
   d. antisocial potential

5. What escalates to aggressive acts beginning with aggression (annoying others, bullying), leading to physical (and gang) fighting, and then to violence (attacking someone, forced theft)?
   a. covert pathway
   b. overt pathway
   c. authority conflict pathway
   d. antisocial potential

6. In his important work, *Making Good: How Ex-Convicts Reform and Rebuild Their Lives*, criminologist Shadd Maruna found that desistance was a(n):
   a. instantaneous event
   b. ideal
   c. mistake
   d. process

7.   Males and females with antisocial behavior have many similar experiences. Which of the following is a **DISSIMILAR** behavior?
   a.   high rates of mortality
   b.   criminal behavior
   c.   poor sexual health
   d.   tendency to commit suicide

8.   What do we call those who follow the path where the prevalence and frequency of antisocial behavior peaks in adolescence and then diminishes?
   a.   adolescent-limited offenders
   b.   life course persisters
   c.   early onsetters
   d.   latent criminals

9.   What theory holds that commitment and attachment to conventional institutions, activities, and beliefs insulate youths from the criminogenic influences of their environment?
   a.   age-graded theory
   b.   latent trait theory
   c.   social development model
   d.   interactional theory

10.   Farrington's ICAP theory, which of the following is **NOT** a factor that protects high-risk youths from beginning criminal careers?
   a.   having few friends (at age 8)
   b.   having a somewhat outgoing personality
   c.   having nondeviant families
   d.   being highly regarded by their mothers

11.   Which of the following is **NOT** a key element of human development that Agnew's general theory of crime and delinquency calls life domains?
   a.   peers
   b.   family
   c.   church
   d.   school

12.   According to Sampson and Laub's age-graded theory, positive relations with individuals and institutions that are life sustaining are called:
   a.   social capital
   b.   life domains
   c.   transitions
   d.   pathways

13.   A personal attribute or characteristic that controls their inclination or propensity to commit crimes is called:
   a.   problem behavior syndrome
   b.   criminal onset
   c.   antisocial potential
   d.   latent trait

14. Which of the following is **NOT** a characteristic of the latent trait view?
    a. latent traits are stable
    b. the opportunity to commit crime is stable
    c. the propensity to commit crime is stable
    d. people age out of crime

15. What theory argues that personal traits, such as genetic makeup, intelligence, and body build, may outweigh the importance of social variables as predictors of criminal activity?
    a. crime and human nature
    b. general theory of crime
    c. age-graded theory
    d. differential coercion theory

16. What theory considers the criminal offender and the criminal act as separate concepts?
    a. crime and human nature
    b. general theory of crime
    c. age-graded theory
    d. differential coercion theory

17. Gottfredson and Hirschi attribute the tendency to commit crimes to a person's level of:
    a. testosterone
    b. self-reliance
    c. self-control
    d. education

18. Gottfredson and Hirschi trace the root cause of poor self-control to:
    a. poor parenting
    b. inadequate childrearing practices
    c. inadequate education
    d. labeling

19. Mark Colvin identifies another master trait that may guide behavioral choices, which he calls:
    a. control
    b. passivity
    c. activity
    d. coercion

20. Coercion that is direct, involving the use or threat of force and intimidation from parents is called:
    a. interpersonal coercion
    b. personal coercion
    c. intrapersonal coercion
    d. impersonal coercion

21. The mind-set in which the world is conceived as full of coercive forces that can only be overcome through the application of equal or even greater coercive responses is called:
   a.   differential coercion
   b.   coercive ideation
   c.   reactive coercion
   d.   active ideation

22. Differential social support and coercion theory posits that what must be consistently applied to eventually negate or counterbalance the crime-producing influence of coercion?
   a.   early intervention
   b.   psychotherapy
   c.   social support
   d.   coercive ideation

23. What theory believes the concept of control has two distinct elements: the amount of control one is subject to by others and the amount of control one can exercise over others?
   a.   crime and human nature
   b.   general theory of crime
   c.   control balance theory
   d.   differential coercion theory

24. The concept that challenges control mechanisms but stops short of physical harm: for example, vandalism, curfew violations, and unconventional sex is called:
   a.   defiance
   b.   predation
   c.   plunder
   d.   exploitation

25. Those that have an excess of control engage in what activity that involves using others to commit crimes?
   a.   defiance
   b.   predation
   c.   plunder
   d.   exploitation

ESSAY QUESTIONS

1.   Discuss the factors that influence the life course.

2. Discuss the social development model. In your answer, discuss how this theory is different from Hirschi's social bond theory.

3. Explain the concept of "turning points in crime."

4. Discuss the influence of social capital on crime.

5. Discuss Gottfredson and Hirschi's general theory of crime.

MATCHING

1. _____ Adolescent-Limited
2. _____ Turning Points
3. _____ Social Development Model
4. _____ Authority Conflict Pathway
5. _____ Social Capital
6. _____ Problem Behavior Syndrome
7. _____ Overt Pathway
8. _____ Covert Pathway
9. _____ Developmental Criminology
10. _____ Life Course Theory

A. A view that a number of community-level risk factors make some people susceptible to develop antisocial behaviors.
B. Pathway to crime that escalates to aggressive acts beginning with aggression, leading to physical fighting and then to violence.
C. A stable feature, characteristic, property or condition, present at birth or soon after, that makes some people crime-prone over the life course.
D. Pathway to crime that begins at an early age with stubborn behavior.
E. Antisocial behavior for most offenders peaks during adolescence and then diminishes.
F. A view that both biological and psychological traits influence the crime-noncrime choice.
G. A small group of offenders who begin their career at an early age and then continue to offend well into adulthood.
H. A view that even as toddlers, people begin relationships and behaviors that will determine their adult life course.
I. Positive relations with individuals and institutions that are life-sustaining.
J. Life events which enable adult offenders to desist from crime.

CHAPTER 9 ANSWER KEY

Fill In The Blank Answers

1. life course theories
2. problem behavior syndrome
3. criminal career
4. continuity of crime
5. life course persisters
6. prosocial bonds
7. interactional theory
8. turning points
9. impersonal coercion
10. plunder

True/False Answers

1.	T	6.	T	11.	T
2.	F	7.	F	12.	F
3.	T	8.	T	13.	T
4.	F	9.	F	14.	T
5.	T	10.	T	15.	F

Multiple Choice Answers

1.	B	11.	C	21.	B
2.	D	12.	A	22.	C
3.	A	13.	D	23.	C
4.	C	14.	B	24.	A
5.	B	15.	A	25.	D
6.	D	16.	B		
7.	D	17.	C		
8.	A	18.	B		
9.	C	19.	D		
10.	B	20.	A		

Essay Questions

1. Pages 289 – 290
2. Pages 296 – 297
3. Pages 304 – 305
4. Page 305
5. Page 303

Matching Answers

1.	J	6.	C
2.	A	7.	F
3.	I	8.	D
4.	B	9.	E
5.	H	10.	G

Chapter 10

Violent Crime

LEARNING OBJECTIVES

1. Be familiar with the various causes of violent crime.

2. Know the concept of the brutalization process.

3. Be able to discuss the history of rape and know the different types of rape.

4. Be able to discuss the legal issues in rape prosecution.

5. Recognize that there are different types of murder.

6. Be able to discuss the differences among serial killing, mass murder, and spree killing.

7. Be familiar with the nature of assault in the home.

8. Understand the careers of armed robbers.

9. Be able to discuss newly emerging forms of violence such as stalking, hate crimes, and workplace violence.

10. Understand the different types of terrorism and what is being done to combat terrorist activities.

KEYWORDS AND DEFINITIONS

Expressive violence: acts that vent rage, anger, or frustration. (page 332)

Instrumental violence: designed to improve the financial or social position of the criminal, for example, through an armed robbery or murder for hire. (332)

Crusted over: children who do not let people inside, nor do they express their feelings. They exploit others and in turn are exploited by those older and stronger; as a result, they develop a sense of hopelessness. They find that parents and teachers focus on their failures and problems, not their achievements. Consequently, they are vulnerable to the lure of delinquent gangs and groups. (337)

Subculture of violence: norms are separate from society's central, dominant value system. In this subculture, a potent theme of violence influences lifestyles, the socialization process, and interpersonal relationships; they expect that violence will be used to solve social conflicts and dilemmas. (337)

Gang rape: forcible rape involving multiple offenders. (341)

Serial rape: engage in multiple rapes. (342)

Acquaintance rape: involves someone known to the victim, including family members and friends. (342)

Statutory rape: rape in which the victim is underage. (342)

Marital rape: rape in which there is forcible sex between people who are legally married to each other. (342)

Marital exemption: a legally married husband could not be charged with raping his wife. (343)

Virility mystique: the belief that males must separate their sexual feelings from needs for love, respect, and affection. (344)

Hypermasculine: men who typically have a callous sexual attitude and believe violence is manly. (344)

Narcissistic personality disorder: a pattern of traits and behaviors that indicate infatuation and fixation with one's self to the exclusion of all others and the egotistic and ruthless pursuit of one's gratification, dominance, and ambition. (344)

Aggravated rape: involving multiple offenders, weapons, and victim injuries. (345)

Consent: It is essential to prove that the attack was forced and that the victim did not give voluntary consent to her attacker. In a sense, the burden of proof is on the victim to show that her character is beyond question and that she in no way encouraged, enticed, or misled the accused rapist. (345)

Shield laws: protect women from being questioned about their sexual history unless it directly bears on the case. In some instances these laws are quite restrictive, whereas in others they grant the trial judge considerable discretion to admit prior sexual conduct in evidence if it is deemed relevant for the defense. (345)

Murder: the unlawful killing of a human being with malice aforethought. (346)

Premeditation: the killing was considered beforehand and suggests that it was motivated by more than a simple desire to engage in an act of violence. (346)

Deliberation: the killing was planned after careful thought rather than carried out on impulse. (346)

Felony murder: a killing accompanying a felony, such as robbery or rape, usually constitutes first-degree murder. (346)

Second-degree murder: requires the killer to have malice aforethought but not premeditation or deliberation. (346)

Manslaughter: homicide without malice. (346)

Nonnegligent manslaughter: a killing committed in the heat of passion or during a sudden quarrel that provoked violence. (346)

Involuntary manslaughter (or negligent manslaughter): a killing that occurs when a person's acts are negligent and without regard for the harm they may cause others. (346)

Feticide: a murder of a fetus that has not yet been delivered. (347)

Infanticide: murders involving very young children. (348)

Eldercide: murders involving senior citizens. (348)

Serial murder: murders committed over a long period of time. (350)

Mass murder: many victims killed in a single, violent outburst. (351)

Road rage: motorists who assault each other. (353)

Child abuse: any physical or emotional trauma to a child for which no reasonable explanation, such as an accident or ordinary disciplinary practices, can be found. (353)

Neglect: not providing a child with the care and shelter to which he or she is entitled. (353)

Sexual abuse: the exploitation of children through rape, incest, and molestation by parents or other adults. (354)

Acquaintance robbery: robberies committed against people the robbers know. (356)

Hate crimes (or Bias crimes): violent acts directed toward a particular person or members of a group merely because the targets share a discernible racial, ethnic, religious, or gender characteristic. (359)

Thrill-seeking hate crimes: in the same way some kids like to get together to shoot hoops, hatemongers join forces to have fun by bashing minorities or destroying property; inflicting pain on others gives them a sadistic thrill. (360)

Reactive (defensive) hate crimes: perpetrators of these crimes rationalize their behavior as defensive stands taken against outsiders whom they believe threaten their community or way of life. (360)

Mission hate crimes: some disturbed individuals see it as their duty to rid the world of evil; they are on a "mission." (360)

Retaliatory hate crimes: These offenses are committed in response to a hate crime, whether real or perceived; whether the original incident actually occurred is irrelevant. (360)

Workplace violence: irate employees or former employees attack coworkers or sabotage machinery and production lines; it is now considered the third leading cause of occupational injury or death. (362)

Sufferance: the aggrieved party may do nothing to rectify the situation; over time, the unresolved conflict may be compounded by other events that cause an eventual eruption. (362)

Terrorism: a political crime, it is an act which must carry with it the intent to disrupt and change the government and must not be merely a common-law crime committed for greed or egotism. (364)

International terrorism: terrorism involving citizens or the territory of more than one country. (364)

Terrorist group: any group that practices, or that has significant subgroups that practice, international terrorism. (364)

Guerilla: are located in rural areas and attack the military, the police, and government officials. Their organizations can grow quite large and eventually take the form of a conventional military force. (364)

Death squads: government troops or civilian groups attempting to destroy political opposition parties. (368)

USA Patriot Act (USAPA): created new laws and made changes to over fifteen different existing statutes. Its aims were to give sweeping new powers to domestic law enforcement and international intelligence agencies in an effort to fight terrorism, to expand the definition of terrorist activities, and to alter sanctions for violent terrorism. (370)

CHAPTER OUTLINE

I. The causes of violence
    A. Personal traits and makeup
        1. Dorothy Otnow Lewis
            a. Major neurological impairment
            b. Low intelligence as measured on standard IQ tests
            c. Psychotic close relatives

        d.   Psychotic symptoms
   2.   Guilty by Reason of Insanity, Lewis finds that death row inmates have a history of
        a.   Mental impairment
        b.   Intellectual dysfunction
B.   Evolutionary factors/human instinct
   1.   Freud maintained that humans possess two opposing instinctual drives that interact to control behavior
        a.   Eros, the life instinct, which drives people toward self-fulfillment and enjoyment
        b.   Thanatos, the death instinct, which produces self-destruction
   2.   Lorenz argued that aggressive energy is produced by inbred instincts that are independent of environmental forces
   3.   Evolutionary theories in criminology suggest that violent behavior is committed predominantly by males
C.   Substance abuse has been linked to violence in one of three ways
   1.   Psychopharmacological relationship – violence may be the direct consequence of ingesting mood-altering substances
   2.   Economic compulsive behavior – drug users/dealers resort to violence to obtain the financial resources to support their habit
   3.   Systemic link – violence escalates when drug-dealing gangs flex their muscle to dominate territory and drive out rivals
D.   Socialization and upbringing are responsible for the onset of violent acts
   1.   Absent or deviant parents
   2.   Inconsistent discipline
   3.   Physical abuse
   4.   Lack of supervision
   5.   Abused children
        a.   Abused later engage in delinquent behaviors, including violence
        b.   Sexual abuse is also a constant factor in father (patricide) and mother (matricide) killings
        c.   Abuse may have the greatest effect if it is persistent and extends from childhood to adolescence
        d.   Abusive childhood experiences may be a key factor in the later development of relationship aggression
   6.   The brutalization process
        a.   Athens finds that people can be classified into three groups based on their aggressive tendencies
            1)   Nonviolent
            2)   Violent (those who attack others physically with the intention of harming them)
            3)   Incipiently violent (those who are willing and ready to attack but limit themselves to violent ultimatums and/or intimidating physical gestures)
        b.   Four distinct types of violent acts
            1)   Physically defensive (in which the perpetrator sees his violent act as one of self-defense)
            2)   Frustrative (in which the offender acts out of anger due to frustration when he cannot get his way)
            3)   Malefic (in which the victim is considered to be extremely evil or malicious)
            4)   Frustrative-malefic (a combined type)

    c.   To become socialized into violence, one must complete the full cycle of the "violentization process"
        1)   Belligerence
        2)   Violent performances
        3)   Virulency
    d.   A significant amount of evidence has shown the association between abuse and violent crime

E.   Exposure to violence
    1.   People who are constantly exposed to violence may adopt violent methods themselves
    2.   People are exposed to violence when they associate with violent peers
    3.   Children living in areas marked by extreme violence may eventually become desensitized to the persistent brutality
    4.   Between 30 and 40 percent of the children who reported exposure to violence also displayed significant violent behavior themselves
    5.   Children living in these conditions become "crusted over"
        a.   They do not let people inside, nor do they express their feelings
        b.   They exploit others and in turn are exploited by those older and stronger
        c.   They develop a sense of hopelessness
        d.   They find that parents and teachers focus on their failures and problems, not their achievements
        e.   They are vulnerable to the lure of delinquent gangs and groups

F.   Cultural values/subculture of violence
    1.   Another theory is that violence is the product of the beliefs, values, and behaviors that develop in the nation's poorest and most disorganized areas
    2.   Some areas contain an independent subculture of violence
    3.   The subculture's norms are separate from society's central, dominant value system
    4.   They expect that violence will be used to solve social conflicts and dilemmas
    5.   Research has shown that the subculture of violence may be found in areas that experience concentrated poverty and social disorganization
    6.   Peer group influences
        a.   Violence rates are highest in urban areas where subcultural values support teenage gangs
        b.   They are also more likely to have peers who are gun owners and are more likely to carry guns outside the home
        c.   Gang violence may be initiated for a variety of reasons
            1)   It enables new members to show toughness during initiation ceremonies
            2)   It can be used to retaliate against rivals for actual or perceived grievances
            3)   It protects ownership, such as when violence erupts when graffiti is defaced by rivals
            4)   It protects turf from incursions by outsiders
        d.   Once in gangs their violent behavior quickly escalates
    7.   Regional values
        a.   Some criminologists have suggested that regional values promote violence
        b.   Not all criminologists agree with the southern subculture concept
    8.   National values – some nations have relatively high violence rates

II. Forcible rape
   A. History of rape
      1. Rape has been a recognized crime throughout history
      2. In early civilization rape was common
   B. Rape and the military
      1. Throughout recorded history, rape has been associated with armies and warfare
      2. Soldiers of conquering armies have considered sexual possession of their enemies' women one of the spoils of war
   C. Incidence of rape
      1. UCR data
         a. About 93, 000 rapes or attempted rapes were reported to U.S. police in 2003
         b. A rate of about 62 per 100,000 females
      2. Population density influences the rape rate
      3. The police make arrests in slightly more than half of all reported rape offenses
      4. Rape is a warm-weather crime
      5. National Crime Victimization Survey (NCVS) – rape is frequently underreported
      6. Rape rate has been in a sharp decline, falling 68 percent between 1993 and 2003
   D. Types of rape and rapists
      1. According to Groth, every rape encounter contains at least one of these three elements
         a. Anger – 55%
         b. Power – 40%
         c. Sadism – 5%
      2. Groth's major contribution – rape is generally a crime of violence, not a sexual act
      3. Gang versus individual rape
         a. As many as 25 percent or more of rapes involve multiple offenders
         b. Little difference in the demographic characteristics of single- or multiple-victim rapes
         c. Women who are attacked by multiple offenders are subject to more violence
         d. Gang rape victims are more likely to
            1) Resist and face injury than those attacked by single offenders
            2) Call police
            3) Seek therapy
            4) Contemplate suicide
      4. Serial rape
         a. Some rapists are one-time offenders; others engage in multiple or serial rapes
         b. Some serial rapists commit "blitz rapes," in which they attack their victims without warning
         c. Others try to "capture" their victims by striking up a conversation or offering them a ride
         d. Others use personal or professional relationships to gain access to their targets
      5. Acquaintance rape involves someone known to the victim
         a. Types
            1) Date rape
            2) Statutory rape
            3) Marital rape
         b. Stranger rapes
            1) Are typically more violent than acquaintance rapes
            2) May be less likely to be prosecuted than acquaintance rapes

      c.   Marital rape
          1)   Marital exemption
          2)   Research – many women are raped each year by their husbands
      d.   Statutory rape
          1)   Sex is not forced or coerced
          2)   Law says young girls are incapable of giving informed consent

E.   The causes of rape
    1.   Evolutionary, biological factors
      a.   The male sexual drive
      b.   Rape is bound up with sexuality as well as violence
    2.   Male socialization
      a.   Some men have been socialized to be aggressive with women and believe that the use of violence or force is legitimate
      b.   Virility mystique
      c.   Gender equality will reduce rape rates because there will be an improved social climate toward women
    3.   Hypermasculinity
      a.   Hypermasculine men typically have a callous sexual attitude and believe violence is manly
      b.   Sexually aggressive males view the female as a legitimate victim of sexual violence
    4.   Psychological abnormality
      a.   Rapists suffer from some type of personality disorder or mental illness
      b.   Evidence linking rape proclivity with narcissistic personality disorder
    5.   Social learning – men learn to commit rapes much as they learn any other behavior
    6.   Sexual motivation
      a.   Most criminologists believe rape is a violent act that is not sexually motivated
      b.   NCVS data reveal
          1)   Victims tend to be young
          2)   Rapists prefer younger, presumably more attractive, victims
          3)   There is an association between the ages of rapists and their victims
          4)   Men choose rape targets of approximately the same age as consensual sex partners
      c.   This pattern indicates that
          1)   Older criminals may rape for motives of power and control
          2)   Younger offenders may be seeking sexual gratification

F.   Rape and the law
    1.   Proving rape
      a.   Proving guilt in a rape case is extremely challenging for prosecutors
      b.   Some male psychiatrists and therapists still maintain
          1)   That women fantasize that a rape has occurred
          2)   They may falsely accuse their alleged attackers
      c.   Defense lawyers may claim that the rape charge against their client was motivated by
          1)   Jealousy
          2)   False marriage proposals
          3)   Pregnancy
      d.   Jurors are sometimes swayed by that the rape was victim precipitated
      e.   There is always fear that a frightened and traumatized victim may identify the wrong man

2. Consent
   a. It is essential to prove that
      1) The attack was forced
      2) That the victim did not give voluntary consent to her attacker
   b. In a sense, the burden of proof is on the victim to show that
      1) Her character is beyond question
      2) She in no way encouraged, enticed, or misled the accused rapist
   c. Proving victim dissent is not a requirement in any other violent crime
3. Reform
   a. Rape laws have been changing around the country
   b. Sexual assault laws outlaw any type of forcible sex, including homosexual rape
   c. Most states and the federal government have developed shield laws
   d. Violence Against Women Act in 1994 – statute allows rape victims to sue in federal court
4. Limits of reform – prosecutors may be influenced in their decision to bring charges by the circumstances of a crime

III. Murder and homicide
   A. Degrees of murder
      1. First-degree murder
         a. Premeditation
         b. Deliberation
         c. Felony murder
      2. Second-degree murder – aforethought, but not premeditation or deliberation
         a. Manslaughter
         b. Voluntary or nonnegligent manslaughter
         c. Involuntary or negligent manslaughter
      3. "Born and alive" – feticide
   B. The nature and extent of murder
      1. Murder tends to be an urban crime
      2. More than half of the homicides occur in cities with a population of 100,000 or more
      3. Almost ¼ of homicides occur in cities with a population of more than 1 million
      4. Murder victims and offenders tend to be males
      5. Approximately 1/3 of murder victims and almost ½ the offenders are under 25
      6. Slightly less than half of all victims are African Americans
      7. Slightly less than half are white
      8. African Americans are disproportionately represented as both homicide victims and offenders
      9. Infanticide
      10. Eldercide
   C. Murderous relations
      1. Spousal relations
         a. The rate of homicide among cohabitating couples has declined significantly during the past two decades
         b. The number of unmarried men killed by their partners has declined
         c. The number of women killed by their partners has increased dramatically
         d. Research indicates that most females who kill their mates do so after suffering repeated violent attacks

2. Personal relations
   a. Most murders occur among people who are acquainted
   b. Homicides follow a sequential pattern
      1) First, the victim makes what the offender considers an offensive move
      2) The offender typically retaliates verbally or physically
      3) An agreement to end things violently is forged with the victim's provocative response
      4) The battle ensues, leaving the victim dead or dying
      5) The offender's escape is shaped by his or her relationship to the victim or the reaction of the audience, if any
3. Stranger relations
   a. Over the past decade, the number of stranger homicides has increased
   b. Today more than half of murderers are strangers to their victims
4. Student relations
   a. Violence in schools has become commonplace
   b. School shootings are relatively rare

D. Serial murder
   1. Serial killers operate over a long period
   2. Mass murderers kill many victims in a single, violent outburst
   3. Fox and Levin have their own typology of serial killers
      a. Thrill killers strive for either sexual sadism or dominance
      b. Mission killers want to reform the world or have a vision that drives them to kill
      c. Expedience killers are out for profit or want to protect themselves from a perceived threat
   4. Fox and Levin define four types of mass murderers
      a. Revenge killers seek to get even with individuals or society at large
      b. Love killers are motivated by a warped sense of devotion
      c. Profit killers are usually trying to cover up a crime, eliminate witnesses, and carry out a criminal conspiracy
      d. Terrorist killers are trying to send a message
   5. Serial murderers and their motivations
      a. The cause of serial murder eludes criminologists
      b. Experts have attempted to classify them
         1) Revenge
         2) Sexual sadist
         3) Mysoped or sadistic child killer
   6. Female serial killers
      a. An estimated 10 to 15 percent of serial killers are women
      b. Males are more likely than females to use extreme violence and torture
      c. Gender-based personality and behavior characteristics
         1) Female killers are
            a) Somewhat older than their male counterparts
            b) Abused both alcohol and drugs
            c) Diagnosed as having histrionic, manic-depressive, borderline, dissociative, and antisocial personality disorders
         2) Males
            a) Not likely to be substance abusers.
            b) More often diagnosed as having antisocial personalities

7. Controlling serial killers
    a. FBI has developed a profiling system to identify potential suspects
    b. the Justice Department's Violent Criminal Apprehension Program (VICAP)

IV. Assault and battery
    A. Nature and extent of assault
        1. The pattern of criminal assault is similar to that of homicide
        2. Road rage
        3. Every citizen is bound by the law of assault, even police officers
        4. In 2003 the FBI recorded 857,000 assaults, a rate of about 295 per 100,000 inhabitants
        5. Young, male (about 80 percent), and white
        6. African Americans arrested for assault (33 percent) in numbers disproportionate to their representation in the population
        7. Assault rates are highest in urban areas, during summer, and in southern and western regions
        8. NCVS indicates that only about ½ of all serious assaults are reported to the police
    B. Assault in the home
        1. Criminologists recognize that intrafamily violence is an enduring social problem
        2. Almost half the women who die due to homicide are killed by their current or former husbands or boyfriends
        3. Child abuse
            a. Child abuse can result from actual physical beatings
            b. Another form of abuse results from neglect
            c. Family violence seems to be perpetuated from one generation to another
            d. Behavior of abusive parents can often be traced to negative experiences in their own childhood
            e. Blended families have also been linked to abuse
            f. Parents may also become abusive if they are isolated from friends, neighbors, or relatives who can help in times of crisis
        4. Sexual abuse – the number of reported cases has been in a significant decline
        5. Parental abuse – Arina Ulman and Murray Straus found
            a. The younger the child, the higher the rate of child-to-parent violence (CPV)
            b. At all ages, more children were violent to mothers than to fathers
            c. Both boys and girls hit mothers more than fathers
            d. At all ages, slightly more boys than girls hit parents
        6. Spousal abuse
            a. Spousal abuse has occurred throughout recorded history
            b. The nature and extent of spousal abuse
                1) 60 to 70 percent of evening calls to the police involve domestic disputes
                2) One view is that batterers are damaged individuals who suffer
                    a) A variety of neuropsychological disorders and cognitive deficits
                    b) May have suffered brain injuries in youth
                3) Evolutionary standpoint – males are aggressive toward their mates because they have evolved with a high degree of sexual proprietariness
                4) Growing support is being given to battered women

V. Robbery
    A. Types of robbers
        1. Professional robbers

188

2. Opportunist robbers
3. Addict robbers
B. Acquaintance robbery
1. Victims were more likely to be injured than in stranger robberies
2. Robberies of family members more likely to have a bigger payoff than stranger robberies
C. Rational robbery
1. Patterns of robbery suggest that it is not merely a random act
2. Robberies seem to peak during the winter months
3. Robbers also choose vulnerable victims
4. Female armed robbers are likely to choose female targets
5. When robbing males, women "set them up" in order to catch them off guard
6. Decker and Wright suggest that robbers are rational decision makers

VI. Emerging forms of interpersonal violence
A. Hate crimes
1. Violent acts directed toward a particular person or members of a group merely because the targets share a discernible racial, ethnic, religious, or gender characteristic
2. Can include the desecration of a house of worship or cemetery, harassment of a minority group family that has moved into a previously all-white neighborhood, or a racially motivated murder
3. Usually involve convenient, vulnerable targets who are incapable of fighting back
4. Factors that produce hate crimes
   a. Poor or uncertain economic conditions
   b. Racial stereotypes in films and on television
   c. Hate-filled discourse on talk shows or in political advertisements
   d. The use of racial code language such as "welfare mothers" and "inner-city thugs"
   e. An individual's personal experiences with members of particular minority groups
   f. Scapegoating
5. The roots of hate
   a. McDevitt and Levin identify three motivations for hate crimes
      1) Thrill-seeking hate crimes
      2) Reactive (defensive) hate crimes
      3) Mission hate crimes
   b. McDevitt and Levin with Susan Bennett uncovered a new category of hate crime: retaliatory hate crimes
   c. Hate crimes can be committed by "dabblers"
6. Nature and extent of hate crime
   a. During 2002, there were 9,222 victims associated with 8,832 hate crimes
   b. Racial bias was the motivation for about half the crimes
   c. Most crimes are motivated by race
   d. Most victims reported that they were acquainted with their attackers
7. Controlling hate crimes
   a. Today, almost every state jurisdiction has enacted some form of legislation designed to combat hate crimes
   b. Some criminals choose their victims randomly

       c.   Bias crimes are different
           1)   More likely to be violent and involve serious physical injury
           2)   Have significant emotional and psychological impact on the victim
           3)   Harm not only the victim but also the "target community"
           4)   Violate the shared value of equality among citizens and racial and religious harmony in a heterogeneous society

8. Legal controls

B. Workplace violence
    1. Creating workplace violence
       a.   A management style that appears cold and insensitive to workers
       b.   refusing romantic relationships with the assailants or reporting them for sexual harassment
       c.   A satisfying work environment provides people with life support, stability, and a sense of achievement
    2. The extent of workplace violence
       a.   Cost of workplace violence runs more than $4 billion annually
       b.   On average violence in the workplace accounts for about 18 percent of all violent crime
    3. Can workplace violence be controlled?
       a.   One approach is to use third parties to mediate disputes
       b.   Restorative justice techniques may work particularly well in the workplace

C. Stalking
    1. Affects an estimated 1.4 million victims annually
    2. Most victims know their stalker
    3. Stalkers behave in ways that induce fear
    4. Stalkers do not always make overt threats against their victims

VII. Terrorism
    A. What is terrorism?
       1. An act must carry with it the intent to disrupt and change the government and must not be merely a common-law crime committed for greed or egotism
       2. Most experts agree that it generally involves the illegal use of force against innocent people to achieve a political objective
       3. International terrorism
       4. Terrorist
       5. Terrorism usually involves a type of political crime that emphasizes violence as a mechanism to promote change
       6. Not all terrorist actions are aimed at political change
       7. Terrorist and guerilla
    B. A brief history of terrorism
    C. Contemporary forms of terrorism
       1. Revolutionary terrorists
       2. Political terrorists
       3. Nationalist terrorism
       4. Cause-based terrorism
       5. Environmental terrorism
       6. State-sponsored terrorism
       7. Criminal terrorism
    D. What motivates terrorists?
       1. Terrorist violence is not so much a political instrument as an end in itself

CHAPTER SUMMARY

The causes of violence are many and varied. Among the explanations for it are personal traits and makeup, evolutionary factors and human instinct, substance, socialization and upbringing, exposure to violence, cultural values, and the subculture of violence.

Forcible rape has been a recognized crime throughout history. The Uniform Crime Report data show that approximately 93, 000 rapes or attempted rapes were reported to U.S. police in 2003, a rate of about 62 per 100,000 females. The National Crime Victimization Survey (NCVS) shows that rape is frequently underreported. The causes of rape include evolutionary or biological factors, male socialization, hypermasculinity, psychological abnormality, social learning, and sexual motivation. Proving guilt in a rape case is extremely challenging for prosecutors. The most difficult issue is consent because it is essential to prove that the attack was forced and that the victim did not give voluntary consent to her attacker.

Murder and homicide tend to be urban crimes and occur in cities with a population of 100,000 or more. Murder victims and offenders tend to be males and under 25. African Americans are disproportionately represented as both homicide victims and offenders. The rate of homicide among cohabiting couples has declined significantly during the past two decades. Most murders occur among people who are acquainted. Over the past decade, the number of stranger homicides has increased and today more than half of murderers are strangers to their victims. Violence in schools has become commonplace, but school shootings are relatively rare. Serial killers operate over a long period, while mass murderers kill many victims in a single, violent outburst. Female killers are somewhat older than their male counterparts; abused both alcohol and drugs; and diagnosed as having histrionic, manic-depressive, borderline, dissociative, and antisocial personality disorders. Males are not likely to be substance abusers. They are more often diagnosed as having antisocial personalities.

The pattern of criminal assault is similar to that of homicide. In 2003, the FBI recorded 857,000 assaults, a rate of about 295 per 100,000 inhabitants. The offenders are typically young, male, and white. However, African Americans are arrested for assault in numbers that are disproportionate to their representation in the population. Assault rates are highest in urban areas, during the summer, and in southern and western regions. The National Crime Victimization Survey indicates that only about ½ of all serious assaults are reported to the police. Criminologists recognize that intrafamily violence is an enduring social problem. Almost half the women who die due to homicide are killed by their current or former husbands or boyfriends. Family violence seems to be perpetuated from one generation to another. Spousal abuse has occurred throughout recorded history. Approximately 60 to 70 percent of evening calls to the police involve domestic disputes.

There are three types of robbers: professional robbers, opportunist robbers, and addict robbers. Patterns of robbery suggest that it is not merely a random act, and it seems to peak during the winter months. Female armed robbers are likely to choose female targets, but when robbing males, women "set them up" in order to catch them off guard. Decker and Wright suggest that robbers are rational decision makers.

Hate crimes are violent acts directed toward a particular person or members of a group merely because the targets share a discernible racial, ethnic, religious, or gender characteristic. Factors that produce hate crimes are poor or uncertain economic conditions, racial stereotypes in films and on television, hate-filled discourse on talk shows or in political advertisements, the use of racial code language such as "welfare mothers" and "inner-city thugs," an individual's personal experiences with members of particular minority groups, or scapegoating. McDevitt and Levin identify three motivations for hate crimes: thrill-seeking hate crimes, reactive (defensive) hate crimes, and mission hate crimes. McDevitt, Levin, and Bennett uncovered a new category of hate crime called retaliatory hate crimes. Hate crimes can also be committed by "dabblers." During 2002, there were 9,222 victims associated with 8,832 hate crimes, with racial bias being the motivation for about half the crimes. Today, almost every state jurisdiction has enacted some form of legislation designed to combat hate crimes.

There are two factors creating workplace violence: a management style that appears cold and insensitive to workers and refusing romantic relationships with the assailants or reporting them for sexual harassment. A satisfying work environment provides people with life support, stability, and a sense of achievement. The cost of workplace violence runs more than $4 billion annually and on average, violence in the workplace accounts for about 18 percent of all violent crime. Stalking affects an estimated 1.4 million victims annually. Most victims know their stalker. Stalkers behave in ways that induce fear, but they do not always make overt threats against their victims.

Terrorism is an act that carries with it the intent to disrupt and change the government and is not merely a common-law crime committed for greed or egotism. Most experts agree that it generally involves the illegal use of force against innocent people to achieve a political objective. Terrorism usually involves a type of political crime that emphasizes violence as a mechanism to promote change.

STUDENT EXERCISES

Exercise 1

Go online to http://www.ojp.usdoj.gov/bjs/homicide/homtrnd.htm and read about homicide trends in the United States. Pick out one topic listed in the contents, browse that topic, and write a one or two page summary on that aspect of homicide trends.

Exercise 2

Go to http://www.ncjrs.org/pdffiles1/nij/grants/193800.pdf and read the paper by Richard Wright and Scott H. Decker. The paper discusses robbery from the point of view of offenders themselves. Make a listing of those points concerning robbery that are different from or not included in what the author of the text has said concerning robbery. Be prepared to present your answer in class.

CRIMINOLOGY WEB LINKS

http://www.ojp.usdoj.gov/BJA/pubs/SniperRpt.pdf
This is website contains a document addressing the problems of managing a multijurisdictional case like the sniper investigation involving John Lee Malvo and John Allen Muhammad. The large document contains a wealth of information on a major case that kept Americans glued to the television for a long period of time.

http://www.ncjrs.org/pdffiles1/bja/205263.pdf
The website provides information concerning Project Safe Neighborhoods, a national program designed to reduce gun violence in America.

http://www.ojp.usdoj.gov/bjs/pub/pdf/vvcs00.pdf
This website contains a Bureau of Justice Statistics document concerning violent victimization of college students.

http://www.mencanstoprape.org/
This is the official website of Men Can Stop Rape, a non-profit organization dedicated to changing the attitudes of men toward rape and sexual violence.

http://www.vaw.umn.edu/documents/vawnet/mrape/mrape.html
This website contains a thoughtful article on marital rape by Raquel Kennedy Bergen.

TEST BANK

FILL-IN THE BLANKS

1. Acts that vent rage, anger, or frustration are called _____ _____.

2. Children who are "_____ _____" do not let people inside, nor do they express their feelings; they exploit others and in turn are exploited by those older and stronger.

3. Date rape is believed to be frequent on _____ _____.

4. _____ means the killing was planned after careful thought rather than carried out on impulse.

5. _____ _____ want to reform the world or have a vision that drives them to kill.

6. At all ages, slightly more boys than girls hit _____.

7. Robbers show evidence of being highly _____ offenders.

8. _____ _____ is now considered the third leading cause of occupational injury or death.

9. _____ terrorism promotes the interests of a minority ethnic or religious group that believes it has been persecuted under majority rule and wishes to carve out its own independent homeland.

10. In the wake of the 9/11 attacks, the United States has moved to freeze the _____ assets of groups they consider to engage in, or support, terrorist activities.

TRUE/FALSE QUESTIONS

1. T/F Sniper attacks may reinforce the impression that the United States is an extremely violent society, especially since violence rates have risen here while they are declining elsewhere around the world.

2. T/F Absent or deviant parents, inconsistent discipline, physical abuse, and lack of supervision have all been linked to persistent violent offending.

3. T/F All criminologists agree with the southern subculture concept.

4. T/F Like other violent crimes, the rape rate has been in a decade-long decline.

5. T/F In some states, defendants can claim they mistakenly assumed their victims were above the age of consent, whereas in others, "mistake-of-age" defenses are ignored.

6. T/F The victim of rape must still establish her intimate, detailed knowledge of the act for her testimony to be believed in court.

7. T/F The rate of homicide among cohabitating couples has risen significantly during the past two decades.

8. T/F The cause of serial murder eludes criminologists.

9. T/F The behavior of abusive parents can often be traced to negative experiences in their own childhood.

10. T/F The typical armed robber is likely to be a professional who carefully studies targets while planning a crime.

11. T/F Hate crimes usually involve convenient, vulnerable targets who are incapable of fighting back.

12. T/F There are specific hate crime laws that actually originated after the Revolutionary War and that were designed to protect the rights of freed slaves.

13. T/F Most victims know their stalker.

14. T/F Contemporary transnational terrorists rely solely on violence to achieve their goals.

15 T/F Many terrorists appear to be uneducated members of the lower class.

MULTIPLE CHOICE QUESTIONS

1. Violence designed to improve the financial or social position of the criminal, for example, through an armed robbery or murder for hire is what kind of violence?
   a. radical
   b. expressive
   c. mission
   d. instrumental

2. Because aggression is instinctual, Freud saw little hope for its:
   a. treatment
   b. extinction
   c. evolution
   d. sexual orientation

3.   Evolutionary theories in criminology suggest that violent behavior is committed predominantly by:
    a.   whites
    b.   females
    c.   males
    d.   minorities

4.   Violence that may be the direct consequence of ingesting mood-altering substances is called:
    a.   psychopharmacological relationship
    b.   economic compulsive behavior
    c.   systemic link
    d.   drug altered violence

5.   Lewis found in her study of juvenile death row inmates that all had long histories of intense:
    a.   drug abuse
    b.   child abuse
    c.   emotions
    d.   relationships

6.   Empirical evidence shows that violence rates are highest in urban areas where subcultural values support:
    a.   school dropouts
    b.   patriarchy
    c.   single female headed households
    d.   teenage gangs

7.   Like other violent crimes, the rape rate has been in a decade-long:
    a.   incline
    b.   steady path
    c.   decline
    d.   steep increase

8.   The type of rape that involves an attacker who does not want to harm his victim as much as he wants to possess her sexually is called:
    a.   anger rape
    b.   power rape
    c.   sadistic rape
    d.   possession rape

9.   What type of rape constitutes the bulk of sexual assaults?
    a.   acquaintance rape
    b.   serial rape
    c.   gang rape
    d.   date rape

10. The belief that males must separate their sexual feelings from needs for love, respect, and affection is called:
    a. hypermasculinity
    b. virility mystique
    c. marital exemption
    d. narcissistic personality disorder

11. What protects women from being questioned about their sexual history unless it directly bears on the case?
    a. rape law
    b. Supreme Court decision
    c. Violence Against Women Act
    d. shield laws

12. What means the killing was planned after careful thought rather than carried out on impulse?
    a. premeditation
    b. felony murder
    c. deliberation
    d. second-degree murder

13. What refers to a killing committed in the heat of passion or during a sudden quarrel that provoked violence?
    a. nonnegligent manslaughter
    b. manslaughter
    c. negligent manslaughter
    d. feticide

14. Today more than half of murderers are what to their victims, a significant increase from years past?
    a. strangers
    b. related
    c. friends
    d. known

15. Sadly, violence in schools has become:
    a. recurring
    b. routine
    c. more violent
    d. commonplace

16. Killers who are out for profit or want to protect themselves from a perceived threat are called:
    a. expedience killers
    b. serial killers
    c. mission killers
    d. thrill killers

17. Killers who are usually trying to cover up a crime, eliminate witnesses, or carry out a criminal conspiracy are called:
    a. revenge killers
    b. love killers
    c. profit killers
    d. terrorist killers

18. What requires offensive touching, such as slapping, hitting, or punching a victim?
    a. assault and battery
    b. assault
    c. battery
    d. simple assault

19. Obsession with a wife's behavior, however trivial, can result in violent assaults, and this is called:
    a. social approval
    b. excessive brooding
    c. estrangement
    d. hostility toward dependency

20. These robbers steal to obtain small amounts of money when an accessible target presents itself are called:
    a. opportunist robbers
    b. professional robbers
    c. addict robbers
    d. alcoholic robbers

21. Those disturbed individuals who see it as their duty to rid the world of evil commit:
    a. mission hate crimes
    b. reactive (defensive) hate crimes
    c. thrill-seeking hate crimes
    d. retaliatory hate crimes

22. Which of the following is **NOT** true for something to be considered terrorism?
    a. It is a political crime.
    b. The act must carry with it the intent to disrupt and change the government.
    c. The act must not be merely a common-law crime committed for greed or egotism.
    d. The act must achieve worldwide press coverage.

23. What kind of terrorists use violence to frighten those in power and their supporters in order to replace the existing government with a regime that holds acceptable political or religious views?
    a. guerrillas
    b. international terrorists
    c. revolutionary terrorists
    d. political terrorists

24. What kind of terrorist direct their terrorist activities against individuals and governments to whom they object?
    a. political terrorist
    b. cause-based terrorist
    c. national terrorist
    d. transnational terrorist

25. Which of the following is **NOT** a mission of the Department of Homeland Security?
    a. coordinating state and local antiterrorism efforts
    b. reducing America's vulnerability to terrorism
    c. minimizing the damage and recovery from attacks that do occur
    d. preventing terrorist attacks within the United States

ESSAY QUESTIONS

1. Discuss the various causes of violent crime.

2. Discuss the history of rape and explain the different types of rape.

3. Discuss the differences among serial killing, mass murder, and spree killing.

4. Discuss the nature of assault in the home.

5. Explain the different types of terrorism and what is being done to combat terrorists.

MATCHING

1. _____ Date Rape
2. _____ Eros
3. _____ Felony Murder
4. _____ Guerilla
5. _____ Hypermasculine
6. _____ Martial Rape
7. _____ Rape
8. _____ Serial Murder
9. _____ Sexual Abuse
10. _____ Shield Laws

A. Laws that protect women from being questioned about their sexual history unless it directly bears on the case.
B. The killing of a large number of people over time by an offender who seeks to escape detection.
C. In common law, "the carnal knowledge of a female forcibly and against her will."
D. Men who typically have a callous sexual attitude and believe violence is manly.
E. A killing accompanying a felony, such as robbery or rape, usually constitutes first-degree murder.
F. Rape involving people in some form of courting relationship.
G. The most basic human drive present at birth; the instinct to preserve and create life.
H. Located in rural areas and attack the military, the police and government officials.
I. Rape of a woman by her husband.
J. The exploitation of children through rape, incest and molestation by parents or other adults.

CHAPTER 10 ANSWER KEY

Fill In The Blank Answers

1. expressive violence
2. crusted over
3. college campuses
4. deliberation
5. mission killers
6. parents
7. rational
8. workplace violence
9. nationalist
10. financial

True/False Answers

1.	F	6.	T	11.	T
2.	T	7.	F	12.	F
3.	F	8.	T	13.	T
4.	T	9.	T	14.	F
5.	T	10.	F	15.	F

Multiple Choice Answers

1.	D	11.	D	21.	A
2.	A	12.	C	22.	D
3.	C	13.	A	23.	C
4.	A	14.	D	24.	B
5.	B	15.	D	25.	A
6.	D	16.	A		
7.	C	17.	C		
8.	B	18.	C		
9.	A	19.	B		
10.	B	20.	A		

Essay Questions

1. Pages 332 – 338
2. Pages 338 – 343
3. Pages 350 – 352
4. Pages 353 – 355
5. Pages 365 – 372

Matching Answers

1.	F	6.	I
2.	G	7.	C
3.	E	8.	B
4.	H	9.	J
5.	D	10.	A

Chapter 11

Property Crime

LEARNING OBJECTIVES

1. Be familiar with the history of theft offenses.

2. Recognize the differences between professional and amateur thieves.

3. Know the similarities and differences between the various types of larceny.

4. Understand the different forms of shoplifting.

5. Be able to discuss the concept of fraud.

6. Know what is meant by a confidence game.

7. Understand what it means to burgle a home.

8. Know what it takes to be a good burglar.

9. Understand the concept of arson.

KEYWORDS AND DEFINITIONS

Fence: a buyer and seller of stolen merchandise. (page 384)

Street crime: illegal acts designed to prey on the public through theft, damage, and violence. (384)

Economic crime: involves organizations devoted to criminal enterprise. (384)

Skilled thieves: typically worked in the larger cities, such as London and Paris. This group included pickpockets, forgers, and counterfeiters, who operated freely. (385)

Flash houses: public meeting places, often taverns that served as headquarters for gangs. Here, deals were made, crimes were plotted, and the sale of stolen goods was negotiated. (385)

Smugglers: They moved freely in sparsely populated areas and transported goods, such as spirits, gems, gold, and spices, without bothering to pay tax or duty. (385)

Poachers: typically lived in the country and supplemented their diet and income with game that belonged to a landlord. (385)

Occasional criminals: do not define themselves by a criminal role or view themselves as committed career criminals. (385)

Professional criminals: make a significant portion of their income from crime. Professionals pursue their craft with vigor, attempting to learn from older, experienced criminals the techniques that will earn them the most money with the least risk. (385)

Situational inducement: short-term influence on a person's behavior, such as financial problems or peer pressure that increases risk taking. (385)

Professional fence: earns his or her living solely by buying and reselling stolen merchandise. (387)

Constructive possession: situations in which persons voluntarily and temporarily give up custody of his or her property but still believe the property is legally theirs. (390)

Petit (petty) larceny: involves small amounts of money or property; it is punished as a misdemeanor. (390)

Grand larceny: involving merchandise of greater value; is considered a felony and is punished by a sentence in the state prison. (390)

Shoplifting: a common form of theft involving taking goods from retail stores. (391)

Boosters (or heels): professional shoplifters who steal with the intention of reselling stolen merchandise to pawnshops or fences, usually at half the original price. (391)

Snitches: usually respectable people who do not conceive of themselves as thieves but are systematic shoplifters who steal merchandise for their own use. They are not simply overcome by an uncontrollable urge to take something that attracts them; they come equipped to steal. (391)

Target removal strategies: putting dummy or disabled goods on display while the real merchandise is kept under lock and key. (392)

Target hardening strategies: locking goods in place or having them monitored by electronic systems. (392)

Naive check forgers: amateurs who do not believe their actions will hurt anyone. Most naive check forgers come from middle-class backgrounds and have little identification with a criminal subculture. (392)

Closure: a term used by Lemert , forgers who come from middle-class backgrounds and have little identification with a criminal subculture. They cash bad checks because of a financial crisis that demands an immediate resolution—perhaps they have lost money at the horse track and have some pressing bills to pay. (392)

Systematic forgers: make a substantial living by passing bad checks. (392)

Carjacking: gunmen who approach a car and force the owner to give up the keys; in some cases, people have been killed when they reacted too slowly. (396)

False pretenses (or fraud): misrepresenting a fact in a way that causes a victim to willingly give his or her property to the wrongdoer, who keeps it. (396)

Confidence games: run by swindlers who aspire to separate a victim (or "sucker") from his or her hard-earned money. (397)

Mark: the target of a con man or woman, interested in some get-rich-quick scheme, which may have illegal overtones. (397)

Pigeon drop: a package or wallet containing money is "found" by a con man or woman. A passing victim is stopped and asked for advice about what to do, since no identification can be found. Another "stranger," who is part of the con, approaches and enters the discussion. The three decide to split the money; but first, to make sure everything is legal, one of the swindlers goes off to consult a lawyer. Upon returning, he or she says that the lawyer claims the money can be split up; first, however, each party must prove he or she has the means to reimburse the original owner, should one show up. The victim then is asked to give some good-faith money for the lawyer to hold. When the victim goes to the lawyer's office to pick up a share of the loot, he or she finds the address bogus and the money gone. (397)

Embezzlement: someone who is so trusted with property fraudulently converts it—that is, keeps it for his or her own use or the use of others. It can be distinguished from fraud on the basis of when the criminal intent was formed. (398)

Good burglar: professional burglars use this title to characterize colleagues who have distinguished themselves as burglars. (401)

Arson for profit: people looking to collect insurance money, but who are afraid or unable to set the fire themselves hire professional arsonists. (403)

Arson fraud: involves a business owner burning his or her property, or hiring someone to do it, to escape financial problems. (403)

Flashover: during the course of an ordinary fire, heat and gas at the ceiling of a room can reach 2,000 degrees. This causes clothes and furniture to burst into flame, duplicating the effects of arsonists' gasoline or explosives. It is possible that many suspected arsons are actually the result of flashover. (403)

CHAPTER OUTLINE

I. A brief history of theft
    A. Self-report studies show that property crime among the young in every social class is widespread
    B. Theft is not a phenomenon unique to modern times
    C. By the eighteenth century, three separate groups of property criminals were active
        1. Skilled thieves
        2. Smugglers
        3. Poachers

II. Modern thieves
    A. Occasional criminals
        1. Most thefts are committed by occasional criminals
        2. Other theft-offenders are in fact skilled professional criminals
        3. The great majority of economic crimes are the work of amateur criminals whose
            a. Decision to steal is spontaneous
            b. Acts are unskilled, impulsive, and haphazard
        4. There are the millions of adults whose behavior may occasionally violate the criminal law
        5. Occasional property crime occurs when there is an opportunity or situational inducement to commit crime
            a. Short-term influences on a person's behavior that increase risk taking
            b. Opportunity and situational inducements are not the cause of crime
            c. They are the occasion for crime
            d. The opportunity to commit crime and the short-run inducements to do so are not randomly situated
            e. Some people, typically poor young males, have an ample supply of both
        6. Occasional criminals have little group support for their acts
    B. Professional criminals
        1. Professional criminals make a significant portion of their income from crime
        2. Professionals pursue their craft with vigor
        3. They attempt to learn from older, experienced criminals
        4. Professional theft traditionally refers to nonviolent forms of criminal behavior
            a. That are undertaken with a high degree of skill for monetary gain
            b. That exploit interests tending
                1) To maximize financial opportunities
                2) To minimize the possibilities of apprehension
        5. Three career patterns of professional thieves and criminals
            a. Youth come under the influence of older, experienced criminals who teach them the trade

b. Juvenile gang members continue their illegal activities at a time when most of their peers have "dropped out" to
   1) Marry
   2) Raise families
   3) Take conventional jobs
c. Youth sent to prison for minor offenses learn the techniques of crime from more experienced thieves

C. Sutherland's professional criminal
   1. The Professional Thief
   2. Conwell and Sutherland's concept of professional theft has two critical dimensions
      a. Professional thieves engage in limited types of crime
      b. The exclusive use of wits, front (a believable demeanor), and talking ability
   3. In their world, "thief" is a title worn with pride
   4. Sutherland and Conwell view professional theft as an occupation with much the same internal organization as legitimate professions
   5. Professional thieves have changed their behavior over time in response to crime control technology

D. The professional fence
   1. Some experts have argued that Sutherland's view of the professional thief may be outdated because
      a. Modern thieves often work alone
      b. They are not part of a criminal subculture
      c. They were not tutored early in their careers by other criminals
   2. Research efforts show that the principles set down by Sutherland still have value
      a. The fence's critical role in criminal transactions has been recognized since the eighteenth century
      b. They act as middlemen who purchase stolen merchandise and resell them to merchants who market them to legitimate customers
   3. According to Goodman, to be successful, a fence must meet the following
      a. Upfront cash
      b. Knowledge of dealing
      c. Connections with suppliers of stolen goods
      d. Connections with buyers
      e. Complicity with law enforcers
   4. Fencing seems to contain many of the elements of professional theft as described by Sutherland

E. The nonprofessional fence
   1. A significant portion of all fencing is performed by amateur or occasional criminals
   2. One type of occasional fence is the part-timer who, unlike professional fences, has other sources of income
   3. Some merchants become actively involved in theft either by specifying the merchandise they want the burglars to steal or by "fingering" victims
   4. Associational fences
   5. Neighborhood hustlers
   6. Amateur receivers

III. Larceny/Theft
    A. Larceny today
        1. Larceny is usually separated by state statute into
            a. Petit (petty) larceny
            b. Grand larceny
        2. Larceny/theft is probably the most common criminal offense
        3. Some larcenies involve complex criminal conspiracies
    B. Shoplifting
        1. Retail security measures add to the already high cost of this crime, all of which is passed on to the consumer
        2. Profile of a shoplifter
            a. Cameron found that about 10 percent of all shoplifters were professionals who derived the majority of their income from shoplifting
            b. Cameron found that the majority of shoplifters are amateur pilferers, called snitches in thieves' argot
            c. Criminologists view shoplifters as people who are likely to reform if apprehended
        3. Controlling shoplifting
            a. Many states encourage the arrest of shoplifters
            b. Many have passed merchant privilege laws designed to protect retailers and their employers from litigation from improper or false arrests of suspected shoplifters
            c. They require
                1) That arrests be made on reasonable grounds or probable cause
                2) That detention be of short duration
                3) That store employees or security guards conduct themselves in a reasonable fashion
        4. Prevention strategies
            a. Target removal strategies
            b. Target hardening strategies
            c. Situational measures
                1) Place the most valuable goods in the least vulnerable places
                2) Use warning signs to deter potential thieves
                3) Use closed-circuit cameras
    C. Bad checks
        1. Lemert
            a. Found that the majority of check forgers are amateurs who do not believe their actions will hurt anyone
            b. He calls them naive check forgers
        2. They cash bad checks because of a financial crisis that demands an immediate resolution
        3. Naive check forgers are often socially isolated people who have been unsuccessful in their personal relationships
        4. They are risk prone when faced with a situation that is unusually stressful for them
        5. Check fraud schemes and techniques
        6. Lemert found that a few professionals (systematic forgers) make a substantial living by passing bad checks
    D. Credit card theft
        1. Fraud has been responsible for a billion-dollar loss in the credit card industry
        2. Compounded by thieves who set up bogus internet sites

E. Auto Theft
   1. Motor vehicle theft is another common larceny offense
   2. Detailed typologies developed by Charles McCaghy and his associates
      a. Joyriding
      b. Short-term transportation
      c. Long-term transportation
      d. Profit
      e. Commission of another crime
   3. Which cars are taken most?
      a. Car thieves show signs of rational choice in their target selections
      b. Typically choose these vehicles because of the high profit potential after stripping the component parts, which are then sold on the black market
      c. Car models that have been in production for a few years without many design changes stand the greatest risk of theft
   4. Carjacking
      a. Both victims and offenders in carjackings tend to be young black men
      b. Weapons were used in about three-quarters of all carjacking victimizations
   5. Combating auto theft
      a. One approach to theft deterrence – increase the risks of apprehension
      b. The Lojack system
      c. Other prevention efforts involve making it more difficult to steal cars
F. False pretenses or fraud
   1. False pretense differs from traditional larceny because the victims willingly give their possessions to the offender
   2. Fraud may also occur when people conspire to cheat a third party or institution
G. Confidence games
H. Embezzlement
   1. First codified in law by the English Parliament during the sixteenth century
   2. Number of people arrested for embezzlement has increased more than 40 percent since 1991
   3. Rash of embezzlement-type crimes around the world

IV. Burglary
   A. The nature and extent of burglary
      1. State jurisdictions have changed the legal requirements of burglary, and most have discarded the necessity of forced entry
      2. Many now protect all structures, not just dwelling houses
      3. The nature and extent of burglary
   B. Residential burglary
      1. Some burglars are crude thieves
      2. Others plan out a strategy
      3. Burglary has been a crime long associated with professional thieves who carefully learn their craft
      4. Gender differences in burglary
   C. Commercial burglary
      1. Some burglars prefer to victimize commercial property rather than private homes
      2. Retail stores are burglars' favorite targets
      3. Establishments located within three blocks of heavily traveled thoroughfares have been found to be less vulnerable to burglary than those located farther away

4. Alarms
   a. Have been found to be an effective deterrent to burglary
   b. Are less effective in isolated areas
   c. Burglary of non-alarmed properties is 4.57 times higher than that of similar property with alarms

D. Careers in burglary
   1. Some criminals make burglary their career
   2. They continually develop new and specialized skills to aid their profession
   3. Characteristics of the good burglar
      a. Technical competence
      b. Maintenance of personal integrity
      c. Specialization in burglary
      d. Financial success
      e. The ability to avoid prison sentences
   4. Shover found that novices must develop four key requirements of the trade
      a. They must learn the many skills needed to commit lucrative burglaries
      b. The good burglar must be able to team up to form a criminal gang
      c. The good burglar must have inside information
      d. The good burglar must cultivate fences or buyers for stolen wares
   5. The burglary "career ladder"
      a. They begin as young novices
      b. The journeyman stage
      c. Finally, they become professional burglars
   6. Repeat burglary
      a. Research suggests that burglars may in fact return to the scene of the crime to repeat their offenses
      b. Research shows that some burglars repeat their acts to steal these replacement goods

V. Arson
   A. There are several motives for arson
      1. Adult arsonists may be motivated by severe emotional turmoil
      2. Some psychologists view fire starting as a function of a disturbed personality
      3. It is alleged that arsonists often experience sexual pleasure from starting fires
      4. Fires are started by angry people looking for revenge against property owners
      5. Fires are started by teenagers out to vandalize property
   B. Juvenile fire setting has long been associated with conduct problems
      1. The "playing with matches" fire setter
      2. The "crying for help" fire setter
      3. The "delinquent" fire setter
      4. The "severely disturbed" fire setter
   C. Arsons are set by professional arsonists who engage in arson for profit
   D. Another form is arson fraud
   E. It is possible that many suspected arsons are actually the result of flashover

CHAPTER SUMMARY

Self-report studies show that property crime among the young in every social class is widespread. Most thefts are committed by occasional criminals, but other theft-offenders are in fact skilled professional criminals. The great majority of economic crimes are the work of amateur criminals whose decision to steal is spontaneous. Their acts are unskilled, impulsive, and haphazard. Professional criminals make a significant portion of their income from crime, so they pursue their craft with vigor. There are three career patterns of professional thieves and criminals. First, youth come under the influence of older, experienced criminals who teach them the trade. Second, juvenile gang members continue their illegal activities at a time when most of their peers have "dropped out" to marry, raise families, and take conventional jobs. Third, youth sent to prison for minor offenses learn the techniques of crime from more experienced thieves. The most renowned work on the professional criminal is Sutherland's The Professional Thief.

Larceny is usually separated by state statute into petit (petty) larceny and grand larceny. Larceny/theft is probably the most common criminal offense. Cameron found that about 10 percent of all shoplifters were professionals who derived the majority of their income from shoplifting. She also found that the majority of shoplifters are amateur pilferers, called snitches in thieves' argot. Criminologists view shoplifters as people who are likely to reform if apprehended. Many states encourage the arrest of shoplifters by passing merchant privilege laws designed to protect retailers and their employers from litigation from improper or false arrests of suspected shoplifters.

Lemert found that the majority of check forgers are amateurs who do not believe their actions will hurt anyone; he calls them naive check forgers. They cash bad checks because of a financial crisis that demands an immediate resolution and they are often socially isolated people who have been unsuccessful in their personal relationships. Lemert also found that a few professionals (systematic forgers) make a substantial living by passing bad checks.

Motor vehicle theft is another common larceny offense. Detailed typologies developed by Charles McCaghy and his associates include joyriding, short-term transportation, long-term transportation, profit, and commission of another crime. Car thieves show signs of rational choice in their target selections as they typically choose those vehicles that have the high profit potential after stripping the component parts, which are then sold on the black market. False pretense differs from traditional larceny because the victims willingly give their possessions to the offender. Fraud may occur when people conspire to cheat a third party or institution. Confidence game is another form of fraud. The number of people arrested for embezzlement has increased more than 40 percent since 1991. In fact, there has been a rash of embezzlement-type crimes around the world.

State jurisdictions have changed the legal requirements of burglary, and most have discarded the necessity of forced entry. Some residential burglars are crude thieves, while others plan out a strategy. Burglary has been a crime long associated with professional thieves who carefully learn their craft. Some burglars prefer to victimize commercial property rather than private homes. Retail stores tend to be burglars' favorite targets. Alarms have been found to be an effective deterrent to burglary, but they are less effective in isolated areas. However, burglary of non-alarmed properties is 4.57 times higher than that of similar property with alarms. The characteristics of the good burglar are technical competence, maintenance of personal integrity, specialization in burglary, financial success, and the ability to avoid prison sentences. Burglars progress through a "career ladder." They begin as young novices, go through the journeyman stage, and finally, they become professional burglars.

There are several motives for arson. First, adult arsonists may be motivated by severe emotional turmoil. Second, some psychologists view fire starting as a function of a disturbed personality. Third, it is alleged that arsonists often experience sexual pleasure from starting fires. Fourth, fires are started by angry people looking for revenge against property owners. And fifth, fires are started by teenagers out to vandalize property. Juvenile fire setting has long been associated with conduct problems such as playing with matches, crying for help, being delinquent, or being severely disturbed. Some arson is committed by professional arsonists who engage in arson for profit. Another form is arson fraud. It is possible that many suspected arsons are actually the result of flashover.

STUDENT EXERCISES

Exercise 1

Go online to policing burglary in Australia. The website for the article to read is at http://jratcliffe.net/papers/Ratcliffe%20(2001)%20Policing%20urban%20burglary.pdf. Be prepared to present in class an analysis of how burglary in Australia compares with burglary as presented in the textbook.

Exercise 2

Go to http://samsara.law.cwru.edu/comp_law/10-shoplifting.html and read the information provided by an anonymous writer concerning how to commit shoplifting. Prepare a one to two page analysis of the article and how it compares with the information provided by the textbook.

CRIMINOLOGY WEB LINKS

http://www.auto-theft.info/
This is the official website for the online Auto-Theft Information Clearing House. Take a look around the website which has a wealth of information on auto theft.

http://www.iii.org/media/hottopics/insurance/test4/
This is the official website by the Insurance Information Institute and provides a great deal of information on auto theft.

http://www.ftc.gov/bcp/conline/pubs/credit/cards.pdf
This website contains a brochure published by the Federal Trade Commission on how to avoid credit and charge card fraud.

http://www.aafp.org/fpm/970900fm/suite_1.html
This is an article on how to prevent embezzlement in a physician's office. It offers some tips that can be of value to anyone who owns their own business and has employees.

http://www.ncjrs.org/pdffiles1/nij/181584.pdf
This website contains a Department of Justice publication on fire and arson investigation.

TEST BANK

FILL-IN THE BLANKS

1.   Though criminologists are not certain, they suspect that the great majority of economic crimes are the work of _____ criminals whose decision to steal is spontaneous.

2.   _____ _____ are short-term influences on a person's behavior that increase risk taking.

3.   _____ _____ act as middlemen who purchase stolen merchandise, ranging from diamonds to auto hubcaps, and resell them to merchants who market them to legitimate customers.

4.   A significant portion of all fencing is performed by _____ or _____ criminals.

5.   _____ was one of the earliest common-law crimes created by English judges to define acts in which one person took for his or her own use the property of another.

6.   Retail security measures add to the already high cost of this crime, all of which is passed on to the _____.

7.   The condition that drives someone to cash bad checks because of a financial crisis that demands an immediate resolution is called _____.

8. _____ do not steal cars for profit or gain but to experience, even briefly, the benefits associated with owning an automobile.

9. _____ _____ are run by swindlers who aspire to separate a victim (or "sucker") from his or her hard-earned money.

10. Most _____ avoid occupied residences, considering them high-risk targets.

TRUE/FALSE QUESTIONS

1. T/F Many theft offenses are committed by school-age youths who are likely to enter into a criminal career.

2. T/F Manual dexterity and physical force are of little importance to professional thieves.

3. T/F According to Goodman, to be successful, a fence must insure that all deals are cash transactions.

4. T/F Petit (petty) larceny is a felony.

5. T/F Cameron found that most shoplifters were professionals.

6. T/F Lemert found that the majority of check forgers are professionals.

7. T/F Most credit card abuse is the work of amateurs who acquire stolen cards through theft or mugging and then use them for two or three days.

8. T/F Motor vehicle theft has increased during the past decade.

9. T/F Fewer cars are being taken today while and similarly fewer stolen cars are being recovered.

10. T/F Both victims and offenders in carjackings tend to be young white men.

11. T/F Embezzlement occurs when someone who is so trusted with property fraudulently converts it, that is, keeps it for his or her own use or the use of others.

12. T/F The FBI's definition of burglary is not restricted to burglary from a person's home; it includes any unlawful entry of a structure to commit theft or felony.

13. T/F Most burglars are deterred by alarms and elaborate locks.

14. T/F Of all business establishments, service centers are burglars' favorite targets.

15 T/F Although some arsonists may be aroused sexually by their activities, there is little evidence that most arsonists are psychosexually motivated.

MULTIPLE CHOICE QUESTIONS

1. Acts in violation of the criminal law designed to bring financial reward to an offender are called:
   a. economic crime
   b. street crime
   c. pandering
   d. poachers

2. Those that do not define themselves by a criminal role or view themselves as committed career criminals are called:
   a. felons
   b. misdemeanants
   c. occasional criminals
   d. embezzlers

3. A professional shoplifter is called a:
   a. heel
   b. booster
   c. con artist
   d. pennyweighter

4. A sneak thief from stores, banks, and offices is called:
   a. heel
   b. booster
   c. con artist
   d. pennyweighter

5. Those who buy and sell stolen property as one of the many ways they make a living are called:
   a. professional hustlers
   b. amateur receivers
   c. associational fences
   d. neighborhood hustlers

6. Those who are approached in a public place by complete strangers offering a great deal on valuable commodities are called:
   a. professional hustlers
   b. amateur receivers
   c. associational fences
   d. neighborhood hustlers

7. The legal fiction applied to situations in which persons voluntarily and temporarily gave up custody of their property but still believed the property was legally theirs is called:
   a. economic crime
   b. situational inducement
   c. constructive possession
   d. petit larceny

8. Professional shoplifters are called:
   a. boosters
   b. heels
   c. con artists
   d. pennyweighters

9. Lemert calls the majority of check forgers who are amateurs and who do not believe their actions will hurt anyone:
   a. closures
   b. naive check forgers
   c. con artists
   d. pennyweighters

10. The process of depositing a check in one bank account into a second bank account without the sufficient funds to cover it is called:
    a. identity assumption
    b. altered checks
    c. systematic forgers
    d. check kiting

11. Thieves stealing cars for their personal use is what type of auto theft transaction?
    a. long-term transportation
    b. joyriding
    c. short-term transportation
    d. profit

12. Car thefts motivated by teenagers' desire to acquire the power, prestige, sexual potency, and recognition associated with an automobile are what type of auto theft transaction?
    a. long-term transportation
    b. joyriding
    c. short-term transportation
    d. profit

13. The auto theft transaction that involves stealing an auto in hope of monetary gain is called:
    a. long-term transportation
    b. joyriding
    c. short-term transportation
    d. profit

14. The auto theft transaction that involves the theft of a car simply to go from one place to another is called:
    a. long-term transportation
    b. joyriding
    c. short-term transportation
    d. profit

15. Which of the following vehicles is most likely to be stolen?
    a. Toyota Camry
    b. Grand Caravan
    c. Ford Taurus
    d. Jeep Grand Cherokee

16. Which of the following is **NOT** a characteristic of a good burglar?
    a. technical competence
    b. maintenance of personal integrity
    c. generalization in crimes
    d. financial success

17. The target of a con game is called a:
    a. pigeon
    b. mark
    c. drop
    d. con

18. Youth who set fires to school property or surrounding areas to retaliate for some slight experienced at school are known as:
    a. "playing with matches" fire setter
    b. "crying for help" fire setter
    c. "delinquent" fire setter
    d. "severely disturbed" fire setter

19. The youngest fire starter, usually between the ages of 4 and 9, who sets fires because parents are careless with matches and lighters is known as:
    a. "playing with matches" fire setter
    b. "crying for help" fire setter
    c. "delinquent" fire setter
    d. "severely disturbed" fire setter

20. The youngster who is obsessed with fires and often dreams about them in "vibrant colors" is known as:
    a. "playing with matches" fire setter
    b. "crying for help" fire setter
    c. "delinquent" fire setter
    d. "severely disturbed" fire setter

21. The type of fire setter who is a 7- to 13-year-old who turns to fire to reduce stress is called:
    a. "playing with matches" fire setter
    b. "crying for help" fire setter
    c. "delinquent" fire setter
    d. "severely disturbed" fire setter

22. Fires set by professionals who engage in arson are known as:
    a. arson for profit
    b. flashover
    c. felony arson
    d. premeditated arson

23. During the course of an ordinary fire, heat and gas at the ceiling of a room can reach 2,000 degrees and this is known as:
    a. flash
    b. crash
    c. flashover
    d. flashunder

24. Which of the following is a reason for individuals to become involved in arson?
    a. obtain money in a crisis
    b. get rid of slow inventory
    c. paying off debt
    d. all of the above

25. Which of the following is a motive for arson?
    a. conduct problems
    b. profit
    c. severe emotional turmoil
    d. all of the above

ESSAY QUESTIONS

1. Explain the differences between professional and amateur thieves.

2. Discuss the different forms of shoplifting.

3. Explain what is meant by a confidence game.

4. Discuss what it takes to be a good burglar.

5. Explain the concept of arson.

MATCHING

1. _____ Systematic Forgers
2. _____ Street Crimes
3. _____ Snitches
4. _____ Situational Inducement
5. _____ Professional Criminals
6. _____ Pigeon Drop
7. _____ Occasional Criminals
8. _____ Naive Check Forgers
9. _____ Joyriding
10. _____ Heels

A. Common theft-related offenses which include larceny, embezzlement and theft by false pretenses.
B. Occasional property crimes occur when there is an opportunity to commit crime.
C. A method of swindling money out of an innocent victim.
D. The majority of check forgers who do not believe their actions will hurt anyone.
E. Professional shoplifters who steal with the intention of reselling stolen merchandise to pawnshops or fences.
F. Professionals who make a substantial living by passing bad checks.
G. Usually respectable persons who do not conceive of themselves as thieves, but are systematic shoplifters who steal merchandise for their own use.
H. Criminals who make a significant portion of their income from crime.
I. Amateur criminals whose decision to steal is spontaneous and whose acts are unskilled, unplanned and haphazard.
J. Car theft usually motivated by a teenager's desire to acquire the power, prestige, sexual potency, and recognition associated with an automobile.

CHAPTER 11 ANSWER KEY

Fill In The Blank Answers

1. amateur
2. situational inducements
3. professional fences
4. amateur; occasional
5. larceny/theft
6. consumer
7. closure
8. joyriders
9. confidence games
10. burglars

True/False Answers

1.	F	6.	F	11.	T
2.	T	7.	T	12.	T
3.	T	8.	F	13.	F
4.	F	9.	T	14.	F
5.	F	10.	F	15.	T

Multiple Choice Answers

1.	A	11.	A	21.	B
2.	C	12.	B	22.	A
3.	B	13.	D	23.	C
4.	A	14.	C	24.	D
5.	D	15.	A	25.	D
6.	B	16.	C		
7.	C	17.	B		
8.	A	18.	C		
9.	B	19.	A		
10.	D	20.	D		

Essay Questions

1. Pages 385 – 387
2. Pages 391 – 392
3. Pages 397 – 398
4. Pages 401 – 402
5. Pages 403 – 404

Matching Answers

1.	F	6.	C
2.	A	7.	I
3.	G	8.	D
4.	B	9.	J
5.	H	10.	E

Chapter 12

Enterprise Crime: White-Collar, Cyber, and Organized Crime

LEARNING OBJECTIVES

1. Understand the concept of enterprise crime.

2. Be familiar with the various types of white-collar crime.

3. Be familiar with the various types of corporate crime.

4. Recognize the extent and various causes of white-collar crime.

5. Be able to discuss the different approaches to combating white-collar crime.

6. Recognize new types of cyber crime.

7. Describe the methods being used to control Internet and computer crime.

8. List the different types of illegal behavior engaged in by organized crime figures.

9. Describe the evolution of organized crime.

10. Explain how the government is fighting organized crime.

KEYWORDS AND DEFINITIONS

Enterprise crime: using illegal tactics to make profit. (page 412)

White-collar crime: illegal activities of people and institutions whose acknowledged purpose is profit through legitimate business transactions. (412)

Cyber crime: people using the instruments of modern technology for criminal purpose. (412)

Organized crime: illegal activities of people and organizations whose acknowledged purpose is profit through illegitimate business enterprise. (412)

Corporate crime: criminal conspiracies designed to improve the market share or profitability of their corporations. (413)

Sting (or swindle): a white-collar crime in which people use their institutional or business position to cheat others out of their money. (414)

Chiseling: regularly cheating an organization, its consumers, or both. (414)

Insider trading: using one's position of trust to profit from inside business information. (415)

Viatical investments: interests in the death benefits of terminally ill patients. (415)

Churning: the repeated, excessive, and unnecessary buying and selling of stock. (415)

Front running: brokers place personal orders ahead of a large customer's order to profit from the market effects of the trade. (415)

Bucketing: skimming customer trading profits by falsifying trade information. (415)

Influence peddling: individuals holding important institutional positions sell power, influence, and information to outsiders who have an interest in influencing or predicting the activities of the institution. (416)

Exploitation: forcing victims to pay for services to which they have a clear right. (416)

Pilferage: systematic theft of company property by employees. (418)

Organizational crime: powerful institutions or their representatives willfully violate the laws that restrain these institutions from doing social harm or require them to do social good. (422)

Actual authority: a corporation knowingly gives authority to an employee. (422)

Apparent authority: a third party, like a customer, reasonably believes the agent has the authority to perform the act in question. (422)

Sherman Antitrust Act: subjects to criminal or civil sanctions any person "who shall make any contract or engage in any combination or conspiracy" in restraint of interstate commerce. (422)

Division of markets: firms divide a region into territories, and each firm agrees not to compete in the others' territories. (423)

Tying arrangement: a corporation requires customers of one of its services to use other services it offers. (423)

Group boycott: an organization or company boycotts retail stores that do not comply with its rules or desires. (423)

Price fixing: conspiracy to set and control the price of a necessary commodity is considered an absolute violation of the act. (423)

Warez: for the past decade, groups of individuals have been working together to illegally obtain software and then "crack" or "rip" its copyright protections, before posting it on the Internet for other members of the group to use. (430)

Phishing: identity information gathered easily because people routinely share their name, address, phone numbers, personal information, credit card account numbers, and Social Security number (SSN) when making routine purchases over the Internet or in stores. (430)

Computer virus: a program that disrupts or destroys existing programs and networks, causing them to perform the task for which the virus was designed. (432)

Computer worm: similar to viruses, but they use computer networks or the Internet to self-replicate and "send themselves" to other users, generally via e-mail without the aid of the operator. (433)

Alien conspiracy theory: the belief, adhered to by the federal government and many respected criminologists, that organized crime is a direct offshoot of a criminal society, the Mafia, that first originated in Italy and Sicily and now controls racketeering in major U.S. cities. (436)

Mafia: first originated in Italy and Sicily and now controls racketeering in major U.S. cities. A major premise of the alien conspiracy theory is that the Mafia is centrally coordinated by a national committee that settles disputes, dictates policy, and assigns territory. (436)

La Cosa Nostra: a national syndicate of 25 or so Italian-dominated crime families. (436)

Racketeer Influenced and Corrupt Organization Act (RICO): Title IX of the Organized Crime Control Act that Congress passed in 1970. (437)

Enterprise theory of investigation (ETI): Rather than investigate crimes after they are committed, under the ETI model the focus is on criminal enterprise and investigation attacks on the structure of the criminal enterprise rather than on criminal acts viewed as isolated incidents. (438)

CHAPTER OUTLINE

I. Enterprise crime
    A. Terms
        1. Insider trading
        2. Enterprise crime
        3. White-collar crime
        4. Cyber crime
    B. Crimes of business enterprise
        1. These organizational crimes taint and corrupt the free market system

2. All three forms of enterprise crime can involve violence
II. White-collar crime
   A. General
      1. Edwin Sutherland first used the phrase "white-collar crime" to describe the criminal activities of the rich and powerful
      2. White-collar crime involved conspiracies by members of the wealthy classes to use their position in commerce & industry for personal gain without regard to law
   B. Redefining white-collar crime
      1. Contemporary definitions of white-collar crime are typically much broader
      2. Corporate crime
      3. White-collar crime often damages property and kills people
      4. Corporate violence
         a. Violations of safety standards
         b. Pollution of the environment
         c. Industrial accidents due to negligence

III. Components of white-collar crime
   A. Stings and swindles
   B. Chiseling
      1. Professional chiseling – Pharmacists have been known to
         a. Alter prescriptions
         b. Substitute low-cost generic drugs for more expensive name brands
      2. Securities fraud
         a. A great deal of chiseling takes place on the commodities and stock markets
         b. California stopped the selling of high-risk viatical investments
         c. Churning, front running, and bucketing
         d. Insider training
   C. Individual exploitation of institutional position
      1. Exploitation in government
      2. Exploitation can also occur in private industry
   D. Influence peddling and bribery
      1. Kickbacks
      2. Bribes
      3. Victim is threatened and forced to pay
      4. Influence peddling in government
         a. Federal officials
         b. State officials
         c. Agents of the criminal justice system have also been involved
      5. Influence peddling in business
   E. Embezzlement and employee fraud
      1. Blue collar fraud
      2. Management fraud
   F. Client fraud
      1. Healthcare fraud
      2. Bank fraud
      3. Tax evasion
   G. Corporate crime
      1. Actual authority
      2. Apparent authority
      3. Illegal restraint of trade and price fixing

4. Sherman Antitrust Act
    a. Division of markets
    b. Tying arrangement
    c. Group boycott
    d. Price fixing
5. Deceptive pricing
6. False claims and advertising
7. Worker safety/environmental crimes

IV. Causes of white-collar crime
    A. Greedy or needy?
        1. Greed
        2. Need
        3. According to Donald Cressey, embezzlement is caused by what he calls a "nonshareable financial problem"
    B. Corporate culture view
    C. Self-control view

V. White-collar law enforcement systems
    A. Controlling white-collar crime
        1. Enforcement generally is reactive rather than proactive
        2. The number of state-funded technical assistance offices to help local prosecutors has increased significantly
        3. In years past, it was rare for a corporate or white-collar criminal to receive a serious criminal penalty
        4. White-collar criminals are often considered nondangerous offenders
        5. Compliance strategies
            a. Set up administrative agencies to oversee business activity
            b. Force corporate boards to police themselves and take oversight responsibility
            c. Enforcing compliance with civil penalties is on the upswing
        6. Deterrence strategies
    B. Is the tide turning?
        a. Sentencing guidelines for convicted criminals has helped deterrence efforts
        b. This get-tough deterrence approach appears to be affecting all classes of white-collar criminals

VI. Cyber crime
    A. Internet crime
        1. Distributing sexual material
        2. Denial of service attack
        3. Illegal copyright infringement
        4. Internet securities fraud
            a. Market manipulation
            b. Fraudulent offerings of securities
            c. Illegal touting
        5. Identity theft
        6. Internet fraud
            a. Ponzi/pyramid schemes
            b. Nondelivery of goods and services
    B. Computer crime

1. Five categories
   a. Theft of services
   b. Use of data in a computer system for personal gain
   c. Unauthorized use of computers employed for various types of financial processing to obtain assets
   d. Theft of property by computer for personal use or conversion to profit
   e. Making the computer itself the subject of a crime
2. The extent of computer crime

C. Controlling cyber crime
   1. Counterfeit Access Device and Computer Fraud and Abuse Law in 1984
   2. National Information Infrastructure Protection Act (NIIPA) of 1996

VII. Organized crime
   A. Characteristics of organized crime
      1. Organized crime is a conspiratorial activity
      2. Organized crime has economic gain as its primary goal, although power and status may also be motivating factors
      3. Organized crime activities are not limited to providing illicit services
      4. Organized crime employs predatory tactics, such as intimidation, violence, and corruption
      5. Organized crime's conspiratorial groups are usually very quick and effective in controlling and disciplining their members, associates, and victims
      6. Organized crime is not synonymous with the Mafia
      7. Organized crime does not include terrorists dedicated to political change
   B. Activities of organized crime
   C. The concept of organized crime
   D. Alien conspiracy theory
   E. Contemporary organized crime groups
      1. A loose confederation of ethnic and regional crime groups, bound together by a commonality of economic and political objectives
      2. One important contemporary change in organized crime is the interweaving of ethnic groups into the traditional structure
      3. Eastern European crime groups
   F. The evolution of organized crime
   G. Controlling organized crime
      1. Organized crime employs ruthless monopolistic tactics to maximize profits
      2. It is also secretive
      3. It is protective of its operations
      4. It is defensive against any outside intrusion
      5. Racketeer Influenced and Corrupt Organization Act (RICO) prohibits acts intended to
         a. Derive income from racketeering or the unlawful collection of debts and use or investment of such income
         b. Acquire, through racketeering, an interest in or control over any enterprise engaged in interstate or foreign commerce
         c. Conduct business through a pattern of racketeering
         d. Conspire to use racketeering as a means of making income, collecting loans, or conducting business
      6. Enterprise theory of investigation (ETI)
   H. The future of organized crime

CHAPTER SUMMARY

Enterprise crime refers to three categories of crime: white-collar crime, cyber crime, and organized crime. Edwin Sutherland first used the phrase "white-collar crime" to describe the criminal activities of the rich and powerful. He argued that white-collar crime involved conspiracies by members of the wealthy classes to use their position in commerce and industry for personal gain without regard to the law. Contemporary definitions of white-collar crime are typically much broader. The components of white-collar crime are stings and swindles, chiseling, individual exploitation of institutional position, influence peddling and bribery, embezzlement and employee fraud, client fraud, and corporate crime. Many criminologists have studied the causes of white-collar crime and asked if the cause was greed or need. The two major views are the corporate culture view and the self-control view.

Law enforcement concerning white collar crime has generally been more reactive rather than proactive. However, the number of state-funded technical assistance offices to help local prosecutors convict white collar criminals has increased significantly. In years past, it was rare for a corporate or white-collar criminal to receive a serious criminal penalty because white-collar criminals were often considered non-dangerous offenders. The major compliance strategies to deter white collar crime have been to set up administrative agencies to oversee business activity, to force corporate boards to police themselves and take oversight responsibility, and to enforce compliance with civil penalties. Research has shown that the tide is turning on white collar crime. Sentencing guidelines for convicted criminals has helped deterrence efforts and this get-tough deterrence approach appears to be affecting all classes of white-collar criminals.

Cyber crime refers to internet crime and computer crime. Internet crime refers to distributing sexual material, denial of service attack, illegal copyright infringement, internet securities fraud, identity theft, and internet fraud. There are five categories of computer crime: theft of services, use of data in a computer system for personal gain, unauthorized use of computers employed for various types of financial processing to obtain assets, theft of property by computer for personal use or conversion to profit, and making the computer itself the subject of a crime. Two major laws designed to control cyber crime are the Counterfeit Access Device and Computer Fraud and Abuse Law of 1984 and the National Information Infrastructure Protection Act (NIIPA) of 1996.

There are seven major characteristics of organized crime. First, organized crime is a conspiratorial activity. Second, it has economic gain as its primary goal, although power and status may also be motivating factors. Third, organized crime activities are not limited to providing illicit services. Fourth, it employs predatory tactics, such as intimidation, violence, and corruption. Fifth, organized crime's conspiratorial groups are usually very quick and effective in controlling and disciplining their members, associates, and victims. Sixth, organized crime is not synonymous with the Mafia. Lastly, it does not include terrorists dedicated to political change. Contemporary organized crime groups are a loose confederation of ethnic and regional crime groups, bound together by a commonality of economic and political objectives.

One important contemporary change in organized crime is the interweaving of ethnic groups into the traditional structure. Organized crime employs ruthless monopolistic tactics to maximize profits, is secretive, protective of its operations, and is defensive against any outside intrusion. The Racketeer Influenced and Corrupt Organization Act (RICO) was put into law and prohibits acts intended to a) derive income from racketeering or the unlawful collection of debts and use or invest such income; b) acquire through racketeering an interest in or control over any enterprise engaged in interstate or foreign commerce; c) conduct business through a pattern of racketeering; and d) conspire to use racketeering as a means of making income, collecting loans, or conducting business.

STUDENT EXERCISES

Exercise 1

Go online to http://www.fbi.gov/ucr/whitecollarforweb.pdf and read the document, The Measurement of White-Collar Crime Using Uniform Crime Reporting (UCR) Data, by Cynthia Barnett. Write a summary of the article.

Exercise 2

Go to http://www.heritage.org/Research/LegalIssues/lm14.cfm and read the article, The Sociological Origins of "White-Collar Crime," by John S. Baker, Jr. Prepare a one to two page analysis of the article and critique of the author's position on who are white collar criminals and how we should prosecute them.

CRIMINOLOGY WEB LINKS

http://www.internetfraud.usdoj.gov/
This is the official website for internet fraud by the Department of Justice. Take a look around the website which has a wealth of information on internet fraud.

http://www.unodc.org/unodc/en/organized_crime.html
This is the official website by the United States on global organized crime and provides a great deal of information on the subject.

http://sfgate.com/cgi-bin/article.cgi?file=/chronicle/archive/2004/03/29/BUG8F5S1011.DTL
This website contains an article from the *San Francisco Chronicle* on phishing and its possible connection to organized crime.

http://www.computerworld.com/securitytopics/security/cybercrime?from=yn
This is the cybercrime website from *ComputerWorld* and contains a wealth of information on the subject, including measures to defend against it.

http://lawprofessors.typepad.com/whitecollarcrime_blog/
This website contains a blog called White Collar Crime Prof Blog which is edited by two law professors, Peter J. Henning and Ellen S. Podgor.

TEST BANK

FILL-IN THE BLANKS

1. The use illegal tactics to make a profit is referred to as _____ _____.

2. Some white-collar criminals use their positions of _____ in business or government to commit crimes.

3. _____ involves forcing victims to pay for services to which they have a clear right.

4. Federal law prohibits physicians and other healthcare providers from referring beneficiaries in federal healthcare programs to clinics or other facilities in which the physician or healthcare provider has a _____ interest.

5. _____ authority is satisfied if a third party, like a customer, reasonably believes the agent has the authority to perform the act in question.

6. The _____ _____ view is that some business organizations promote white-collar criminality in the same way that lower-class culture encourages the development of juvenile gangs and street crime.

7. White-collar criminals have _____ _____ and are inclined to follow momentary impulses without considering the long-term costs of such behavior.

8. For the past decade, groups of individuals have been working together to illegally obtain software and then "crack" or "rip" its copyright protections, before posting it on the Internet for other members of the group to use; this is called _____.

9. _____ _____ are similar to viruses but use computer networks or the Internet to self-replicate and "send themselves" to other users, generally via e-mail without the aid of the operator.

10. RICO's success has shaped the way the FBI attacks organized crime groups; they now use the _____ _____ of investigation.

TRUE/FALSE QUESTIONS

1.   T/F Martha Stewart, who dumped her shares of ImClone stock just prior to the negative press announcement concerning FDA approval of the cancer drug, was accused of insider trading.

2.   T/F A sting is a white-collar crime in which people use their institutional or business position to cheat others out of their money.

3.   T/F Viatical investments are interests in the death benefits of terminally ill patients.

4.   T/F Exploitation can not occur in private industry.

5.   T/F "Gang visits" means referring patients to other physicians in the same office.

6.   T/F Many white collar offenders feel free to engage in business crime because they can easily rationalize its effects.

7.   T/F According to the corporate culture view, new employees learn the attitudes and techniques needed to commit white-collar crime from their business peers.

8.   T/F Local prosecutors pursue white-collar criminals more vigorously if they are part of a team effort involving a network of law enforcement agencies.

9.   T/F Compliance strategies aim for law conformity, but require detecting, processing, or penalizing individual violators.

10. T/F Leniency is given as part of a confession or plea arrangement in a white collar crime case.

11. T/F The salami slice is a computer crime in which an employee sets up a dummy account in the company's computerized records and a small amount, even a few pennies, is subtracted from customers' accounts and added to the account of the thief.

12. T/F Specialized enforcement agencies to fight computer crime have not been created by the U.S. government.

13. T/F Organized crime activities are limited to providing illicit services.

14. T/F The traditional sources of income are for organized crime derived from providing illicit materials and using force to enter into and maximize profits in legitimate businesses.

15. T/F In sum, the alien conspiracy theory sees organized crime as being run by an ordered group of ethnocentric criminal syndicates, maintaining unified leadership and shared values.

MULTIPLE CHOICE QUESTIONS

1. Selling stock based on privileged knowledge not available to the general public is known as:
   a. white collar crime
   b. cybercrime
   c. enterprise crime
   d. insider trading

2. Illegal activities of people and institutions whose acknowledged purpose is profit through legitimate business transactions are called:
   a. organized crime
   b. cybercrime
   c. enterprise crime
   d. insider trading

3. Using the instruments of modern technology for criminal purpose is known as:
   a. organized crime
   b. cybercrime
   c. enterprise crime
   d. insider trading

4. Illegal activities of people and organizations whose acknowledged purpose is profit through illegitimate business enterprise are known as:
   a. organized crime
   b. cybercrime
   c. enterprise crime
   d. insider trading

5. Using illegal tactics to make profit is known as:
   a. organized crime
   b. cybercrime
   c. enterprise crime
   d. insider trading

6. The first person to use the term "white collar crime" was:
   a. Michael Gottfredson
   b. Travis Hirschi
   c. Mark Moore
   d. Edwin Sutherland

7. The type of white-collar crime, which includes antitrust violations, price fixing, and false advertising, is known as:
   a. organized crime
   b. corporate crime
   c. enterprise crime
   d. insider trading

8. A white-collar crime in which people use their institutional or business position to cheat others out of their money is known as:
   a. sting
   b. bucketing
   c. chiseling
   d. churning

9. Regularly cheating an organization, its consumers, or both is known as:
   a. sting
   b. bucketing
   c. chiseling
   d. churning

10. Repeated, excessive, and unnecessary buying and selling of stock is known as:
    a. front running
    b. bucketing
    c. chiseling
    d. churning

11. The act in which brokers place personal orders ahead of a large customer's order to profit from the market effects of the trade is called:
    a. front running
    b. bucketing
    c. chiseling
    d. churning

12. Skimming customer trading profits by falsifying trade information is known as:
    a. front running
    b. bucketing
    c. chiseling
    d. churning

13. Exploitation involves forcing victims to pay for services to which they have:
    a. a definite interest
    b. no right
    c. no interest
    d. a clear right

14. Referring patients to other physicians in the same office is known as:
    a. "gang visits"
    b. "steering"
    c. "ping-ponging"
    d. "pilferage"

15. Billing for multiple medical services is known as:
    a. "gang visits"
    b. "steering"
    c. "ping-ponging"
    d. "pilferage"

16. Directing patients to particular pharmacies is known as:
    a. "gang visits"
    b. "steering"
    c. "ping-ponging"
    d. "pilferage"

17. Systematic theft of company property by employees is known as:
    a. "gang visits"
    b. "steering"
    c. "ping-ponging"
    d. "pilferage"

18. The process by which firms divide a region into territories, and each firm agrees not to compete in the others' territories is known as:
    a. price fixing
    b. group boycott
    c. division of markets
    d. tying arrangements

19. The process by which a corporation requires customers of one of its services to use other services it offers is known as:
    a. price fixing
    b. group boycott
    c. division of markets
    d. tying arrangements

20. The process by which an organization or company boycotts retail stores that do not comply with its rules or desires is known as:
    a. price fixing
    b. group boycott
    c. division of markets
    d. tying arrangements

21. The process by which some Internet criminals threaten to or actually flood an Internet site with millions of bogus messages or orders so that their services will be tied up and unable to perform as promised is known as:
    a. warez
    b. phishing
    c. denial of service attack
    d. ponzi scheme

22. The process by which groups of individuals work together to illegally obtain software and then "crack" or "rip" its copyright protections, before posting it on the Internet for other members of the group to use is known as:
    a. warez
    b. phishing
    c. denial of service attack
    d. ponzi scheme

23. Identity information gathered easily because people routinely share their name, address, phone numbers, personal information, credit card account numbers, and Social Security number (SSN) when making routine purchases over the Internet or in stores is known as:
    a. warez
    b. phishing
    c. denial of service attack
    d. ponzi scheme

24. The investment fraud in which investors are promised abnormally high profits on their investments; no investment is actually made and early investors are paid returns with the investment money received from the later investors is known as:
    a. warez
    b. phishing
    c. denial of service attack
    d. ponzi scheme

25. The Racketeer Influenced and Corrupt Organization Act (RICO) created:
    a. new law enforcement agencies
    b. new categories of crimes in racketeering activity
    c. new categories of offenses in racketeering activity
    d. new courts for prosecuting organized crime

ESSAY QUESTIONS

1. Explain the concept of enterprise crime.

2. Discuss the various causes of white-collar crime.

3. Explain the different approaches to combating white-collar crime.

4. Describe the methods being used to control Internet and computer crime.

5.   Explain how the government is fighting organized crime.

MATCHING

1. _____   Pilferage
2. _____   Organized Crime
3. _____   Computer Worms
4. _____   Forfeiture
5. _____   Entrepreneurship
6. _____   Enterprise
7. _____   Alien Conspiracy Theory
8. _____   Compliance
9. _____   Churning
10. _____   Arbitrage

A.   The practice of buying large blocks of stock in companies that are believed to be the target of corporate buyouts or takeovers.
B.   Strategies that aim for law conformity without the necessity of detecting, processing, or penalizing individual violators.
C.   An organized crime group that profits from the sale of illegal goods and services, such as narcotics, pornography and prostitution.
D.   Use computer networks or the Internet to self-replicate and "send themselves" to other users, generally via e-mail without the aid of the operator.
E.   A conspiratorial activity, involving the coordination of numerous persons in the planning and execution of illegal acts or in the pursuit of a legitimate objective by lawful means.
F.   The seizure of personal property by the state as a civil or criminal penalty.
G.   Theft by employees through stealth or deception.
H.   One willing to take risks for profit in the marketplace.
I.   Organized crime is made up of a national syndicate of 25 or so Italian-dominated crime families that call themselves La Cosa Nostra.
J.   A white-collar crime in which a stockbroker makes repeated trades to fraudulently increase his/her commissions.

CHAPTER 12 ANSWER KEY

Fill In The Blank Answers

1. enterprise crime
2. trust
3. exploitation
4. financial
5. apparent
6. corporate culture
7. low self-control
8. warez
9. computer worms
10. enterprise theory

True/False Answers

1.	F	6.	T	11.	T
2.	T	7.	T	12.	F
3.	T	8.	T	13.	F
4.	F	9.	F	14.	T
5.	F	10.	F	15.	T

Multiple Choice Answers

1.	D	11.	A	21.	C
2.	A	12.	B	22.	A
3.	B	13.	D	23.	B
4.	A	14.	C	24.	D
5.	C	15.	A	25.	C
6.	D	16.	B		
7.	B	17.	D		
8.	A	18.	C		
9.	C	19.	D		
10.	D	20.	B		

Essay Questions

1. Page 412
2. Pages 424 – 425
3. Pages 427 – 428
4. Page 433
5. Pages 437 – 438

Matching Answers

1.	G	6.	C
2.	E	7.	I
3.	D	8.	B
4.	F	9.	J
5.	H	10.	A

Chapter 13

Public Order Crime

LEARNING OBJECTIVES

1. Be familiar with the association between law and morality.

2. Be able to discuss the legal problems faced by gay people.

3. Know what is meant by paraphilias.

4. Be able to discuss the various types of prostitution.

5. Describe the relationship between obscenity and pornography.

6. Know the various techniques being used to control pornography.

7. Discuss the history and extent of drug abuse.

8. Be able to discuss the cause of substance abuse.

9. Describe the different types of drug users.

10. Identify the various drug control strategies.

KEYWORDS AND DEFINITIONS

Public order crimes (or victimless crimes): crimes for which laws have been enacted to control behaviors involving sexuality and morality. (page 448)

Social harm: A view that behaviors harmful to other people and society in general must be controlled. Acts that are believed to be extremely harmful to the general public are usually outlawed; those that may only harm the actor are more likely to be tolerated. Some acts that cause enormous amounts of social harm are perfectly legal, such as tobacco and alcohol. (450)

Vigilantes: Do-gooders who take it on themselves to enforce the law, battle evil, and personally deal with those whom they consider immoral. (450)

Moral crusaders: rule creators who have an absolute certainty that their way is right and that any means are justified to get their way; "the crusader is fervent and righteous, often self-righteous." (450)

Gay bashing: Violent acts directed at people because of their sexual orientation. (451)

Homosexuality: Erotic interest in members of one's own sex. (451)

Sodomy: Deviant intercourse. (451)

Homophobia: Extremely negative overreaction to homosexuals. (451)

Paraphilias: Bizarre or abnormal sexual practices involving recurrent sexual urges focused on (1) nonhuman objects (such as underwear, shoes, or leather), (2) humiliation or the experience of receiving or giving pain (such as in sadomasochism or bondage), or (3) children or others who cannot grant consent. (453)

Brothels: A house of prostitution, typically run by a madam who sets prices and handles "business" arrangements. (453)

Prostitution: Granting nonmarital sexual access, established by mutual agreement of the prostitutes, their clients, and their employers, for remuneration. (454)

Madam: A woman who employs prostitutes, supervises their behavior, and receives a fee for her services; her cut is usually 40 to 60 percent of the prostitute's earnings. (455)

Call girls: Prostitutes who make dates via the phone and then service customers in hotel rooms or apartments. Call girls typically have a steady clientele who are repeat customers. (455)

Skeezers: On the street, women who barter drugs for sex. (455)

Pornography: Sexually explicit books, magazines, films, or tapes intended to provide sexual titillation and excitement for paying customers. (459)

Obscenity: Material deeply offensive to morality or decency and designed to incite to lust or depravity. (459)

Temperance movement: A drive that was mustered to prohibit the sale of alcohol. (463)

Gateway model: Regardless of its cause, most people fall into drug abuse slowly, beginning with alcohol and then following with marijuana and more serious drugs as the need for a more powerful high intensifies. (469)

CHAPTER OUTLINE

I. Law and morality
    A. Debating morality
        1. Some scholars argue that acts like pornography, prostitution, and drug use erode the moral fabric of society and therefore should be prohibited and punished
        2. According to this view, so-called victimless crimes are prohibited because one of the functions of criminal law is to express a shared sense of public morality
        3. Some influential legal scholars have questioned the propriety of legislating morals
        4. Gusfield argues that the purpose of outlawing immoral acts is to show the moral superiority of those who condemn the acts over those who partake of them
        5. Cultural clashes may ensue when behavior that is considered normative in one society is deplored by those living in another
    B. Social harm
        1. Immoral acts can be distinguished from crimes on the basis of the social harm they cause
        2. Acts that are believed to be extremely harmful to the general public are usually outlawed
        3. Those acts that may only harm the actor are more likely to be tolerated
        4. Some acts that cause enormous amounts of social harm are perfectly legal
    C. Moral crusaders
        1. Vigilantes held a strict standard of morality that, when they caught their prey, resulted in sure and swift justice
        2. The assumption that it is okay to take matters into your own hands if the cause is right and the target is immoral
        3. Moral crusaders run the risk of engaging in immoral conduct in their efforts to protect society from those they consider immoral

II. Homosexuality
    A. Attitudes toward homosexuality
        1. Throughout much of Western history, homosexuals have been subject to discrimination, sanction, and violence
        2. Intolerance continues today
    B. Homosexuality and the law
        1. Homosexuality is no longer a crime in the United States
        2. The Defense of Marriage Act
            a. Massachusetts allows same-sex marriage
            b. States are not obligated to recognize single-sex marriages performed in other states
    C. Is the tide turning?
        1. All sodomy laws in the United States are now unconstitutional and unenforceable
        2. Romer and Lawrence decisions have heralded a new era of legal and civil rights for gay men and women

III. Paraphilias
    A. Bizarre or abnormal sexual practices involving recurrent sexual urges focused on
        1. Nonhuman objects (such as underwear, shoes, or leather)
        2. Humiliation or the experience of receiving or giving pain (such as in sadomasochism or bondage)
        3. Children or others who cannot grant consent
    B. Behaviors subject to criminal penalties
        1. Asphyxiophilia
        2. Frotteurism
        3. Voyeurism
        4. Exhibitionism
        5. Sadomasochism
        6. Pedophilia
    C. Paraphilias that involve unwilling or underage victims are illegal

IV. Prostitution
    A. General
        1. Prostitution has been known for thousands of years
        2. These conditions are usually present in a commercial sexual transaction
            a. Activity that has sexual significance for the customer
            b. Economic transaction
            c. Emotional indifference
    B. Incidence of prostitution
        1. Rate of arrests for prostitution have declined
        2. The sexual revolution has liberalized sexuality so that men are less likely to use prostitutes because legitimate alternatives for sexuality are now available
    C. International sex trade
        1. Sex tourism
        2. There has also been a soaring demand for pornography, strip clubs, lap dancing, escorts, and telephone sex in developing countries
        3. Countries with large sex industries create the demand for women
        4. Countries where traffickers easily recruit women provide the supply
        5. In the sex industry today, the most popular and valuable women are from Russia and the Ukraine
    D. Types of prostitutes
        1. Street walkers
            a. Many are young runaways who gravitate to major cities to find a new, exciting life and escape from sexual and physical abuse at home
            b. The street life is very dangerous
        2. Bar girls
            a. B-girls are served diluted drinks or water colored with dye or tea, for which the customer is charged an exorbitant price
            b. It is common to find B-girls in towns with military bases and large transient populations
        3. Brothel prostitutes
            a. Madam is in charge of the brothel
            b. Despite their decline, some madams and their brothels have achieved national prominence

4. Call girls
   a. The aristocrats of prostitution
   b. They either entertain clients in their own apartments or visit clients' hotels and apartments
5. Escort services/Call houses
   a. Some escort services are fronts for prostitution rings
   b. Both male and female sex workers can be sent out after the client calls an ad in the yellow pages
   c. A relatively new phenomenon, call houses, combines elements of the brothel and call girl rings
6. Circuit travelers
   a. Prostitutes known as circuit travelers move around in groups of two or three to lumber, labor, and agricultural camps
   b. Sometimes young girls are forced to become circuit travelers by unscrupulous pimps
7. Skeezers
   a. A significant portion of female prostitutes have substance abuse problems
   b. Not all drug-addicted prostitutes barter sex for drugs
8. Massage parlors/photo studios
9. Cyber prostitute

E. Becoming a prostitute
   1. Both male and female street-level sex workers often come from troubled homes
      a. Marked by extreme conflict and hostility
      b. From poor urban areas or rural communities
   2. Most prostitutes grew up in homes with absent fathers
   3. Women engaging in prostitution have limited educational backgrounds
   4. Most did not complete high school
   5. Lower-class girls who get into "the life" report
      a. Conflict with school authorities
      b. Poor grades
      c. An overly regimented school experience
   6. A significant portion of lower class girls have long histories of drug abuse
   7. Young girls who frequently use drugs and begin using at an early age are most at risk for prostitution to support their habits
   8. Child sexual abuse and prostitution
      a. Child prostitution is not a recent development
      b. In contemporary society, child prostitution has been linked to sexual trauma experienced at an early age
      c. Many prostitutes
         1) Were initiated into sex by family members at ages as young as 10 to 12 years
         2) Have long histories of sexual exploitation and abuse

F. Controlling prostitution
   1. Prostitution is considered a misdemeanor, punishable by a fine or a short jail sentence
   2. Law enforcement is uneven and aims at confining illegal activities to particular areas in the city
   3. Prostitution is illegal in all states except Nevada
   4. The Child Sexual Abuse Prevention Act made it a criminal offense to travel abroad for the purpose of engaging in sexual activity with a minor

G. Legalize prostitution?
   1. Feminists have staked out conflicting views of prostitution
      a. One position is that women must become emancipated from male oppression and reach sexual equality
      b. The sexual equality view considers the prostitute a victim of male dominance
      c. The free choice view is that prostitution, if freely chosen, expresses women's equality and is not a symptom of subjugation
   2. Advocates of both positions
      a. Argue that the penalties for prostitution should be reduced (decriminalized)
      b. Neither side advocates outright legalization

V. Pornography
   A. General
      1. The Internet contains at least 200,000 websites offering pornographic material
      2. The purpose of this material is to provide sexual titillation and excitement for paying customers
   B. Child pornography
      1. Child pornography has become widespread on the Internet
      2. Most sites are short-lived entities whose addresses are passed around to users
   C. Does pornography cause violence?
      1. Some studies indicate that viewing sexually explicit material actually has little effect on sexual violence
      2. Even high levels of exposure to pornography do not turn nonaggressive men into sexual predators
      3. The pornography–violence link seems modest
      4. Men exposed to violent pornography are more likely to act aggressively and hold aggressive attitudes toward women
      5. James Fox and Jack Levin find it common for serial killers to collect and watch violent pornography
   D. Pornography and the law
      1. All states and the federal government prohibit the sale and production of pornographic material
      2. Obscene material and the First Amendment
      3. The basic guidelines for obscenity
         a. Whether the average person applying contemporary community standards would find that the work taken as a whole appeals to the prurient interest
         b. Whether the work depicts or describes, in a patently offensive way, sexual conduct specifically defined by the applicable state law
         c. Whether the work, taken as a whole, lacks serious literary, artistic, political or scientific value
   E. Controlling pornography
      1. Controlling sex for profit is difficult because of the public's desire to purchase sexually related material and services
      2. An alternative approach has been to restrict the sale of pornography within acceptable boundaries
      3. The state has the right to regulate adult films as long as the public has the right to view them
   F. Technological change
      1. The First Amendment right to free speech makes legal control of pornography, even kiddie porn, quite difficult

2. Problems with the Child Pornography Prevention Act (CPPA)

VI. Substance abuse
   A. When did drug use begin?
   B. Alcohol and its prohibition
      1. The temperance movement was fueled by the belief that the purity of the U.S. agrarian culture was being destroyed by the growth of the city
      2. What doomed Prohibition?
         a. One factor was the use of organized crime to supply illicit liquor
         b. The law made it illegal only to sell alcohol, not to purchase it
         c. Law enforcement agencies were inadequate and officials were likely to be corrupted by wealthy bootleggers
   C. The extent of substance abuse
      1. Monitoring the Future
         a. Conducted by the Institute of Social Research (ISR) at the University of Michigan
         b. Survey is based on the self-report responses of nearly 50,000 high school students in the 8th, 10th, and 12th grades in almost 400 schools across the United States
         c. Drug use declined from a high point around 1980 until 1990, when it began once again to increase until 1996; since then teenage drug use has either stabilized or declined
      2. National Survey on Drug Use and Health
         a. Conducted by the Substance Abuse and Mental Health Services Administration (SAMHSA), a division of the Department of Health and Human Services
         b. The NSDUH collects information from all U.S. residents of households, noninstitutional group quarters, and civilians living on military bases
         c. In 2003, an estimated 19.5 million Americans aged 12 or older (about 8 percent of the population) were current illicit drug users
      3. National Center on Addiction and Substance Abuse (CASA) Survey
         a. Alcohol abuse begins at an early age and remains an extremely serious problem over the life course
         b. The age at which children begin drinking is dropping
      4. Are surveys accurate?
         a. Self-report evidence is subject to error
         b. National surveys overlook important segments of the drug-using population
         c. There is evidence that reporting may be affected by social and personal traits
         d. These surveys also use statistical estimating methods to project national use trends from relatively small samples
   D. AIDS and drug use
      1. Intravenous (IV) drug use is closely tied to the threat of AIDS
      2. It is now estimated that as many as one-third of all IV drug users are AIDS carriers
      3. One reason for the AIDS–drug use relationship is the widespread habit of needle sharing among IV users
      4. Needle sharing has been encouraged by efforts to control drugs by outlawing the over-the-counter sale of hypodermic needles
      5. The threat of AIDS may be changing the behavior of recreational and middle-class users

E. What causes substance abuse?
1. Subcultural view
   a. The onset of drug use can be tied to such factors as racial prejudice, devalued identities, low self-esteem, poor socioeconomic status, and the high level of mistrust, negativism, and defiance found in impoverished areas
   b. Residents feel trapped in a cycle of violence, drug abuse, and despair
   c. Research shows that peer influence is a significant predictor of drug careers that actually grow stronger as people mature
2. Psychological view
   a. Not all drug abusers reside in lower-class slum areas; the problem of middle-class substance abuse is very real
   b. Some experts have linked substance abuse to psychological deficits that can strike people in any economic class such as
      1) Impaired cognitive functioning
      2) Personality disturbance
      3) Emotional problems
   c. Drugs may help people deal with unconscious needs and impulses and relieve dependence and depression
   d. Research does in fact reveal the presence of a significant degree of personal pathology
3. Genetic factors
   a. Research shows that substance abuse may have a genetic basis
   b. People whose parents were alcoholic or drug dependent have a greater chance of developing a problem than the children of non-abusers
   c. This relationship occurs regardless of parenting style or the quality of the parent–child relationship
4. Social learning
   a. Social psychologists suggest that drug abuse may also result from observing parental drug use
   b. People who learn that drugs provide pleasurable sensations may be the most likely to experiment with illegal substances
   c. A habit may develop if the user experiences lower anxiety, fear, and tension levels
5. Problem behavior syndrome
   a. Longitudinal studies show that drug abusers are maladjusted, alienated, and emotionally distressed
   b. Having a deviant lifestyle begins early in life and is punctuated with
      1) Criminal relationships
      2) Family history of substance abuse
      3) Educational failure
      4) Alienation
   c. There is robust support for the interconnection of problem drinking and drug abuse and other similar social problems
6. Rational choice
   a. Some may use drugs and alcohol because they want to enjoy their effects
   b. Substance abuse may be a function of the rational but mistaken belief that drugs can benefit the user
   c. Adolescents may begin using drugs because they believe their peers expect them to do so

246

F. Is there a drug gateway?
   1. A number of research efforts have confirmed the gateway model
   2. Drinking with an adult present, presumably a parent, was a significant precursor of future substance abuse and delinquency
   3. The most serious drug users have a history of alcohol abuse
   4. Not all research efforts find that users progress to ever-more potent drugs
   5. Some research shows that many hard-core drug abusers never actually smoked pot or used alcohol
G. Types of drug users
   1. Adolescents who distribute small amounts of drugs
   2. Adolescents who frequently sell drugs
   3. Teenage drug dealers who commit other delinquent acts
   4. Adolescents who cycle in and out of the justice system
   5. Drug-involved youth who continue to commit crimes as adults
   6. Outwardly respectable adults who are top-level dealers
   7. Smugglers
   8. Adult predatory drug users who are frequently arrested
   9. Adult predatory drug users who are rarely arrested
   10. Less predatory drug-involved adult offenders
   11. Women who are drug-involved offenders
H. Drugs and crime
   1. One of the main reasons for the criminalization of particular substances is the assumed association between drug abuse and crime
   2. Research suggests that many criminal offenders have extensive experience with drug use
   3. Drug users commit an enormous amount of crime
   4. The true relationship between them is still uncertain
   5. Many users have had a history of criminal activity before the onset of their substance abuse
   6. User surveys
      a. People who take drugs have extensive involvement in crime
      b. Violent adolescents report histories of alcohol abuse
      c. Adults with long histories of drinking are also more likely to report violent offending patterns
   7. Surveys of known criminals
      a. Youths who self-reported delinquent behavior during the past year were also more likely to use illicit drugs in the past month than other youths
      b. Surveys of prison inmates disclose that many (80 percent) are lifelong substance abusers
      c. Arrestee Drug Abuse Monitoring Program (ADAM)
         1) Approximately two-thirds of both female and male arrestees tested positive for at least one drug
         2) Marijuana was the drug most commonly used by male arrestees
         3) Cocaine was the drug most commonly used by female arrestees
      d. The drug-crime connection
         1) Most criminals are not actually drug users
         2) A second interpretation is that most criminals are in fact substance abusers

        3) Even if the crime rate of drug users were actually half that reported in the research literature, users would be responsible for a significant portion of the total criminal activity in the United States

I. Drugs and the law
1. The federal government first initiated legal action to curtail the use of some drugs early in the twentieth century
2. Since then, various federal laws have attempted to increase penalties imposed on drug smugglers and limit the manufacture and sale of newly developed substances

J. Drug control strategies
1. Source control
   a. One approach to drug control is to deter the sale and importation of drugs
   b. Designed to capture and punish known international drug dealers and deter those who are considering entering the drug trade
   c. The drug trade is an important source of foreign revenue
   d. United States has little influence in some key drug-producing areas such as Vietnam, Cambodia, and Myanmar
2. Interdiction strategies
   a. Law enforcement efforts have also been directed at intercepting drug supplies as they enter the country
   b. Border patrols and military personnel using sophisticated hardware have been involved in massive interdiction efforts
3. Law enforcement strategies
   a. Local, state, and federal law enforcement agencies have been actively fighting against drugs
   b. The long-term consequence has been to decentralize drug dealing and encourage young independent dealers to become major suppliers
4. Punishment strategies
   a. Once convicted, drug dealers can get very long sentences
   b. Courts are so backlogged that prosecutors are anxious to plea bargain
   c. Prisons have become jammed with inmates
5. Community strategies
   a. Another type of drug-control effort relies on the involvement of local community groups to lead the fight against drugs
   b. Citizen-sponsored programs attempt to restore a sense of community in drug-infested areas, reduce fear, and promote conventional norms and values
   c. Another tactic is to use the civil justice system to harass offenders
   d. There are also community-based treatment efforts in which citizen volunteers participate in self-help support programs
   e. Drug prevention efforts designed to enhance the quality of life, improve interpersonal relationships, and upgrade the neighborhood's physical environment
   f. D.A.R.E.
6. Drug testing programs
   a. Drug testing of private employees, government workers, and criminal offenders is believed to deter substance abuse
   b. Drug testing is also common in government and criminal justice agencies
   c. Criminal defendants are now routinely tested at all stages of the justice system, from arrest to parole

7. Treatment strategies
   a. One approach rests on the assumption that users have low self-esteem and treatment efforts must focus on building a sense of self
   b. There are also residential programs for the more heavily involved, and a large network of drug treatment centers has been developed
   c. Other therapeutic programs attempt to deal with the psychological causes of drug use
   d. Supporters of treatment argue that many addicts are helped by intensive in- and out-patient treatment
8. Employment programs
   a. Research indicates that drug abusers who obtain and keep employment will end or reduce the incidence of their substance abuse
   b. One approach is the supported work program, which typically involves job-site training, ongoing assessment, and job-site intervention

K. Drug legalization
   1. Despite the massive effort to control drugs through prevention, deterrence, education, and treatment strategies, the fight against substance abuse has not proved successful
   2. Legalization is warranted because the use of mood-altering substances is customary in almost all human societies
   3. Banning drugs creates networks of manufacturers and distributors, many of whom use violence as part of their standard operating procedures
   4. When drugs were legal and freely available in the early twentieth century, the proportion of Americans using drugs was not much greater than today
   5. If drugs were legalized, the government could control price and distribution
   6. The consequences of legalization
      a. Critics argue that legalization
         1) Might have the short-term effect of reducing the association between drug use and crime
         2) Might also have grave social consequences
      b. Drug users might significantly increase their daily intake
   7. The lesson of alcohol
      a. The problems of alcoholism should serve as a warning of what can happen when controlled substances are made readily available
      b. Drunk-driving fatalities might be matched by deaths due to driving under the influence of pot or crack

CHAPTER SUMMARY

When discussing the issue of law and morality, some scholars argue that acts like pornography, prostitution, and drug use erode the moral fabric of society and therefore should be prohibited and punished. According to this view, so-called victimless crimes are prohibited because one of the functions of criminal law is to express a shared sense of public morality. Throughout much of Western history, homosexuals have been subject to discrimination, sanction, and violence. In fact, much intolerance continues today even though homosexuality is no longer a crime in the United States. Massachusetts is the only state that allows same-sex marriage, but under The Defense of Marriage Act, individual states are not obligated to recognize single-sex marriages performed in other states. All sodomy laws in the United States are now unconstitutional and unenforceable and Supreme Court decisions such as those in Romer and Lawrence have heralded a new era of legal and civil rights for gay men and women.

Paraphilias means bizarre or abnormal sexual practices involving recurrent sexual urges focused on nonhuman objects (such as underwear, shoes, or leather), humiliation or the experience of receiving or giving pain (such as in sadomasochism or bondage), or children or others who cannot grant consent. Behaviors subject to criminal penalties include asphyxiophilia, frotteurism, voyeurism, exhibitionism, sadomasochism, and pedophilia. Paraphilias that involve unwilling or underage victims are also illegal.

Prostitution has been known for thousands of years. The following conditions are usually present in a commercial sexual transaction: the activity that has sexual significance for the customer, economic transaction, and emotional indifference. In the international sex trade, sex tourism is a booming business. There has also been a soaring demand for pornography, strip clubs, lap dancing, escorts, and telephone sex in developing countries. Both male and female street-level sex workers often come from troubled homes marked by extreme conflict and hostility and from poor urban areas or rural communities. In contemporary society, child prostitution has been linked to sexual trauma experienced at an early age. Prostitution is illegal in all states except Nevada. The Child Sexual Abuse Prevention Act made it a criminal offense to travel abroad for the purpose of engaging in sexual activity with a minor.

The Internet contains at least 200,000 websites offering pornographic material. The purpose of this material is to provide sexual titillation and excitement for paying customers. Child pornography has become widespread on the Internet. Some studies indicate that viewing sexually explicit material has little effect on sexual violence. Men exposed to violent pornography are more likely to act aggressively and hold aggressive attitudes toward women. According to the Supreme Court, the basic guidelines for obscenity include 1) whether the average person applying contemporary community standards would find that the work taken as a whole appeals to the prurient interest, 2) whether the work depicts or describes, in a patently offensive way, sexual conduct specifically defined by the applicable state law, and 3) whether the work, taken as a whole, lacks serious literary, artistic, political or scientific value.

Several studies concerning the extent of substance abuse in the United States are conducted throughout the year. Among those studies are Monitoring the Future, the National Survey on Drug Use and Health, and the National Center on Addiction and Substance Abuse (CASA) Survey. Intravenous (IV) drug use is closely tied to the threat of AIDS and it is now estimated that as many as one-third of all IV drug users are AIDS carriers. One reason for the AIDS–drug use relationship is the widespread habit of needle sharing among IV users. There are six major theories concerning what causes substance abuse. They include the subcultural view, the psychological view, genetic factors, social learning, problem behavior syndrome, and rational choice. A number of research efforts have confirmed that there is a drug gateway. The most serious drug users have a history of alcohol abuse, but not all research efforts find that users progress to ever-more potent drugs. One of the main reasons for the criminalization of particular substances is the assumed association between drug abuse and crime. Even if the crime rate of drug users were actually half that reported in the research literature, users would be responsible for a significant portion of the total criminal activity in the United States. Despite the massive effort to control drugs through prevention, deterrence, education, and treatment strategies, the fight against substance abuse has not proved successful and so some scholars propose legalization as a solution.

STUDENT EXERCISES

Exercise 1

Go online to http://www.city-journal.org/html/7_2_a1.html and read the document, *Don't Legalize Drugs*, by Theodore Dalrymple. Next, go to http://www.lp.org/issues/relegalize.html and read the document, *Should We Re-Legalize Drugs?*, by the Libertarian Party. Now write a short paper on which drugs should be legalized and which should be not. Justify your answer.

Exercise 2

Go online to http://www.whitehousedrugpolicy.gov/publications/policy/ndcs04/2004ndcs.pdf and scan the *2004 National Drug Control Strategy*. Prepare a one to two page analysis of our government's strategy to deal with drugs. In your response, address the major law enforcement, treatment, and international efforts that are being taken.

CRIMINOLOGY WEB LINKS

http://www.psychdirect.com/forensic/Criminology/para/paraphilia.htm#types
This is the official website for PsychDirect. Take a look around the website which has a wealth of information on paraphilias.

http://www.dianarussell.com/porntoc.html
This is an article by Diana Russell on the relationship between pornography and rape.

http://www.impactresearch.org/documents/sistersspeakout.pdf
This publication by Jody Raphael and Deborah L. Shapiro from the Center for Impact Research is a study on prostitutes in Chicago. It provides "helpful information for understanding the lives of women in prostitution, and what can be done to assist them."

http://www.ojp.usdoj.gov/ovc/publications/bulletins/internet_2_2001/NCJ184931.pdf
This is a publication from the Office for Victims of Crime that deals with internet crimes against children. Although only eight pages long, it provides a great deal of information.

This website contains a document from the Office of Juvenile Justice and Delinquency Prevention called *Prostitution of Juveniles: Patterns from NIBRS*. It provides demographic data on juveniles arrested by the police for prostitution.

TEST BANK

FILL-IN THE BLANKS

1. _____ _____ _____ involve acts that interfere with the operations of society and the ability of people to function efficiently.

2. In our society, _____ _____ can be distinguished from crimes on the basis of the social harm they cause.

3. _____ is rubbing against or touching a nonconsenting person in a crowd, elevator, or other public area.

4. Modern commercial sex appears to have its roots in ancient _____.

5. A _____ is a woman who employs prostitutes, supervises their behavior, and receives a fee for her services.

6. Philip Jenkins suggests that kiddie porn is best combated by more effective law enforcement; instead of focusing on users, efforts should be directed against _____.

7. The eventual prohibition of the sale of alcoholic beverages brought about by ratification of the _____ Amendment in 1919.

8. There is evidence that reporting may be affected by _____ and personal traits.

9. For many people, substance abuse is just one of many _____ behaviors.

10. Although the drug–crime connection is powerful, the true relationship between them is still _____ because many users have had a history of criminal activity before the onset of their substance abuse.

TRUE/FALSE QUESTIONS

1. T/F There is little debate that the purpose of criminal law is to protect society and reduce social harm.

2. T/F Acts that are believed to be extremely harmful to the general public are always outlawed.

3. T/F It is possible to be a homosexual but not to engage in sexual conduct with members of the same sex.

4. T/F All paraphilias activity is outlawed.

5. T/F The sexual exchange in prostitution is simply for economic consideration.

6. T/F The aristocrats of prostitution are brothel prostitutes.

7. T/F The free choice view considers the prostitute a victim of male dominance.

8. T/F Allowing individual judgments on what is obscene makes the Constitution's guarantee of free speech unworkable.

9. T/F In the case of Young v. American Mini Theaters, the Supreme Court permitted a zoning ordinance that restricted theaters showing erotic movies to one area of the city, even though it did not find that any of the movies shown were obscene.

10. T/F Marijuana accounted for most of the increase in overall illicit drug use during the 1990s, but use is now in decline and more kids view it as dangerous.

11. T/F One of the strengths of national surveys on drug usage is that they include all the important segments of the drug-using population.

12. T/F Needle sharing has been encouraged by efforts to control drugs by outlawing the over-the-counter sale of hypodermic needles.

13. T/F Research shows that substance abuse may have a genetic basis.

14. T/F Most all research shows that most people fall into drug abuse slowly, beginning with alcohol and then following with marijuana and more serious drugs as the need for a more powerful high intensifies.

15 T/F Women are far less likely than men to use addictive drugs.

MULTIPLE CHOICE QUESTIONS

1. Crimes for which laws have been enacted to control behaviors involving sexuality and morality are often referred to as:
    a. misdemeanors
    b. public order crimes
    c. social harm
    d. felonies

2. Rule creators who have an absolute certainty that their way is right and that any means are justified to get their way are known as:
    a. vigilantes
    b. entrepreneurs
    c. law makers
    d. moral crusaders

3. Violent acts directed at people because of their sexual orientation are called:
    a. gay bashing
    b. homophobia
    c. paraphilias
    d. sodomy

4. The U.S. Supreme Court determined that people could not be criminally prosecuted because of their status (such as drug addict or homosexual) in which of the following case?
    a. *Romer v. Evans*
    b. *Robinson v. California*
    c. *Bowers v. Hardwick*
    d. *Lawrence v. Texas*

5. In which case did the U.S. Supreme Court rule six to three that Colorado's Amendment 2, which prohibited state and local governments from protecting the civil rights of gay people, was unconstitutional?
    a. *Romer v. Evans*
    b. *Robinson v. California*
    c. *Bowers v. Hardwick*
    d. *Lawrence v. Texas*

6. Which Supreme Court case made it impermissible for states to criminalize oral and anal sex and all other forms of intercourse that are not heterosexual under statutes prohibiting sodomy, deviant sexuality, or buggery?
    a. *Romer v. Evans*
    b. *Robinson v. California*
    c. *Bowers v. Hardwick*
    d. *Lawrence v. Texas*

7. Rubbing against or touching a nonconsenting person in a crowd, elevator, or other public area is known as:
   a. asphyxiophilia
   b. exhibitionism
   c. frotteurism
   d. voyeurism

8. Obtaining sexual pleasure from spying on a stranger while he or she disrobes or engages in sexual behavior with another is known as:
   a. asphyxiophilia
   b. exhibitionism
   c. frotteurism
   d. voyeurism

9. Which of the following conditions are usually **NOT** present in a commercial sexual transaction?
   a. sexual significance for the customer
   b. curiosity
   c. economic transaction
   d. emotional indifference

10. Which of the following is correct concerning prostitution?
    a. The number of arrests for prostitution has remained stable for the past two decades.
    b. The number of men who hire prostitutes has increased sharply.
    c. The prevalence of sexually transmitted diseases has not caused many men to avoid visiting prostitutes.
    d. We have accurate statistics on the number of prostitutes operating in the U.S.

11. Women who barter drugs for sex are called:
    a. boozers
    b. ticketeros
    c. skeezers
    d. working girls

12. One recent survey of street-level sex workers in Phoenix found that women engaging in prostitution have all of the following characteristics **EXCEPT**:
    a. limited educational backgrounds
    b. did not complete high school
    c. high rates of physical abuse in childhood
    d. low rates of sexual abuse in childhood

13. Which of the following is **NOT** correct concerning pornography and violence?
    a. The pornography–violence link is strong.
    b. People exposed to material that portrays violence, sadism, and women enjoying being raped and degraded are also likely to be sexually aggressive toward female victims.
    c. Men exposed to violent pornography are more likely to act aggressively and hold aggressive attitudes toward women.
    d. Fox and Levin find it common for serial killers to collect and watch violent pornography.

14. Which Supreme Court decision is currently the standard for the concept of obscenity?
    a. *Memoirs v. Massachusetts*
    b. *Miller v. California*
    c. *Roth v. United States*
    d. *Alberts v. California*

15. Which law restricted importation, manufacture, sale, and dispensing of narcotics?
    a. Harrison Narcotics Act
    b. Boggs Act of 1951
    c. Marijuana Tax Act
    d. Durham-Humphrey Act of 1951

16. Which law made it illegal to dispense barbiturates and amphetamines without a prescription?
    a. Harrison Narcotics Act
    b. Boggs Act of 1951
    c. Marijuana Tax Act
    d. Durham-Humphrey Act of 1951

17. The annual self-report survey of drug abuse among high school students conducted by the Institute of Social Research (ISR) at the University of Michigan that is an important source of information on drug use is called:
    a. National Survey on Drug Use and Health (NSDUH)
    b. National Center on Addiction and Substance Abuse (CASA) Survey
    c. Arrestee Drug Abuse Monitoring Program (ADAM)
    d. Monitoring the Future (MTF)

18. The view that drug abuse as having an environmental basis is called:
    a. problem behavior syndrome
    b. rational choice
    c. subcultural view
    d. social learning

19. Those who suggest that drug abuse may result from observing parental drug use follow which view?
    a. problem behavior syndrome
    b. rational choice
    c. subcultural view
    d. social learning

20. Those who argue that some may use drugs and alcohol because they want to enjoy their effects subscribe to which view?
    a. problem behavior syndrome
    b. rational choice
    c. subcultural view
    d. social learning

21. Another important source of data on the drug abuse–crime connection is:
    a. National Survey on Drug Use and Health (NSDUH)
    b. National Center on Addiction and Substance Abuse (CASA) Survey
    c. Arrestee Drug Abuse Monitoring Program (ADAM)
    d. Monitoring the Future (MTF)

22. The approach to drug control that deters the sale and importation of drugs through the systematic apprehension of large-volume drug dealers, coupled with the enforcement of strict drug laws that carry heavy penalties is called:
    a. source control
    b. interdiction strategy
    c. community strategy
    d. law enforcement strategy

23. Directing efforts at large-scale drug rings is a:
    a. source control
    b. interdiction strategy
    c. community strategy
    d. law enforcement strategy

24. A drug prevention effort designed to enhance the quality of life, improve interpersonal relationships, and upgrade the neighborhood's physical environment is called:
    a. source control
    b. interdiction strategy
    c. community strategy
    d. law enforcement strategy

25. Which of the following is **NOT** part of the D.A.R.E. program?
    a. teaching students techniques to resist peer pressure
    b. teaching students to report drug users
    c. teaching students respect for the law and law enforcers
    d. giving students ideas for alternatives to drug use

ESSAY QUESTIONS

1. Explain the association between law and morality.

2. Discuss the various types of prostitution.

3. Explain the various techniques being used to control pornography.

4. Describe the cause of substance abuse.

5. Explain the various drug control strategies.

MATCHING

1. _____ Addict
2. _____ Brothels
3. _____ Call Girls
4. _____ Paraphilias
5. _____ Gay Bashing
6. _____ Homosexuality
7. _____ Madam
8. _____ Mann Act
9. _____ Massage Parlors
10. _____ Moral Crusades

A. Base of some prostitutes where massage and some prostitution services are for sale.
B. A woman who employs prostitutes, supervises their behavior, and receives a fee for her services.
C. Violent acts directed at people because of their sexual orientation.
D. Prostitutes who service upper-class customers and earn large sums of money.
E. A person with an overpowering physical and psychological need to continue taking a particular substance or drug by any means possible.
F. Efforts by interest-group members to stamp out behavior they find objectionable.
G. The Federal Act which prohibited bringing women into the country or transporting them across state lines for the purposes of prostitution.
H. Refers to erotic interest in members of one's own sex.
I. Bizarre or abnormal sexual practices involving recurrent sexual urges focused on nonhuman objects, humiliation or the experience of receiving or giving pain, or children or others who cannot grant consent.
J. Also known as bordellos, cathouses, sporting houses and houses of ill repute.

CHAPTER 13 ANSWER KEY

Fill In The Blank Answers

1. public order crimes
2. immoral acts
3. frotteurism
4. Greece
5. madam
6. suppliers
7. Eighteenth
8. social
9. problem
10. uncertain

True/False Answers

1.	T	6.	F	11.	F
2.	F	7.	F	12.	T
3.	T	8.	T	13.	T
4.	F	9.	T	14.	F
5.	T	10.	T	15.	T

Multiple Choice Answers

1.	B	11.	C	21.	C
2.	D	12.	D	22.	A
3.	A	13.	A	23.	D
4.	B	14.	B	24.	C
5.	A	15.	A	25.	B
6.	D	16.	D		
7.	C	17.	D		
8.	D	18.	C		
9.	B	19.	D		
10.	A	20.	B		

Essay Questions

1. Pages 448 – 451
2. Pages 454 – 456
3. Pages 461 – 462
4. Pages 468 – 469
5. Pages 473 – 477

Matching Answers

1.	E	6.	H
2.	J	7.	B
3.	D	8.	G
4.	I	9.	A
5.	C	10.	F

Chapter 14

The Criminal Justice System

LEARNING OBJECTIVES

1. Be familiar with the history of the criminal justice system.

2. Be familiar with the various stages in the process of justice.

3. Understand how criminal justice is shaped by the rule of law.

4. Know the elements of the crime control model.

5. Know what is meant by the justice model.

6. Discuss the elements of due process.

7. Be able to argue the merits of the rehabilitation model.

8. Understand the concept of nonintervention.

9. Know the elements of the restorative justice model.

KEYWORDS AND DEFINITIONS

Criminal justice system: the agencies of government charged with enforcing law, adjudicating crime, and correcting criminal conduct. (page 492)

Arrest: occurs when the police take a person into custody for allegedly committing a criminal act. (495)

Probable cause: there is sufficient evidence that a crime is being or has been committed and that the suspect committed the crime. (495)

Booking: the person is taken to the police station to be fingerprinted and photographed and to have personal information recorded. (495)

Lineup: witnesses are brought in to view the suspect in a group of people with similar characteristics and asked to pick out the suspect. (495)

Interrogation: questioning by police to get the suspect's side of the story. (495)

Complaint: a sworn allegation made in writing to a court or judge that an individual is guilty of some designated offense. (495)

Indictment: a charging document asking the court to bring a case forward to be tried. (495)

Grand jury: considers the case in a closed hearing, in which only the prosecutor presents evidence. (495)

Information: a charging document that is filed before an impartial lower court judge, who decides whether the case should go forward. (495)

Preliminary hearing (or probable cause hearing): a hearing at which the defendant may appear and dispute the prosecutor's charges. If the prosecution's evidence is accepted as factual and sufficient, the suspect is called to stand trial for the crime. (498)

Arraignment: brings the accused before the court that will actually try the case. The formal charges are read, and defendants are informed of their constitutional rights (such as the right to legal counsel). Bail is considered, and a trial date is set. (498)

Bail: a money bond, the amount of which is set by judicial authority; it is intended to ensure the presence of suspects at trial while allowing them their freedom until that time. Suspects who do not show up for trial forfeit their bail. (498)

Recognizance: allows defendants awaiting trial to be released on their own. (499)

Plea bargaining: the accused pleads guilty as charged, thus ending the criminal trial process. In return for the plea, the prosecutor may reduce charges, request a lenient sentence, or grant the defendant some other consideration. (499)

Criminal trial: a full-scale inquiry into the facts of the case before a judge, a jury, or both. (500)

Hung jury: the jury fails to reach a decision. (500)

Disposition: involves a fine, a term of community supervision (probation), a period of incarceration in a penal institution, or some combination of these penalties. In the most serious capital cases, it is possible to sentence the offender to death. Dispositions are usually made after a presentencing investigation is conducted by the court's probation staff. (500)

Incarceration: confinement in a penal institution. (500)

Presentencing investigation: a report conducted by the court's probation staff. (500)

Appeal: if the defendant believes he or she was not treated fairly by the justice system, the individual may seek to have the finding overturned by a higher appellate court. (500)

Discretion: decisions made by agencies of criminal justice whether to send the case further down the line or "kick it" from the system. (500)

Courtroom work group: The pattern of cooperation in the criminal justice system that is actually dominated by judges, prosecutors, and public defenders who work in concert to get cases processed quickly and efficiently. (502)

Hands-off doctrine: The policy of U.S. courts in which they exercised little control over the operations of criminal justice agencies, believing that their actions were not an area of judicial concern. (502)

Law of criminal procedure: sets out and guarantees citizens certain rights and privileges when they are accused of crime. (502)

Right to counsel: the right guaranteed by the U.S. Constitution that a suspect must have advice of a lawyer during certain pretrial and trial activities. (502)

Bill of Rights: the first ten amendments to the U.S. Constitution, ratified in 1791. (502)

Exclusionary rule: the rule that protects defendants from illegal searches and seizures and overly aggressive police interrogations. Information or evidence obtained illegally cannot be used in a trial. (502)

Crime control model: the overriding purpose of the justice system is to protect the public, deter criminal behavior, and incapacitate known criminals. (503)

Justice model: it is futile to rehabilitate criminals, both because treatment programs are ineffective and because they deny people equal protection under the law. (504)

Determinate sentencing: all offenders in a particular crime category would receive the same sentence. (504)

Due process model: combines elements of liberal/positivist criminology with the legal concept of procedural fairness for the accused. Those who adhere to due process principles believe in individualized justice, treatment, and rehabilitation of offenders. If discretion exists in the criminal justice system, it should be used to evaluate the treatment needs of offenders. (504)

Rehabilitation model: embraces the notion that given the proper care and treatment, criminals can be changed into productive, law-abiding citizens. Influenced by positivist criminology, the rehabilitation school suggests that people commit crimes through no fault of their own. Instead, criminals themselves are the victims of social injustice, poverty, and racism; their acts are a response to a society that has betrayed them. (506)

Nonintervention model: calls for limiting government intrusion into people's lives, especially minors who run afoul of the law. Noninterventionists advocate deinstitutionalization of nonserious offenders, diversion from formal court processes into informal treatment programs, and decriminalization of nonserious offenses, such as possessing small amounts of marijuana. (506)

Restorative justice model: the true purpose of the criminal justice system is to promote a peaceful, just society; they advocate peacemaking, not punishment. (507)

CHAPTER OUTLINE

I. Origins of the American criminal justice system
   A. General
      1. Criminal justice agencies have existed for only 150 years or so
      2. Wickersham Commission analyzed the American justice system in detail and helped usher in the era of treatment and rehabilitation
   B. Modern era of criminal justice study
      1. American Bar Foundation studies
      2. 1967 – President's Commission on Law Enforcement and the Administration of Justice
      3. Safe Streets and Crime Control Act of 1968, which provided federal funds for state and local crime control efforts
      4. Funded the Law Enforcement Assistance Administration (LEAA)

II. What is the criminal justice system?
   A. General
      1. The criminal justice system is essentially an instrument of social control
      2. Only the criminal justice system has the power to control crime and punish criminals
   B. The major components of the criminal justice system
      1. Police
      2. Courts
      3. Correctional agencies

III. The process of justice
   A. General
      1. It is possible to see the criminal justice system as a series of decision points through which offenders flow
      2. The process is so routine than some commentators refer to it as "assembly-line justice"
   B. Critical stages of the criminal justice process
      1. Initial contact
      2. Investigation
      3. Arrest
      4. Custody
         a. Booking
         b. Lineup
         c. Interrogation

5. Complaint/charging
    a. Complaint – misdemeanor
    b. Information – felony
    c. Indictment – felony
6. Preliminary hearing/grand jury
    a. Half the states and in the federal system, the decision of whether to bring a suspect to trial (indictment) is made by a grand jury
    b. Remaining states use the charging document called information
        1) Is filed before an impartial lower court judge, who decides whether the case should go forward
        2) Known as a preliminary hearing or probable cause hearing
            a) Defendant may appear at a preliminary hearing
            b) Defendant may dispute the prosecutor's charges
7. Arraignment
    a. Brings the accused before the court that will actually try the case
    b. Formal charges are read
    c. Defendants are informed of their constitutional rights
    d. Bail is considered
    e. A trial date is set
8. Bail or detention
9. Plea bargaining
10. Trial/Adjudication
11. Disposition
12. Postconviction remedies
    a. Appeal
    b. Outright release
13. Correctional treatment
14. Release
15. Postrelease/aftercare
C. Going through the justice process
    1. At every stage of the process, a decision is made by an agency of criminal justice whether to send the case further down the line or "kick it" from the system
    2. These decisions transform the identity of the individual passing through the system from an accused to a defendant, convicted criminal, inmate, and ex-con
    3. The criminal justice system acts like a funnel in which a great majority of cases are screened out before trial
    4. Celebrity cases
        a. Celebrity cases are few and far between
        b. Trials are rare
        c. Courtroom work group

IV. Criminal justice and the rule of law
A. Hands-off doctrine
B. Law of criminal procedure
    1. Procedural laws control the actions of the agencies of justice and define the rights of criminal defendants
    2. Procedural laws have several different sources
        a. Bill of Rights
        b. Procedural rights protect defendants from illegal searches and seizures and overly aggressive police interrogations

V. Concepts of justice
   A. Crime control model
      1. The overriding purpose of the justice system
         a. Protect the public
         b. Deter criminal behavior
         c. Incapacitate known criminals
      2. Speedy, efficient justice is the goal
      3. Emphasizes protecting society and compensating victims
      4. Dominant force in American justice
      5. There is some evidence that strict crime control measures can in fact have a deterrent effect
   B. Justice model
      1. It is futile to rehabilitate criminals
         a. Treatment programs are ineffective
         b. They deny people equal protection under the law
      2. The consequence is a sense of injustice in the criminal justice system
      3. Question the crime control perspective's reliance on deterrence
      4. Concerned with unfairness in the system
      5. The justice model calls for fairness in criminal procedure
      6. The justice model has had an important influence on criminal justice policy
   C. Due process model
      1. Combines elements of liberal/positivist criminology with the legal concept of procedural fairness for the accused
      2. Believe in individualized justice, treatment, and rehabilitation of offenders
      3. Discretion should be used to evaluate the treatment needs of offenders
      4. Have demanded that competent defense counsel, jury trials, and other procedural safeguards be offered to every criminal defendant
      5. Due process advocates see themselves as protectors of civil rights
      6. Due process exists to protect citizens
      7. The due process orientation has not fared well in recent years
   D. Rehabilitation model
      1. Embraces the notion that given the proper care and treatment, criminals can be changed into productive, law-abiding citizens
      2. The general public
         a. Wants protection from crime
         b. Also favors programs designed to help unfortunate people who commit crime because of emotional or social problems
      3. Dealing effectively with crime requires attacking its root causes
      4. Also known as the medical model
      5. Research evidence suggests that correctional treatment can have an important influence on offenders
      6. Calls for limiting government intrusion into people's lives, especially minors who run afoul of the law
      7. Advocate deinstitutionalization of nonserious offenders
      8. Programs instituted under this model include mediation, diversion, and community-based corrections
      9. There is little evidence that alternative programs actually reduce recidivism rates

E. Nonintervention model
 1. Calls for limiting government intrusion into people's lives, especially minors who run afoul of the law
 2. Noninterventionists advocate
  a. Deinstitutionalization of nonserious offenders
  b. Diversion from formal court processes into informal treatment programs
  c. Decriminalization of nonserious offenses
 3. Justice system should interact as little as possible with offenders
 4. There has also been criticism of the nonintervention philosophy
  a. Little evidence that alternative programs actually reduce recidivism rates
  b. Alternative programs actually result in "widening the net"
F. Restorative justice model
 1. The true purpose of the criminal justice system is to promote a peaceful, just society
 2. The violent punishing acts of the state are not dissimilar from the violent acts of individuals
 3. There is no single definition of what constitutes restorative justice

VI. Concepts of justice today
 A. General
 B. The various philosophies of justice compete today for dominance in the criminal justice system
 C. There is a growing emphasis on protecting the public by increasing criminal sentences and swelling prison populations
 D. Advocates of the rehabilitation model claim that the recent imprisonment binge may be a false panacea

CHAPTER SUMMARY

Criminal justice agencies have existed for only 150 years or so. In 1931 the Wickersham Commission analyzed the American justice system in detail and helped usher in the era of treatment and rehabilitation. The modern era of criminal justice study began with the American Bar Foundation studies. The most significant impact on criminal justice came from the President's Commission on Law Enforcement and the Administration of Justice in 1967. One major piece of legislation that came from that commission was the Safe Streets and Crime Control Act of 1968, which provided federal funds for state and local crime control efforts. This act also funded the Law Enforcement Assistance Administration (LEAA).

What is the criminal justice system? The criminal justice system is essentially an instrument of social control because only the criminal justice system has the power to control crime and punish criminals. The major components of the criminal justice system include police, courts, and correctional agencies.

When one looks at the process of justice, it is possible to see the criminal justice system as a series of decision points through which offenders flow. The process is so routine than some commentators refer to it as "assembly-line justice." There are fifteen critical stages of the criminal justice process. At every one of those critical stages of the process, a decision is made by an agency of criminal justice whether to send the case further down the line or "kick it" from the system. These decisions transform the identity of the individual passing through the system from an accused to a defendant, convicted criminal, inmate, and ex-con. The criminal justice system acts like a funnel in which a great majority of cases are screened out before trial. Celebrity cases are few and far between; trials are rare.

Procedural laws control the actions of the agencies of justice and define the rights of criminal defendants. The source of procedural laws is the Bill of Rights (the first ten amendments to the U.S. Constitution). Procedural rights protect defendants from illegal searches and seizures and overly aggressive police interrogations.

Many competing views of justice exist simultaneously in U.S. culture. The first of these is the crime control model. It sees the overriding purpose of the justice system as protecting the public, deterring criminal behavior, and incapacitating known criminals. According to this view, the goal of the criminal justice system is speedy, efficient justice. The justice model claims questions the crime control perspective's reliance on deterrence and is concerned with unfairness in the system. The justice model has had an important influence on criminal justice policy. The due process model combines elements of liberal/positivist criminology with the legal concept of procedural fairness for the accused. The model believes in individualized justice, treatment, and rehabilitation of offenders. Due process advocates see themselves as protectors of civil rights. The due process orientation has not fared well in recent years. The rehabilitation model embraces the notion that given the proper care and treatment, criminals can be changed into productive, law-abiding citizens. The model state that the general public wants protection from crime, but it also favors programs designed to help unfortunate people who commit crime because of emotional or social problems. The rehabilitation model is also known as the medical model.

The nonintervention model calls for limiting government intrusion into people's lives, especially minors who run afoul of the law. Noninterventionists advocate deinstitutionalization of nonserious offenders, diversion from formal court processes into informal treatment programs, and decriminalization of nonserious offenses. They argue that the justice system should interact as little as possible with offenders. There has been criticism of the nonintervention philosophy because there is little evidence that alternative programs actually reduce recidivism rates and that they actually result in "widening the net." The restorative justice model proposes that the true purpose of the criminal justice system is to promote a peaceful, just society. There is no single definition of what constitutes restorative justice. The various philosophies of justice compete today for dominance in the criminal justice system.

STUDENT EXERCISES

Exercise 1

Write a one to two page paper answering the following question. To which of the six competing views of the criminal justice system do you subscribe? Which of the six do you find to be the weakest? Justify your answer.

Exercise 2

Go online to http://www.ojp.usdoj.gov/reports/98Guides/lblf/panel2c.htm and read the article, Continuity and Change in American Crime: Lessons from Three Decades by Jeffrey Fagan. Write a one to two page summary of the lessons that can be learned about American crime from the work of the President's Commission on Law Enforcement and Administration of Justice.

CRIMINOLOGY WEB LINKS

http://www.ojp.usdoj.gov/reports/98Guides/lblf/welcome.html
This is a summary of the Symposium on the 30th Anniversary of the President's Commission on Law Enforcement and Administration of Justice. It is an excellent review of the President's Commission's work thirty years after it published its findings.

http://www.restorativejustice.org/
This is the official website of Restorative Justice Online from the PFI Centre for Justice and Reconciliation. It contains links to a wealth of information on restorative justice.

http://www.nccd-crc.org/nccd/pubs/2004_corrections_attitudes.pdf
This publication by Barry Krisberg, Jessica Craine, and Susan Marchionna from the National Council on Crime and delinquency is a study on *Attitudes of Californians toward Effective Correctional Policies*. It provides an insight into the views of criminal justice that exist among Californians.

http://www.civitas.org.uk/pdf/Rehab.pdf
This is a publication from Civitas that deals with rehabilitation. The study is entitled *Making Rehabilitation Work: American Experience of Rehabilitating Prisoners* by Iain Murray.

TEST BANK

FILL-IN THE BLANKS

1.   At first criminal justice institutions operated _____, with little recognition that their functions could be coordinated or share common ground.

2.   In 1931, President Herbert Hoover appointed the National Commission of Law Observance and Enforcement, commonly known today as the _____ Commission.

3.   Federal intervention through the LEAA established the concept that its component agencies actually make up a _____.

4.   The _____ _____ _____ refers to the agencies of government charged with enforcing law, adjudicating crime, and correcting criminal conduct.

5.   Nineteenth-century reformers, today known as _____ _____, lobbied to separate young offenders from serious adult criminals.

6.   An _____ occurs when the police take a person into custody for allegedly committing a criminal act.

7.   An _____ brings the accused before the court that will actually try the case.

8.   The criminal justice system acts like a _____ in which a great majority of cases are screened out before trial.

9.   Those espousing the _____ _____ model believe that the overriding purpose of the justice system is to protect the public, deter criminal behavior, and incapacitate known criminals.

10. The _____ model calls for limiting government intrusion into people's lives, especially minors who run afoul of the law.

270

TRUE/FALSE QUESTIONS

1. T/F The modern era of criminal justice study began with a series of explorations of the criminal justice process conducted under the auspices of the American Bar Foundation.

2. T/F Although it appears that way, the criminal justice system is not an instrument of social control.

3. T/F The correctional system population is at an all-time low.

4. T/F The policy of treating juveniles who commit criminal acts separately from adults is relatively new.

5. T/F The police officer is required to use the word arrest or a similar word to initiate an arrest.

6. T/F The law allows suspects to have their lawyers present when police conduct in-custody interrogations.

7. T/F The grand jury considers the case in a closed hearing, in which only the prosecutor presents evidence.

8. T/F Defendants are informed of their constitutional rights (such as the right to legal counsel) at a preliminary hearing.

9. T/F Successful completion of the postrelease period marks the end of the criminal justice process.

10. T/F The courtroom workgroup consists of the prosecutors and public defenders who work in concert to get cases processed quickly and efficiently.

11. T/F The law of criminal procedure sets out and guarantees citizens certain rights and privileges when they are accused of crime.

12. T/F The due process philosophy emphasizes protecting society and compensating victims.

13. T/F According to the justice model, it is futile to rehabilitate criminals, both because treatment programs are ineffective and because they deny people equal protection under the law.

14. T/F The nonintervention model of the justice system portrays it as a method for dispensing "treatment" to needy "patients."

15. T/F According to the restorative justice model, mutual aid rather than coercive punishment is the key to a harmonious society.

MULTIPLE CHOICE QUESTIONS

1. This national study group formed by President Hoover to analyze the American justice system in detail and helped usher in the era of treatment and rehabilitation was:
    a. American Bar Foundation
    b. Wickersham Commission
    c. President's Commission on Law Enforcement and Administration of Justice
    d. Law Enforcement Assistance Administration

2. What helped launch a massive campaign to restructure the justice system by funding the Law Enforcement Assistance Administration (LEAA), an agency that provided hundreds of millions of dollars in aid to local and state justice agencies?
    a. Safe Streets and Crime Control Act of 1968
    b. Wickersham Commission
    c. President's Commission on Law Enforcement and Administration of Justice
    d. Omnibus Crime Bill of 1973

3. What is true concerning both the adult criminal justice system and the juvenile justice system?
    a. independent
    b. correlated
    c. unified
    d. interrelated

4. The Supreme Court decision in In Re Gault granted juveniles all of the following rights **EXCEPT**:
    a. procedural rights
    b. right to a jury
    c. due process rights
    d. right to legal counsel

5. Which of the following is **NOT** true concerning the juvenile justice system?
    a. Plea bargaining exists in juvenile court.
    b. Juvenile proceedings are considered criminal.
    c. Pretrial motions are allowed in juvenile court.
    d. Juveniles can be placed in pretrial detention.

6. Which of the following pertains **ONLY** to the juvenile court system?
    a. Upon conviction, the defendant is sentenced.
    b. Must release information about the defendant.
    c. Purpose of the procedure is treatment.
    d. Can be sentenced to a county jail.

7. Which of the following is **NOT** required to have a legal arrest?
   a. The officer believes there is sufficient evidence (probable cause) that a crime is being or has been committed and that the suspect committed the crime.
   b. The officer says "I am placing you under arrest."
   c. The officer deprives the individual of freedom.
   d. The suspect believes that he or she is in the custody of a police officer and cannot voluntarily leave.

8. The procedure where a person may be taken to the police station to be fingerprinted and photographed and to have personal information recorded is known as:
   a. arraignment
   b. custody
   c. lineup
   d. booking

9. Which of the following is used to charge someone in a misdemeanor?
   a. complaint
   b. bill of indictment
   c. information
   d. bill of charge

10. Half the states and in the federal system, the decision of whether to bring a suspect to trial (indictment) is accomplished by a(n):
    a. grand jury
    b. information
    c. preliminary hearing
    d. probable cause hearing

11. The formal charges are read, and defendants are informed of their constitutional rights (such as the right to legal counsel) during the:
    a. charging
    b. preliminary hearing
    c. arraignment
    d. plea bargaining

12. Bail is set during the:
    a. booking
    b. preliminary hearing
    c. arraignment
    d. plea bargaining

13. If the jury fails to reach a decision, there is a:
    a. mistrial
    b. hung jury
    c. retrial
    d. acquittal

14. The pattern of cooperation among judges, prosecutors, and public defenders who work in concert to get cases processed quickly and efficiently is referred to as the:
    a.   courtroom players
    b.   court hierarchy
    c.   judicial group
    d.   courtroom work group

15. Those who embrace what view see the justice system as a barrier between destructive criminal elements and conventional society?
    a.   justice model
    b.   due process model
    c.   crime control model
    d.   rehabilitation model

16. Which criminal justice view calls for fairness in criminal procedure?
    a.   justice model
    b.   due process model
    c.   crime control model
    d.   rehabilitation model

17. Which group lobbies for abolition of the exclusionary rule and applaud when the Supreme Court hands down rulings that increase police power?
    a.   justice model
    b.   due process model
    c.   crime control model
    d.   rehabilitation model

18. Which criminal justice view adheres to due process principles believe in individualized justice, treatment, and rehabilitation of offenders?
    a.   justice model
    b.   due process model
    c.   crime control model
    d.   rehabilitation model

19. Which criminal justice view argues that discretion should be used to evaluate the treatment needs of offenders?
    a.   justice model
    b.   due process model
    c.   crime control model
    d.   rehabilitation model

20. Which criminal justice view embraces the notion that given the proper care and treatment, criminals can be changed into productive, law-abiding citizens?
    a.   justice model
    b.   due process model
    c.   crime control model
    d.   rehabilitation model

21. Which criminal justice view argues that dealing effectively with crime requires attacking its root causes?
    a. restorative justice model
    b. rehabilitation model
    c. nonintervention model
    d. due process model

22. Which criminal justice view advocates of the due process model have demanded that competent defense counsel, jury trials, and other procedural safeguards be offered to every criminal defendant?
    a. restorative justice model
    b. rehabilitation model
    c. nonintervention model
    d. due process model

23. Which criminal justice view calls for limiting government intrusion into people's lives, especially minors who run afoul of the law?
    a. restorative justice model
    b. rehabilitation model
    c. nonintervention model
    d. due process model

24. Which criminal justice view advocates that studies show that punitive methods of correction (such as jail and prison) are no more effective than more humanitarian efforts (such as probation with treatment)?
    a. restorative justice model
    b. rehabilitation model
    c. nonintervention model
    d. due process model

25. Which model views the justice system as a wise and caring parent?
    a. restorative justice model
    b. rehabilitation model
    c. nonintervention model
    d. due process model

ESSAY QUESTIONS

1. List the various stages in the process of justice.

2. Explain the elements of the crime control model.

3. Explain the elements of due process model.

4. Describe the merits of the rehabilitation model.

5. Explain the elements of the restorative justice model.

MATCHING

1. _____ Parens Patriae
2. _____ President Hoover
3. _____ In Re Gault
4. _____ Probable Cause
5. _____ Booking
6. _____ Hung Jury
7. _____ American Bar Foundation
8. _____ President's Commission on Law Enforcement and Administration of Justice
9. _____ Hands-Off Doctrine
10. _____ Lineup

A. Fail to reach a decision.
B. Officer believes there is sufficient evidence that a crime is being or has been committed and that the suspect committed the crime.
C. Witnesses are brought in to view the suspect.
D. With a series of explorations of the criminal justice process that they conducted, the modern era of criminal justice study began.
E. State was acting in the best interests of children.
F. U.S. courts exercised little control over the operations of criminal justice agencies, believing that their actions were not an area of judicial concern.
G. Granted procedural and due process rights, such as the right to legal counsel, to juveniles at trial.
H. The person may be taken to the police station to be fingerprinted and photographed and to have personal information recorded.
I. The Challenge of Crime in a Free Society.
J. Wickersham Commission

CHAPTER 14 ANSWER KEY

Fill In The Blank Answers

1. independently
2. Wickersham
3. system
4. criminal justice system
5. child savers
6. arrest
7. arraignment
8. funnel
9. crime control
10. nonintervention

True/False Answers

1.	T	6.	T	11.	T
2.	F	7.	T	12.	F
3.	F	8.	F	13.	T
4.	T	9.	T	14.	F
5.	F	10.	F	15.	T

Multiple Choice Answers

1.	B	11.	C	21.	B
2.	A	12.	C	22.	D
3.	D	13.	B	23.	C
4.	C	14.	D	24.	A
5.	B	15.	C	25.	B
6.	C	16.	A		
7.	B	17.	C		
8.	D	18.	B		
9.	A	19.	B		
10.	A	20.	D		

Essay Questions

1. Pages 495 – 500
2. Pages 503 – 504
3. Pages 504 – 505
4. Page 506
5. Page 507

Matching Answers

1.	E	6.	A
2.	J	7.	D
3.	G	8.	I
4.	B	9.	F
5.	H	10.	C

Chapter 15

Police and Law Enforcement

LEARNING OBJECTIVES

1. Be familiar with the history of American Policing.

2. Understand how reform movements created the ideal of police professionalism.

3. Recognize that there are law enforcement agencies on the federal, state, and local level.

4. Comment on the efforts to improve patrol and investigative effectiveness.

5. Discuss the changing role of police.

6. Be able to comment on how the courts have set limits on the extent of police interrogations, and search and seizure evidence.

7. Understand the police personality and its effect on performance and discretion.

8. Talk about how women and minority officers are changing police.

9. Become familiar with the issues surrounding police use of force.

KEYWORDS AND DEFINITIONS

Gatekeepers: police initiate contact with law violators and decide whether to formally arrest them and start their journey through the criminal justice system, settle the issue informally (such as by issuing a warning), or simply take no action at all. (page 514)

Racial profiling: selecting suspects on the basis of their ethnic or racial background. (514)

Pledge system: every man living in the villages scattered throughout the countryside was responsible for aiding his neighbors and protecting the settlement from thieves and marauders. (514)

Tithing: people were grouped into a collective of ten families. (514)

Constable: the supervisor of ten tithings that were grouped into a hundred. The constable, who might be considered the first real police officer, dealt with more serious breaches of the law. (514)

Shire: the hundreds were grouped into shires resembling the counties of today. (514)

Reeve: appointed by the crown to supervise a certain territory, such as a shire, and to assure the local nobleman that order would be kept. (514)

Watch system: created to help protect property in England's larger cities and towns. Watchmen patrolled at night and helped protect against robberies, fires, and disturbances. They reported to the area constable. (514)

Justice of the peace: created to assist the shire reeve in controlling the county. Eventually the justices took on judicial functions in addition to their primary duty as peacekeeper. (514)

Sheriff: the most important law enforcement agent in the county. (515)

Wickersham Commission: created by President Herbert Hoover to study police issues on a national scale. In its 1931 report, the commission identified many of the problems of policing, including a weak command structure and overly complex job requirements. (516)

Federal Bureau of Investigation (FBI): an investigative agency, with jurisdiction over all matters in which the United States is, or may be, an interested party. It limits its jurisdiction to federal laws, including all federal statutes not specifically assigned to other agencies. These include statutes dealing with espionage, sabotage, treason, civil rights violations, the murder and assault of federal officers, mail fraud, robbery and burglary of federally insured banks, kidnapping, and interstate transportation of stolen vehicles and property. (517)

Drug Enforcement Administration (DEA): investigates illegal drug use and carries out independent surveillance and enforcement activities to control the importation of narcotics. (518)

U.S. marshals: court officers who help implement federal court rulings, transport prisoners, and enforce court orders. (518)

Bureau of Alcohol, Tobacco, Firearms, and Explosives (ATF): has jurisdiction over the sales and distribution of firearms, explosives, alcohol, and tobacco products. (518)

Internal Revenue Service (IRS): enforces violations of income, excise, stamp, and other tax laws. (518)

Department of Homeland Security (DHS): a new cabinet-level agency charged with preventing terrorist attacks within the United States, reducing America's vulnerability to terrorism, and minimizing the damage and helping recover from attacks that do occur. (518)

State police: a law enforcement agency with statewide jurisdiction. (519)

Foot patrols: each officer has a particular area, or beat, to walk; the police officer is the symbol of state authority in that area. (521)

Aggressive preventive patrol: a patrol technique designed to suppress crime before it occurs. (521)

Mug shots: pictures that victims or witnesses are asked to look at to identify offenders. (522)

Modus operandi (MO): the working methods of particular offenders. (522)

Sting: detectives pose as fences with thieves interested in selling stolen merchandise. Transactions are videotaped to provide prosecutors with strong cases. (523)

Morals squad (or vice squad): usually staffed by plainclothes officers or detectives specializing in victimless crimes such as prostitution or gambling. (523)

Community-oriented policing (COP): police maintained a presence in the community, walked beats, got to know citizens, and inspired feelings of public safety. (524)

Reactive policing: merely responding to calls for help. (524)

Problem-oriented policing: police play an active role in identifying particular community problems – street-level drug dealers, prostitution rings, gang hangouts—and developing strategies to counteract them. (524)

Miranda warning: the Supreme Court maintained that before the police can question a person who has been arrested or is in custody, they must inform the individual of the Fifth Amendment right to be free from self-incrimination. This is accomplished by the police informing the suspect that 1) he or she has the right to remain silent; 2) if he or she makes a statement, it can be used against him or her in court; 3) he or she has the right to consult an attorney and to have the attorney present at the time of the interrogation; and 4) if he or she cannot afford an attorney, one will be appointed by the state. (527)

Inevitable discovery rule: information provided by a suspect that leads to the seizure of incriminating evidence is permissible if the evidence would have been obtained anyway by other means or sources. (528)

Public safety doctrine: admissible evidence can be obtained without a Miranda warning if the information the police seek is needed to protect public safety; for example, in an emergency, suspects can be asked where they hid their weapons. Their answer can be used in a court of law even though they had not received the Miranda warning. (528)

Search warrant: a judicial order, based on probable cause, allowing police officers to search for evidence in a particular place, seize that evidence, and carry it away. If seized with a valid warrant, the evidence can be used against the suspect at trial. (528)

Blue curtain subculture: negative values and attitudes are believed to cause police officers to be secretive and isolated from the rest of society. (530)

Deadly force: the actions of a police officer who shoots and kills a suspect who is fleeing from arrest, assaulting a victim, or attacking the officer. (538)

CHAPTER OUTLINE

I.   History of police
   A.   General
      1.   Police are the gatekeepers of the criminal justice process
      2.   They initiate contact with law violators
      3.   They decide whether to
         a.   Formally arrest them and start their journey through the criminal justice system
         b.   Settle the issue informally (such as by issuing a warning)
         c.   Simply take no action at all
      4.   The origin of U.S. police agencies can be traced back to early English society
      5.   Pledge system
         a.   Tithing
         b.   Constable
         c.   Shire
         d.   Reeve
      6.   Watch system
      7.   Justice of the peace
   B.   The London Police
      1.   Sir Robert Peel
      2.   The first organized police force in London
      3.   Its members wore a distinctive uniform and were led by two magistrates, who were later given the title of commissioner
      4.   By 1856 every borough and county in England was required to form its own police force
   C.   Policing the American colonies
      1.   Law enforcement in colonial America paralleled the British model
      2.   The county sheriff became the most important law enforcement agent
         a.   Peacekeeping and crime fighting
         b.   Collected taxes
         c.   Supervised elections
         d.   Handled a great deal of other legal business
         e.   Did not patrol or seek out crime
         f.   Reacted to citizens' complaints and investigated crimes that had already occurred
         g.   Salary was related to his effectiveness
         h.   Sheriffs were paid by the fee system
      3.   In the cities
         a.   Law enforcement was the province of the town marshal

      b.   Aided, often unwillingly, by a variety of constables, night watchmen, police justices, and city council members

      c.   If trouble arose, citizens might be called on to form a posse to chase offenders or break up an angry mob

D.   Early American police agencies

   1.   The modern police department was born out of

      a.   Fear of disorder

      b.   The influx of immigrants

      c.   The desire of the wealthy to restructure what they feared was becoming a chaotic society

      d.   Boston created the nation's first formal police department in 1838

      e.   The new police departments replaced the night watch system

   2.   Politics dominated the departments and determined the recruitment of new officers and promotion of supervisors

   3.   At mid-nineteenth century, the detective bureau was created in the Boston police

   4.   Police during the nineteenth century were generally

      a.   Incompetent

      b.   Corrupt

      c.   Disliked by the people they served

E.   Reform movements

   1.   Uniforms were introduced in 1853 in New York

   2.   Technological innovations, such as linking precincts to central headquarters by telegraph, appeared in the late 1850s

   3.   Somewhat later, call boxes allowed patrol officers on the beat to communicate with their commanders

   4.   Nonpolice functions, such as care of the streets, began to be abandoned after the Civil War

   5.   Another reform movement was the takeover of some big city police agencies by state legislators

   6.   The Boston police strike of 1914 heightened interest in police reform

   7.   The Wickersham Commission was created by President Herbert Hoover to study police issues on a national scale

F.   The advent of professionalism

   1.   The onset of police professionalism might be traced to the 1920s and the influence of August Vollmer

   2.   Vollmer's disciples included O. W. Wilson, who pioneered the use of advanced training for officers

   3.   Wilson also was instrumental in applying modern management and administrative techniques to policing

   4.   One important aspect of professionalism was the technological breakthroughs

      a.   The first innovation came in the area of communications – telegraph boxes

      b.   Detroit police department outfitted some of its patrol officers with bicycles

      c.   The first police car was used in Akron, Ohio, in 1910

      d.   The police wagon became popular in Cincinnati in 1912

      e.   In the early 1960s police professionalism was interpreted as being a tough, highly trained, rule-oriented law enforcement department organized along militaristic lines

II. Law enforcement agencies today
   A. Federal law enforcement
      1. Federal Bureau of Investigation (FBI)
         a. An investigative agency
         b. Jurisdiction over all matters in which the United States is, or may be, an interested party
         c. It limits its jurisdiction to federal laws, including all federal statutes not specifically assigned to other agencies
         d. FBI offers important services to local law enforcement agencies
      2. Drug Enforcement Administration (DEA)
      3. U.S. Marshals
      4. Bureau of Alcohol, Tobacco, Firearms, and Explosives (ATF)
      5. Internal Revenue Service (IRS)
      6. Department of Homeland Security
         a. Assigned the mission of
            1) Preventing terrorist attacks within the United States
            2) Reducing America's vulnerability to terrorism
            3) Minimizing the damage and helping recover from attacks that do occur
         b. The Border and Transportation Security directorate
            1) The U.S. Customs Service (Treasury)
            2) The Immigration and Naturalization Service (part) (Justice)
            3) The Federal Protective Service
            4) The Transportation Security Administration (Transportation)
            5) Federal Law Enforcement Training Center (Treasury)
            6) Animal and Plant Health Inspection Service (part) (Agriculture)
            7) Office for Domestic Preparedness (Justice)
         c. The Emergency Preparedness and Response directorate
            1) The Federal Emergency Management Agency (FEMA)
            2) Strategic National Stockpile and the National Disaster Medical System (HHS)
            3) Nuclear Incident Response Team (Energy)
            4) Domestic Emergency Support Teams (Justice)
            5) National Domestic Preparedness Office (FBI)
         d. The Science and Technology directorate
            1) CBRN Countermeasures Programs (Energy)
            2) Environmental Measurements Laboratory (Energy)
            3) National BW Defense Analysis Center (Defense)
            4) Plum Island Animal Disease Center (Agriculture)
         e. The Information Analysis and Infrastructure Protection directorate
            1) Federal Computer Incident Response Center (GSA)
            2) National Communications System (Defense)
            3) National Infrastructure Protection Center (FBI)
            4) Energy Security and Assurance Program (Energy)
   B. County law enforcement
      1. The county police department is an independent agency whose senior officer, the sheriff, is usually elected
      2. Typically, the sheriff's law enforcement functions today are carried out
         a. Only in unincorporated areas within a county
         b. Or in response to city departments' requests for aid in such matters as patrol or investigation

284

C. State police
   1. The Texas Rangers, organized in 1835, are considered by some the first state police force
   2. The impetus for creating state police agencies
      a. The low regard of the public for the crime-fighting ability of local police agencies
      b. The increasingly greater mobility of law violators
   3. In states with large, powerful county sheriff's departments, the state police function is usually restricted to highway patrol
   4. Where the county sheriff's law enforcement role is limited
      a. State police usually maintain a more active investigative and enforcement role
      b. Aid cities and town police departments in criminal investigation
D. Metropolitan police
   1. Metropolitan police agencies make up the vast majority of the law enforcement community's members
   2. Most larger urban departments are independent agencies operating without specific administrative control from any higher governmental authority
   3. Organized at the executive level of government
   4. Common for the city mayor (or the equivalent) to control the hiring and firing of the police chief and, consequently, determine departmental policies
   5. Core functions
      a. Law enforcement
      b. Order maintenance
      c. Service

III. Police functions
   A. Patrol function
      1. Patrol entails police officers' visible presence on the streets and public places of their jurisdiction
      2. The purpose of patrol is to
         a. Deter crime
         b. Maintain order
         c. Enforce laws
         d. Aid in service functions
      3. In early police forces, foot patrols were used almost exclusively
      4. Today patrol cars, motorcycles, helicopters, and other types of mechanized transportation have all but ended walking the beat
      5. The patrol car
         a. Allows police to supervise more territory with fewer officers
         b. Has removed and isolated patrol officers from the communities they serve
      6. Police departments have initiated a number of programs and policies to try to improve patrol effectiveness
         a. Proactive policing
         b. Full enforcement/zero tolerance
         c. Targeting crimes
         d. Making arrests
         e. Adding patrol officers
   B. Investigation function
      1. The second prominent police role is investigation and crime detection

2. Detective branches are organized on the individual precinct level or out of a central headquarters and perform various functions
3. Sometimes they obtain fingerprints from a crime scene and match them with those on file
4. Detectives also solve a crime by being familiar with the modus operandi of the offender
5. Detectives can use their own initiative in solving a case
6. Some jurisdictions maintain morals or vice squads
7. Are investigations effective?
   a. The Rand Corporation, in a classic 1975 study, found that
      1) A great deal of detectives' time was spent in nonproductive work
      2) Investigative expertise did little to help them solve cases
   b. Replications of the Rand study have found that when a suspect was identified, it usually occurred before the case was assigned to a detective
   c. Efforts have been made to revamp investigation procedures

IV. Changing the police role
   A. Community-oriented policing (COP)
      1. "Broken Windows: The Police and Neighborhood Safety," criminologists James Q. Wilson and George Kelling
      2. They asked police to get their officers out of depersonalizing patrol cars
      3. Police administrators should station their officers where they can do the most to promote public confidence and elicit citizen cooperation
      4. Community preservation, public safety, and order maintenance, not crime fighting, should become the primary focus of police
      5. Police should
         a. Play an active role in the community
         b. Identify neighborhood problems and needs
         c. Set a course of action for an effective response
      6. Implementing COP
         a. The current COP movement began when foot patrols were reintroduced in a limited number of jurisdictions
         b. Foot patrol was believed to be an effective device that could help police monitor community concerns
         c. Officers on foot are more approachable and offer a comforting presence to citizens
         d. There has been an effort
            1) To actively pursue citizen involvement in police activities
            2) To orient police strategies toward the neighborhood or block level
            3) To identify community-level problems and seek their solutions
      7. Community policing in action – federal government has encouraged it
      8. Neighborhood policing
         a. To achieve the goals of COP, some agencies have tried to decentralize
         b. Neighborhood initiatives may be an ideal way to fight crime
   B. Problem-oriented policing
      1. Police have been reactive, responding to calls for help
      2. They should play an active role in identifying particular community problems
      3. Problems are better defined narrowly
      4. Solutions draw on the creative talents found in two important resources
         a. The community

       b.   The line officers who are familiar with community problems
    5.   Criminal acts/criminal places
        a.   Problem-oriented strategies are being developed that focus on specific criminal problem areas and/or specific criminal acts
        b.   Combating auto theft – car thieves are no longer able to steal cars with as much ease as before
        c.   Reducing violence
        d.   Operation Ceasefire

C.   Does community policing work?
    1.   Many police experts and administrators have embraced the community and problem-oriented policing
    2.   Not all criminologists agree that a return to the older model of policing is a panacea
    3.   Most police officers do not have the social service skills required of effective community agents
    4.   Police administrators are reluctant to give up the autonomy and authority that power sharing with the public demands
    5.   There is significant evidence that COP programs improve community relations, upgrade the image of local police, and reduce levels of community fear

V. Police and the rule of law
  A.   Custodial interrogation
    1.   The Fifth Amendment guarantees people the right to be free from self-incrimination
    2.   Miranda v. Arizona created objective standards for questioning by police after a defendant has been taken into custody
        a.   He or she has the right to remain silent.
        b.   If he or she makes a statement, it can be used against him or her in court.
        c.   He or she has the right to consult an attorney and to have the attorney present at the time of the interrogation.
        d.   If he or she cannot afford an attorney, one will be appointed by the state.
    3.   The Miranda rule today
        a.   Inevitable discovery rule
        b.   Public safety doctrine
    4.   Dickerson v. United States – the Supreme Court established Miranda as an indisputable cornerstone of the justice process

B.   Search and seizure
    1.   Under normal circumstances police must obtain a search warrant allowing the police
        a.   To search for evidence in a particular place
        b.   To seize that evidence
        c.   To carry it away
    2.   Examples of when police may conduct a legal search without a warrant
        a.   Threshold inquiry (stop-and-frisk)
        b.   Search incident to an arrest
        c.   Automobile search
        d.   Motorist search
        e.   Consent search
        f.   Plain view
        g.   Seizure of nonphysical evidence

        h.   Hot pursuit/ exigency

VI. Issues in policing
    A. Police personality and subculture
        1. The typical police personality is thought to include
            a.   Authoritarianism
            b.   Suspicion
            c.   Racism
            d.   Hostility
            e.   Insecurity
            f.   Conservatism
            g.   Cynicism
        2. Blue curtain subculture
        3. There are two opposing viewpoints on the cause of this phenomenon
            a.   One position holds that police departments attract recruits who are by nature cynical, authoritarian, secretive, and so on
            b.   Other experts maintain that socialization and experience on the police force cause these character traits to develop in police officers
            c.   Research evidence supportive of both viewpoints has been produced
        4. The police subculture
            a.   Police expert William Westly argued that most police officers develop into cynics because of their daily duties
            b.   Westly maintained that
                 1) Police officers learn to mistrust the citizens they protect because they are constantly faced with keeping people in line
                 2) Police come to believe that most people are out to break the law or harm a police officer
                 3) Most officers band together in a police subculture characterized by
                     a.   Clannishness
                     b.   Secrecy
                     c.   Insulation from others in society
            c.   Both the daily routines of police work as well as their close peer relations support the subculture
            d.   The police subculture encourages its members to draw a sharp distinction between good and evil
            e.   Shared group norms may take precedence over individual style in handling daily activities
        5. Police styles
    B. Discretion
        1. The law enforcement function of police involves an enormous amount of personal discretion as to whether to invoke the power of arrest
        2. Police discretion involves the selective enforcement of the law by duly authorized police agents
        3. Police officers are neither regulated in their daily procedures by administrative scrutiny nor subjected to judicial review
        4. The exercise of discretion by police may sometimes deteriorate into violence, discrimination, and other abusive practices
        5. Factors affecting discretion
            a.   Environmental factors – community culture and values
            b.   Departmental factors - policies and orders

  c. Situational factors – suspect demeanor
  d. Victim factors – victim–criminal relationship
  e. Supervision factors – supervisors' style and control
  f. Peer factors – peer influences and culture
  g. Legal factors – crime seriousness, prior record
  h. Extralegal factors – race, gender, age

6. Limiting police discretion
  a. Numerous efforts have been made to limit police discretion
  b. Most experts believe that written rules, either directing or prohibiting action, can be highly effective at controlling police discretion
  c. Perhaps limiting police discretion can be carried out only by outside review

C. Minority and female police officers

1. U.S. police departments have made a concerted effort to attract women and minority police officers

2. A culturally diverse police force dispels the view that police departments are generally bigoted or biased organizations

3. Another important reason for recruiting female and minority police officers is the need to comply with various federal guidelines on hiring

4. United States v. Paradise – the Supreme Court upheld the use of racial quotas to counter the effects of past discrimination

5. Minority police officers
  a. Part of this recruitment effort is to shore up relations between the local police department and the minority community
  b. African Americans have served on police forces since the mid-nineteenth century
  c. Nicholas Alex found that black police officers suffered "double marginality"
    1. African American officers must deal with the expectation that they will give members of their own race a break
    2. On the other hand, they often experience overt racism from police colleagues
    3. African American and white police officers share similar attitudes toward community policing
    4. The number of black officers in some of the nation's largest cities is now proportionate to minority representation in the population

6. Female police officers
  a. The first female police officers were appointed in New York as early as 1845, as "matrons"
  b. How effective are female police officers?
    1) Evaluations of policewomen show them to be equal or superior to male officers in most areas of police work
    2) Female officers seem to have the ability to avoid violent encounters with citizens and to de-escalate potentially violent arrest situations
    3) They are typically the target of fewer citizen complaints
    4) Female police officers have not received general support from their colleagues
  c. Black female police
    1) Black women, who account for only about 2 percent of police officers
    2) They perceive significantly more racial discrimination than either other female officers or black male officers

D. The police and violence
   1. Police officers are empowered to use force and violence in their daily tasks
   2. Police violence first became a major topic for discussion in the 1940s
   3. How common is the use of force today?
       a. Research does in fact show that the least intrusive types of force, like handcuffing, are used much more often than the most intrusive, like lethal violence
       b. There is still debate over whether police are more likely to get rough with minority suspects
   4. Deadly force
       a. A more recent area of concern has been the use of deadly force in apprehending fleeing or violent offenders
       b. The following factors are related to police violence
           1) Exposure to threat and stress
           2) Police workload
           3) Firearm availability
           4) Population type and density
           5) Race and class discrimination
           6) Lack of proper training and preparation
   5. Controlling force
       a. The Supreme Court moved to restrict police use of deadly force when, in Tennessee v. Garner
       b. There are other methods of controlling police shootings
           1) Administrative policies that stress limiting the use of deadly force
           2) Containing armed offenders until specially trained backup teams are sent to take charge of the situation
           3) New York police department also created the Firearm Discharge Review Board
   6. Killing police
   7. Nonlethal weapons
       a. Local police forces have started using some sort of less-than-lethal weapon designed to subdue suspects
       b. Recent research efforts indicate that nonlethal weapons may help reduce police use of force

CHAPTER SUMMARY

Police are considered to be the gatekeepers of the criminal justice process who initiate contact with law violators. They decide whether to formally arrest them and start their journey through the criminal justice system, settle the issue informally, or simply take no action at all. The origin of U.S. police agencies can be traced back to early English society. Sir Robert Peel created the first organized police force in London, and by 1856 law enforcement in colonial America paralleled the British model. Boston created the nation's first formal police department in 1838, and soon other cities did likewise. Politics dominated the departments and determined the recruitment of new officers and promotion of supervisors. Police during the nineteenth century were considered to be generally incompetent, corrupt, and disliked by the people they served. The onset of police professionalism might be traced to the 1920s and the influence of August Vollmer. Vollmer's disciples included O. W. Wilson, who was instrumental in applying modern management and administrative techniques to policing.

Today, at the federal level we have several agencies such as the Federal Bureau of Investigation (FBI), the Drug Enforcement Administration (DEA), U.S. Marshals, the Bureau of Alcohol, Tobacco, Firearms, and Explosives (ATF), the Internal Revenue Service (IRS), and the Department of Homeland Security. At the county level we find the county sheriff's office is an independent agency whose senior officer, the sheriff, is usually elected. At the state level are the state police. Metropolitan police agencies make up the vast majority of the law enforcement community's members. It is common for the city mayor (or the equivalent) to control the hiring and firing of the police chief and, consequently, determine departmental policies. The core functions of the metropolitan police are law enforcement, order maintenance, and service. In "Broken Windows: The Police and Neighborhood Safety," criminologists James Q. Wilson and George Kelling argued that community preservation, public safety, and order maintenance, not crime fighting, should become the primary focus of police. Samuel Walker developed the concept of problem-oriented policing. He noted that should play an active role in identifying particular community problems.

The Fifth Amendment guarantees people the right to be free from self-incrimination. Miranda v. Arizona created objective standards for questioning by police after a defendant has been taken into custody. The Miranda rule has been somewhat weakened today, but in Dickerson v. United States the Supreme Court established Miranda as an indisputable cornerstone of the justice process. Under normal circumstances police must obtain a search warrant allowing the police to search for evidence in a particular place, to seize that evidence, and to carry it away.

The typical police personality is thought to include authoritarianism, suspicion, racism, hostility, insecurity, conservatism, and cynicism. Out of this has grown the blue curtain subculture. There are two opposing viewpoints on the cause of this phenomenon. One position holds that police departments attract recruits who are by nature cynical, authoritarian, secretive, and so on. Other experts maintain that socialization and experience on the police force cause these character traits to develop in police officers. Research evidence supportive of both viewpoints has been produced. The law enforcement function of police involves an enormous amount of personal discretion as to whether to invoke the power of arrest.

U.S. police departments have made a concerted effort to attract women and minority police officers. A culturally diverse police force dispels the view that police departments are generally bigoted or biased organizations. Another important reason for recruiting female and minority police officers is the need to comply with various federal guidelines on hiring. The number of black officers in some of the nation's largest cities is now proportionate to minority representation in the population. Evaluations of policewomen show them to be equal or superior to male officers in most areas of police work.

Police officers are empowered to use force and violence in their daily tasks. Research does in fact show that the least intrusive types of force, like handcuffing, are used much more often than the most intrusive, like lethal violence. The Supreme Court moved to restrict police use of deadly force when, in Tennessee v. Garner. There are other methods of controlling police shootings such as administrative policies that stress limiting the use of deadly force and containing armed offenders until specially trained backup teams are sent to take charge of the situation. Local police forces have started using some sort of less-than-lethal weapon designed to subdue suspects. Recent research efforts indicate that nonlethal weapons may help reduce police use of force.

STUDENT EXERCISES

Exercise 1

Go online to http://www.ncjrs.org/pdffiles1/jr000244c.pdf and read the article on *Keeping the Peace: Police Discretion and Mentally Ill Persons* by Linda A. Teplin. Write a one to two page paper summary of how police officers should handle mentally ill persons.

Exercise 2

Go online to http://www.ncjrs.org/pdffiles1/nij/grants/198029.pdf and read the prologue of the article, *The Evolving Strategy of Policing: Case Studies of Strategic Change* by George L. Kelling and Mary Ann Wycoff. The prologue provides a discussion of the work of O. W. Wilson. Write a one page summary of the work of O. W. Wilson.

CRIMINOLOGY WEB LINKS

http://www.dhs.gov/dhspublic/
This is the official website of the Department of Homeland Security.

http://www.met.police.uk/index.shtml
This is the official website of the Metropolitan Police of London. Scan the website and you will find some interesting facts about the police department founded by Sir Robert Peel.

http://www.communitypolicing.org/
This is the official website of the Community Policing Consortium. Scan the website and you will find the latest information on community policing.

http://www.popcenter.org/default.htm
This is the official website on problem-oriented policing operated by the Department of Justice.

http://www.fletc.gov/

This is the official website of the Federal Law Enforcement Center (FLETC). The FLETC, a bureau of the Department of Homeland Security, is the nation's lead organization for interagency training of Federal law enforcement personnel. Basic and advanced training is provided at the FLETC for personnel from over 70 partner organizations.

TEST BANK

FILL-IN THE BLANKS

1.   Police are the _____ of the criminal justice process.

2.   The hundreds were grouped into _____ resembling the counties of today.

3.   The _____ _____ _____
_____ is not a police agency but an investigative agency, with jurisdiction over all matters in which the United States is, or may be, an interested party.

4.   _____ entails police officers' visible presence on the streets and public places of their jurisdiction.

5.   James Q. Wilson and George Kelling called for a return to a nineteenth-century style of _____-_____ _____ in which police maintained a presence in the community, walked beats, got to know citizens, and inspired feelings of public safety.

6.   The _____ _____ guarantees people the right to be free from self-incrimination.

7.   People and their property may be searched without a warrant if they willingly _____ to the search.

8.   One approach is to limiting police discretion is to develop _____
_____ _____ that monitor police behavior and tactics and investigate civilian complaints.

9.   Viewed in its most positive light, such recruitment of minority and female officers reflects the police departments' desire to field a more balanced force that truly represents the _____ it serves.

10. Research also shows that female officers are actually less likely to use _____ than male officers.

TRUE/FALSE QUESTIONS

1. T/F The origin of U.S. police agencies can be traced back to early English society.

2. T/F Law enforcement in colonial America paralleled the German model.

3. T/F The shire reeve was appointed by the crown to supervise a certain territory and assure the local nobleman that order would be kept.

4. T/F In 1326 the office of constable was created to assist the shire reeve in controlling the county.

5. T/F In 1829 Sir Robert Peel, England's home secretary, guided through Parliament the "Act for Improving the Police In and Near the Metropolis" that established the first organized police force in London.

6. T/F Police during the nineteenth century were generally competent, honest and liked by the people they served.

7. T/F The onset of police professionalism might be traced to the 1920s and the influence of August Vollmer.

8. T/F Law enforcement duties are distributed across local, county, state and federal jurisdictions.

9. T/F County police agencies make up the vast majority of the law enforcement community's members.

10. T/F When the old-style beat officer needed assistance, he would pound the pavement with his stick to summon his colleagues from nearby areas.

11. T/F Today's FBI is a police agency not an investigative agency.

12. T/F There are research studies showing that contact with the police may cause some offenders to forgo repeat criminal behavior and deter future criminality.

13. T/F James Q. Wilson and George Kelling called for a return to a nineteenth-century style of problem-oriented policing.

14. T/F All criminologists agree that a return to the older model of policing is a panacea.

15 T/F The Supreme Court established Miranda as an indisputable cornerstone of the justice process.

MULTIPLE CHOICE QUESTIONS

1. In early English society, every man living in the villages scattered throughout the countryside was responsible for aiding his neighbors and protecting the settlement from thieves and marauders in a system known as:
   a. watch system
   b. reeve system
   c. tithing system
   d. pledge system

2. What system was created in the thirteenth century, during the reign of King Edward I, to help protect property in England's larger cities and towns?
   a. watch system
   b. reeve system
   c. tithing system
   d. pledge system

3. In 1326 what office was created to assist the shire reeve in controlling the county?
   a. constable
   b. justice of the peace
   c. coroner
   d. marshal

4. In the colonies, who became the most important law enforcement agent?
   a. chief of police
   b. marshal
   c. sheriff
   d. constable

5. After the American Revolution night watchmen were referred to as:
   a. knuckleheads
   b. jarheads
   c. warheads
   d leatherheads

6. President Herbert Hoover appointed whom to study police issues on a national scale?
   a. August Vollmer
   b. Wickersham Commission
   c. O. W. Wilson
   d. President's Commission on Law Enforcement and Administration of Justice

7. Who instituted university training as an important part of his development of young officers?
   a. August Vollmer
   b. Sir Robert Peel
   c. O. W. Wilson
   d. Herbert Hoover

8. Who operates the National Crime Information Center that is a computerized network linked to local police departments by terminals?
   a. ATF
   b. DEA
   c. FBI
   d. IRS

9. Which agency is composed of court officers who help implement federal court rulings, transport prisoners, and enforce court orders?
   a. Bureau of Prisons
   b. U.S. Marshals
   c. FBI
   d. ATF

10. Which agency is considered to be the first state police organization?
    a. Pennsylvania State Police
    b. Georgia State Patrol
    c. Massachusetts State Police
    d. Texas Rangers

11. Resolving conflict, keeping the peace, and maintaining a sense of community security are which of the following core functions of the police?
    a. law enforcement
    b. order maintenance
    c. service functions
    d. none of the above

12. Aiding individuals in danger or in need of assistance and public education and outreach are which of the following core functions of the police?
    a. law enforcement
    b. order maintenance
    c. service functions
    d. none of the above

13. In early police forces, which patrols were used almost exclusively?
    a. foot
    b. bicycle
    c. automobile
    d. van

14. Targeting even minor or lifestyle crimes such as vandalism, panhandling, and graffiti is known as:
    a. proactive policing
    b. full enforcement/zero tolerance
    c. targeting crimes
    d. routine police work

15. James Q. Wilson's pioneering work, *Varieties of Police Behavior*, viewed the major police role as:
    a. law enforcement
    b. order maintenance
    c. service function
    d. handling the situation

16. Implied in the Wilson and Kelling model of community policing is what kind of police role?
    a. active
    b. proactive
    c. reactive
    d. passive

17. Which Amendment to the U.S. Constitution guarantees people the right to be free from self-incrimination?
    a. First
    b. Fourth
    c. Fifth
    d. Sixth

18. In which case did the Supreme Court create objective standards for questioning by police after a defendant has been taken into custody?
    a. *Miranda v. Arizona*
    b. *Kirk v. Louisiana*
    c. *Tennessee v. Garner*
    d. *Dickerson v. United States*

19. Information provided by a suspect that leads to the seizure of incriminating evidence is permissible if the evidence would have been obtained anyway by other means or sources; this is now referred to as the:
    a. public safety doctrine
    b. inevitable discovery rule
    c. harmless error rule
    d. plenary rule

20. Police may conduct a legal search without a warrant being issued under all of the following **EXCEPT**:
    a. threshold inquiry (stop-and-frisk)
    b. search incident to an arrest
    c. consent search
    d. traffic stop

21. Isolation and conflict may contribute to what occupational hazard of police work?
    a. ulcers
    b. stress
    c. camaraderie
    d. hate

22. Selective enforcement of the law by duly authorized police agents is known as:
    a. investigation
    b. discretion
    c. prevention
    d. authority

23. In which important case did the Supreme Court uphold the use of racial quotas to counter the effects of past discrimination?
    a. *United States v. Paradise*
    b. *Kirk v. Louisiana*
    c. *Tennessee v. Garner*
    d. *Dickerson v. United States*

24. In which case did the Supreme Court establish Miranda as an indisputable cornerstone of the justice process?
    a. *United States v. Paradise*
    b. *Kirk v. Louisiana*
    c. *Tennessee v. Garner*
    d. *Dickerson v. United States*

25. Which Supreme Court decision banned the shooting of unarmed or nondangerous fleeing felons?
    a. *United States v. Paradise*
    b. *Kirk v. Louisiana*
    c. *Tennessee v. Garner*
    d. *Dickerson v. United States*

ESSAY QUESTIONS

1. Give a short review of the history of American policing.

2. Explain how reform movements created the ideal of police professionalism.

3. Explain the changing role of the police.

4. Describe how the courts have set limits on the extent of police interrogations and the search for and seizure of evidence.

5. Explain the issues surrounding police use of force.

MATCHING

1. _____ Selective Enforcement
2. _____ Sting
3. _____ Modus Operandi
4. _____ Mug Shots
5. _____ Vice Squad
6. _____ Public Safety Doctrine
7. _____ Morals Squad
8. _____ Aggressive Preventive Patrol
9. _____ Foot Patrol
10. _____ Shire Reeve

A. Area or beat that an officer walks.
B. Admissible evidence can be obtained without a Miranda warning if the information the police seek is needed to protect public safety.
C. The working methods of particular offenders.
D. The policy of police officers to concentrate on some crimes, but handling the majority in an informal manner.
E. Forerunner of today's sheriff.
F. Method of patrol designed to deter crime.
G. Another name for vice squad.
H. An operation where police pose as fences with thieves interested in selling stolen merchandise.
I. Photographs of offenders taken by law enforcement for victims to use in identifying offenders.
J. Detectives assigned to investigate crimes of vice such as prostitution.

CHAPTER 15 ANSWER KEY

Fill In The Blank Answers

1. gatekeepers
2. shires
3. Federal Bureau of Investigation
4. patrol
5. community-oriented police
6. Fifth Amendment
7. consent
8. civilian review boards
9. community
10. force

True/False Answers

1.	T	6.	F	11.	F
2.	F	7.	T	12.	T
3.	T	8.	T	13.	F
4.	F	9.	F	14.	F
5.	T	10.	T	15.	T

Multiple Choice Answers

1.	D	11.	B	21.	B
2.	A	12.	C	22.	B
3.	B	13.	A	23.	A
4.	C	14.	B	24.	D
5.	D	15.	D	25.	C
6.	B	16.	B		
7.	A	17.	C		
8.	C	18.	A		
9.	B	19.	B		
10.	D	20.	D		

Essay Questions

1. Pages 514 – 517
2. Page 517
3. Pages 523 – 527
4. Pages 527 – 529
5. Pages 537 – 540

Matching Answers

1.	D	6.	B
2.	H	7.	G
3.	C	8.	F
4.	I	9.	A
5.	J	10.	E

Chapter 16

The Judicatory Process

LEARNING OBJECTIVES

1.   Be familiar with the state and federal court structure.

2.   Discuss the duties of a judge, defense counsel, and prosecutor.

3.   Discuss the various pretrial procedures.

4.   Discuss the plea bargaining process.

5.   Be familiar with the process of the jury trial.

6.   Review legal rights during trial.

7.   Understand the various forms of sentencing used in the United States.

8.   Know the difference between three strikes laws and truth in sentencing.

9.   Discuss the sentencing process and outcomes and how people are sentenced.

10. Be familiar with arguments for and against the death penalty.

KEYWORDS AND DEFINITIONS

U.S. district courts: the trial courts of the federal system; they have jurisdiction over cases involving violations of federal law, such as interstate transportation of stolen vehicles and racketeering. (page 550)

Federal courts of appeal: courts which hear appeals from the district court. (550)

U.S. Supreme Court: the court of last resort for all cases tried in the various federal and state courts. (550)

Writ of certiorari: the document that is granted when the Supreme Court decides to hear a case and to request a transcript of the case proceedings for review. (550)

Precedent: The Supreme Court can word a decision so that it becomes a decision that must be honored by all lower courts. (550)

Landmark decision: a precedent that must be honored by all lower courts. For example, if the Court grants a particular right, then all people in similar situations must be given the same right. (550)

Judge: acts as an impartial arbiter of procedure, ensuring that neither side violates the rules of trial conduct. (552)

Prosecutor: represents the state's interests. (552)

Adversarial process: the prosecution and the defense fight over the facts of the case at hand, with the prosecutor arguing the case for the state and the defense counsel using all possible means to aid the client. (552)

Nolle prosequi: the prosecutor can also attempt to prosecute and then decide to drop the case. (554)

Assigned counsel system: the appointment from a list of private bar members who accept cases on a judge-by-judge, court-by-court, or case-by-case basis. This may include an administrative component and a set of rules and guidelines governing the appointment and processing of cases handled by the private bar members. (557)

Public defender system: a salaried staff of full-time or part-time attorneys that renders indigent criminal defense services through a public or private nonprofit organization, or as direct government paid employees. (557)

Contract attorney system: nonsalaried private attorneys, bar associations, law firms, consortiums or groups of attorneys, or nonprofit corporations that contract with a funding source to provide court-appointed representation in a jurisdiction. (557)

Missouri Plan: a plan to select judges. This three-part approach consists of (1) a judicial commission to nominate candidates for the bench, (2) an elected official (usually from the executive branch) to make appointments from the list submitted by the commission, and (3) subsequent nonpartisan, noncompetitive elections in which incumbent judges run on their records. (559)

Criminal charge: a formal written document identifying the criminal activity, the facts of the case, and the circumstances of the arrest. (559)

Indictment: the charge is called a bill of indictment (if it is to be considered by a grand jury). (559)

Information: the charge is called an information (if that particular jurisdiction uses the preliminary hearing system). (559)

Complaint: the process by which misdemeanants are charged. (559)

Bail: represents money or some other security provided to the court to ensure the appearance of the defendant at trial. (560)

Preventive detention: those denied bail because of the danger they present to the community. (561)

Bail bonding agent: puts up 90 percent of a bond fee and the defendant the remaining 10 percent (this is called a surety bond). When the defendant appears at trial, the bail is returned and the bonding agent keeps the entire amount; the defendant's 10 percent serves as the bonding agent's commission. If the defendant does not show up for trial, the bonding agent must pay the entire bail. (562)

Surety bond: the remaining 10 percent that is put up by the defendant to secure a bond from a bail bonding agent. (562)

Skip tracers (or recovery agents): the bonding agent may hire people to track down the fugitive in order to recover the lost bond, if a bailee fails to return for trial. (562)

Release on recognizance (ROR): the defendant is released on a promise to appear, without any requirement of money bond. This form of release is unconditional – that is, without imposition of special conditions, supervision, or specially provided services. The defendant must simply appear in court for scheduled hearings. (563)

Deposit bail system: designed to replace the bonding agents. The defendant deposits a percentage of the bail amount, typically 10 percent, with the court. When the defendant appears in court, the deposit is returned, sometimes minus an administrative fee. If the defendant fails to appear, he or she is liable for the full amount of bail. (563)

Bail guidelines: set standard bail amounts based on such factors as criminal history and the current charge. (563)

Plea bargaining: defendants, aware of the prosecutor's strong case, plead guilty to minimize their sentences and avoid the harmful effects of a criminal conviction. Some may even plead guilty to protect accomplices or confederates by "taking the rap" themselves. (563)

Venire (or jury array): The initial list of people chosen provides the state with a group of citizens potentially capable of serving on a jury. (566)

Voir dire: once the prospective jurors have been chosen, all people selected are questioned by both the prosecution and the defense to determine their appropriateness to sit on the jury. They are examined under oath by the government, the defense, and sometimes the judge about their backgrounds, occupations, residences, and possible knowledge about or interest in the case. (566)

Removed for cause: a juror who acknowledges any bias for or prejudice against the defendant and is eliminated from the jury. (566)

Peremptory challenges: both the prosecution and the defense are allowed to excuse jurors for no particular reason or an undisclosed reason. (566)

Direct examination: the prosecutor questions the witness to reveal the facts believed pertinent to the government case. Testimony involves what the witness actually saw, heard, or touched; it does not include opinions. (567)

Redirect examination: the prosecutor may ask additional questions about information brought out during cross-examination. (567)

Cross-examination: after the prosecutor finishes questioning a witness, the defense cross-examines the same witness by asking questions in an attempt to clarify the defendant's role in the crime. (567)

Directed verdict: the judge directs the jury to acquit the defendant because the prosecution did not present enough evidence to prove all the elements of the alleged crime. (567)

Rebuttal evidence: this normally involves bringing forward evidence that was not used when the prosecution initially presented its case. (567)

Double jeopardy: the Fifth Amendment provides that no person shall "be subject for the same offense to be twice put in jeopardy of life or limb." The right to be protected from **double jeopardy** was made applicable to the states through the Fourteenth Amendment in the case of *Benton v. Maryland*. (569)

Dual sovereignty doctrine: if a single act violates the laws of two states, the offender may be punished for each offense under the dual sovereignty doctrine: Legal jurisdictions have the right to enforce their own laws, and a single act can violate the laws of two separate jurisdictions. (569)

Fine: payment of money is usually exacted for a minor crime and may also be combined with other sentencing alternatives, such as probation or confinement. (571)

Probation: allows the offender to live in the community subject to compliance with legally imposed conditions. (571)

Alternative sanctions: involve probation plus some other sanction, such as house arrest, electronic monitoring, or forfeiture of property. (571)

Incarceration: confinement is imposed when it has been decided that the general public needs to be protected from further criminal activity by the defendant. (571)

Capital punishment: the death penalty; reserved for people who commit first-degree murder under aggravated circumstances, such as with extreme cruelty, violence, or torture. (571)

Mandatory prison term: prison terms dictated by the law. (571)

Impact statement: allows victims to make statements that are considered at sentencing hearings, although these often have little influence on sentencing outcomes. (571)

Concurrent sentence: both sentences are served at the same time, and the term of imprisonment is completed after the longest term has been served. (571)

Consecutive sentence: upon completion of one sentence, the other term of incarceration begins. (571)

Indeterminate sentence: a sentence with very brief minimums and very long maximums, allowing inmates to be released as soon as a parole board concluded they were rehabilitated. (572)

Determinate sentence: as originally constructed, the judge could impose a sentence, based on personal and professional judgment, which fell within limits set by statute. (572)

Sentencing guidelines: develop guidelines to control and structure the sentencing process and make it more rational. (572)

Truth-in-sentencing laws: require offenders to serve a substantial portion of their prison sentences behind bars. (574)

Sentencing disparity: people convicted of similar criminal acts receive widely different sentences. (575)

Brutalization effect: executions may actually increase the likelihood of murders being committed; the basis of this theory is that potential criminals may begin to model their behavior after state authorities: If the government can kill its enemies, so can they. (577)

CHAPTER OUTLINE

I.   Court structure
    A.   State courts
        1.   Most states employ a multitiered court structure
        2.   Lower courts try misdemeanors and conduct the preliminary processing of felony offenses
        3.   Superior trial courts try felony cases
        4.   Appellate courts review the criminal procedures of trial courts to determine whether the offenders were treated fairly
        5.   Superior appellate courts or state supreme courts, used in about half the states, review lower appellate court decisions
        6.   A recent trend has been to develop specialized courts to handle specific justice-related problems
    B.   Federal Courts
        1.   The U.S. district courts are the trial courts of the system
        2.   Appeals from the district court are heard in one of the intermediate federal courts of appeal
        3.   The U.S. Supreme Court, is the court of last resort for all cases tried in the various federal and state courts
            a.   Supreme Court can word a decision so that it becomes a precedent that must be honored by all lower courts
            b.   Precedent in the legal system gives the Supreme Court power to influence and mold the everyday operating procedures of the criminal justice system
    C.   Court case flow
II. Actors in the judicatory process
    A.   Prosecutor
        1.   Represents the state in criminal matters that come before the courts

2. Types of prosecutors
    a. Federal system
        1) The chief prosecuting officer is the U.S. attorney
        2) They represent the government in federal district courts
        3) The chief prosecutor is usually an administrator
        4) Assistants normally handle the actual preparation and trial work
    b. State level
        1) Office titles include
            a) District attorney
            b) County attorney
            c) Prosecuting attorney
            d) Commonwealth attorney
            e) State's attorney
        2) Typically elected officials
        3) Most attorneys who work for prosecutors at state and county levels are political appointees
        4) Many young lawyers serve in this capacity to gain trial experience
3. Prosecutorial discretion
    a. Prosecutors maintain broad discretion
    b. *Nolle prosequi*
    c. About half of all arrests are dismissed before they reach the trial stage
    d. Of those carried forward to trial, the great majority end with a plea bargain
    e. Prosecutor can concentrate on bringing to trial those who commit more serious criminal offenses
4. Factors influencing decision making
    a. Criminal history
    b. Victim's behavior
    c. Politics
    d. Resources
B. Defense attorney
    1. Represent the accused in the criminal process
    2. Investigate the incident
    3. Interview clients, police, and witnesses
    4. Principal forms of indigent defense
        a. Public defender
        b. Assigned counsel
        c. Contract
    5. Conflicts of defense
        a. Criminal defense attorneys face many role conflicts
        b. A defensive advocate
        c. An officer of the court
        d. *Nix v. Whiteside* – the Court sustained an attorney's right to refuse to represent a client whom he suspected would commit perjury
        e. Ethical issues
            1) Is it proper to cross-examine for the purpose of discrediting the reliability or credibility of an adversarial witness whom you know to be telling the truth?
            2) Is it proper to put a witness on the stand when you know he or she will commit perjury?

3) Is it proper to give your client legal advice when you have reason to believe that the knowledge you give your client will tempt him or her to commit perjury?
    f.   Attorney–client privilege

C. Judge
    1.   Senior officer in a court of criminal law
    2.   Rules on the appropriateness of conduct
    3.   Settles questions of evidence and procedure
    4.   Guides the questioning of witnesses
    5.   Instruct jury members on which evidence can be examined and which should be ignored
    6.   If a defendant is found guilty, the judge decides on the sentence
    7.   Judges must be wary of the legal controls placed on the trial process by the appellate court system
    8.   Judicial selection – several methods
        a)   The governor simply appoints judges
        b)   In others, judicial recommendations must be confirmed by
            1)   The state senate
            2)   The governor's council
            3)   A special confirmation committee
            4)   An executive council elected by the state assembly
            5)   An elected review board
        c)   Some states employ screening bodies that submit names to the governor for approval
        d)   Missouri Plan
            1)   A judicial commission to nominate candidates for the bench
            2)   An elected official (usually from the executive branch) makes appointments from the list submitted by the commission
            3)   Subsequent nonpartisan, noncompetitive elections in which incumbent judges run on their records
    9.   Judicial overload
        a.   In most states, people appointed to the bench have had little or no training in the role of judge
        b.   Once they are appointed to the bench, judges are given an overwhelming amount of work that has risen dramatically over the years
        c.   Several agencies have been created to improve the quality of the judiciary
            1)   The National Conference of State Court Judges
            2)   The National College of Juvenile Justice

III. Pretrial procedures
  A.   General
    1.   Arrest
    2.   Charge
        a.   If the crime is a felony, the charge is called a bill of indictment (if it is to be considered by a grand jury)
        b.   An information (if that particular jurisdiction uses the preliminary hearing system)
        c.   Misdemeanants are charged with a complaint
    3.   If sufficient evidence is found in either procedure, the accused is brought before the trial court for arraignment
        a.   The judge informs the defendant of the charge

      b.   Judge ensures that the accused is properly represented by counsel

      c.   Judge determines whether the accused should be released on bail or handled in some alternative manner pending a hearing or trial

  4.   The defendant who is arraigned on an indictment or information can ordinarily plead

      a.   Guilty

      b.   Not guilty

      c.   *Nolo contendere* – equivalent to a guilty plea but cannot be used as evidence in subsequent cases

B.   Bail

  1.   The amount of bail is set by a magistrate

  2.   Defendants who cannot afford or who are denied bail are detained, usually in a county jail or lockup, until their trial date

  3.   Those who make bail are free to pursue their defense before trial

  4.   The bail system goes back to English common law

  5.   Under the U.S. system of justice, the right to bail comes from the Eighth Amendment of the Constitution

  6.   Sixty-two percent of all defendants were released by the court prior to the disposition of their case

  7.   Making bail

      a.   Not all defendants make bail

      b.   Some defendants are detained because

         1)   They cannot afford to make bail

         2)   Others are denied bail because of the danger they present to the community (called preventive detention)

      c.   The likelihood of making bail is directly related to the criminal charge

  8.   Problems of bail

      a.   Bail penalizes the indigent offender who does not have the means to pay the bond

      b.   The bail system is also costly because the state must pay for the detention of offenders who are unable to raise bail

      c.   Most significant problems

         1)   Increases punishment risk

         2)   Bonding and recovery agents

            a)   Normally the bail bonding agent puts up 90 percent of a bond fee

            b)   The defendant the remaining 10 percent

            c)   If a bailee fails to return for trial, the bonding agent may hire skip tracers or recovery agents

  9.   Bail reform

      a.   Vera Institute pioneered the concept of release on recognizance (ROR)

      b.   The project proved to be a great success

 10. Bail systems

      a.   Release on recognizance

      b.   Conditional release

      c.   Unsecured bail

      d.   Privately secured bail

      e.   Deposit bail

      f.   Surety bail

      g.   Cash bail

 11. Preventive detention

C.   Plea bargaining

1. Majority of defendants in criminal trials are convicted by their own guilty pleas
2. Plea bargaining usually occurs between arraignment and the onset of trial
3. Different motivations for plea bargaining
   a. plea bargain to minimize their sentences and avoid the harmful effects of a criminal conviction
   b. Some may even plead guilty to protect accomplices or confederates by "taking the rap" themselves
   c. Defense attorney may bargain to limit own involvement in the case
   d. The prosecution also can benefit from a plea bargain
      1) Prosecutor's case may be weaker than hoped for
      2) Prosecutor may believe arresting officers made a serious procedural error
4. Plea bargaining issues
   a. Benefits
      1) Overall financial costs of criminal prosecution are reduced.
      2) Administrative efficiency of the courts is greatly improved.
      3) Prosecution can devote more time to cases of greater seriousness and importance
      4) Defendant avoids possible detention and extended trial and may receive a reduced sentence
   b. Weaknesses
      1) Defendants waive their constitutional right to a trial
      2) Prosecutors are given too much leeway to convince defendants to plea bargain, thus circumventing law
      3) Plea bargaining raises the danger that innocent people will be convicted of a crime
5. Control of plea bargaining – reforms include
   a. Development of uniform plea practices
   b. Presence of counsel during plea negotiations
   c. Establishment of time limits on plea negotiations

IV. The criminal trial
   A. Jury selection
      1. The first stage of the trial process involves jury selection
      2. Jurors are selected randomly in both civil and criminal cases, usually from voter registration lists within each court's jurisdiction
      3. The initial list of people chosen, which is called a venire or jury array
      4. Once the prospective jurors have been chosen, the process of voir dire begins
      5. Removal for cause
      6. Peremptory challenges
      7. Impartial juries
         a. *Ham v. South Carolina* – held the defense counsel of an African-American civil rights leader was entitled to question each juror on the issue of radical prejudice
         b. *Turner v. Murray* – held that African-American defendants accused of murdering whites are entitled to have jurors questioned about their racial bias
         c. *Taylor v. Louisiana* – overturned the conviction of a man by an all-male jury because a Louisiana statute allowed women but not men to exempt themselves from jury duty
   B. The trial process
      1. Opening statements
      2. The prosecution's case

3. Cross-examination
   a. Prosecutor may seek a redirect examination
   b. Defense attorney may question or cross-examine the witness once again
4. The defense's case
   a. Defense may ask the presiding judge to rule on a motion for a directed verdict
   b. If the judge fails to sustain the motion, the defense presents its case
5. Rebuttal
   a. Government may present rebuttal evidence
   b. The defense may examine the rebuttal witnesses and introduce new witnesses in a process called surrebuttal
6. Closing arguments
7. Instructions to the jury
8. Verdict
9. Sentence
   a. If found not guilty, the defendant is released
   b. If the defendant is convicted, the judge normally orders a presentence investigation by the probation department preparatory to imposing a sentence
   c. Sentencing usually occurs a short time after trial
10. Appeal

C. Trials and the rule of law
   1. Right to a speedy and public trial
      a. The Sixth Amendment guarantees a defendant the right to a speedy trial
      b. The right to a speedy trial was made applicable to state courts through the due process clause of the Fourteenth Amendment
   2. Right to a jury trial
      a. *Duncan v. Louisiana*, made the guarantee applicable to the states through the Fourteenth Amendment
      b. *Blanton v. City of North Las Vegas*, the Court upheld the 6 month–plus jail sentence requirement for a jury trial
      c. Sixth Amendment does not specify a jury size
      d. In the case of *Williams v. Florida*, the Supreme Court held that a six-person jury fulfilled a defendant's right to a trial by jury
      e. However, a unanimous verdict is required when a six-person jury is used
      f. In *Apodica v. Oregon*, the Court found constitutional an Oregon statute that required a finding of guilt by ten out of twelve jurors
   3. Right to be free from double jeopardy
      a. The Fifth Amendment provides that no person shall "be subject for the same offense to be twice put in jeopardy of life or limb"
      b. Made applicable to the states through the Fourteenth Amendment in the case of *Benton v. Maryland*
      c. *Heath v. Alabama* – the offender may be punished for each offense under the dual sovereignty doctrine
   4. Right to legal counsel
      a. Sixth Amendment provides the right to be represented by an attorney in criminal trials
      b. *Powell v. Alabama* – an an attorney is essential in capital cases where the defendant's life was at stake
      c. *Gideon v. Wainwright* – the Court granted the absolute right to counsel in all felony cases
      d. *Argersinger v. Hamlin* – the defendant's right to counsel in misdemeanor cases was established

      e.   U.S. Supreme Court stated that in the event he or she cannot pay for counsel, the state provides free legal services

   5.   The right to be competent at trial - in order to stand trial, a criminal defendant must be considered mentally competent

   6.   Right to confront witnesses

      a.   An important confrontation issue is the ability to shield child witnesses from the trauma of a court appearance

      b.   *Maryland v. Craig*

V. Sentencing

   A. Purposes of sentencing – four goals

     1.   Deterrence

     2.   Incapacitation

     3.   Rehabilitation

     4.   Desert/retribution

   B. Sentencing dispositions

     1.   Types of sentences

       a.   Fines

       b.   Probation

       c.   Alternative or intermediate sanctions

       d.   Incarceration

       e.   Capital punishment

     2.   Imposing the sentence

       a.   Mandatory prison terms

       b.   Impact statements

       c.   Concurrent sentence

       d.   Consecutive sentence

   C. Sentencing structures

     1.   Indeterminate sentence

     2.   Determinate sentences

     3.   Structured sentencing

       a.   Sentencing guidelines

       b.   Guidelines eliminate discretionary parole

     4.   How are guidelines used?

       a.   Today there are seventeen states that use some form of structured sentencing

       b.   Prescriptive guidelines are created by appointed sentencing commissions

     5.   Configuring guidelines – one method is to create a grid with prior record and current offense as the two coordinates and set out specific punishments

     6.   Future of structured sentencing

     7. Mandatory sentences

       a.   Another effort to limit judicial discretion

       b.   Mandatory sentencing generally limits the judge's discretionary power to impose any disposition but that authorized by the legislature

     8.   Truth in sentencing

     9.   Three strikes law

       a.   Three strikes laws may in fact help put some chronic offenders behind bars

       b.   Three strikes policy will enlarge an already overburdened prison system

   D. How people are sentenced

     1.   Sentencing disparity

       a.   It is common for people convicted of similar criminal acts to receive widely different sentences

b. Few defendants actually serve their entire sentences, causing even greater disparity

VI. The death penalty
   A. The death penalty debate
      1. Arguments for the death penalty
         a. Executions have always been used, and capital punishment is inherent in human nature
         b. The Bible describes methods of executing criminals
         c. The death penalty also seems to be in keeping with the current mode of dispensing punishment
         d. The death penalty is sometimes the only real threat available to deter crime
         e. Death is the ultimate incapacitation
         f. The death penalty is cost effective
         g. Despite some allegations of racism, more whites are on death row than minorities
      2. Arguments against the death penalty
         a. The death penalty has little deterrent effect
         b. Brutalization effect
         c. Capital punishment may be tarnished by gender, racial, ethnic, and other biases
         d. Capital punishment may cause more crime than it deters
         e. The death penalty is brutal and demeaning
         f. Critics also question whether the general public gives blanket approval to the application of capital punishment
         g. Opponents also object to the finality of the death penalty
         h. The death penalty is capricious; receiving death is similar to losing a lottery
         i. Abolitionists claim that capital punishment has never been proven to be a deterrent, any more than has life in prison
         j. Denmark and Sweden have long abandoned the death penalty
   B. Legality of the death penalty
      1. *Furman v. Georgia*
      2. *Gregg v. Georgia*

CHAPTER SUMMARY

Most states employ a multitiered court structure. Lower courts try misdemeanors and conduct the preliminary processing of felony offenses while superior trial courts try felony cases. Appellate courts review the criminal procedures of trial courts to determine whether the offenders were treated fairly, while superior appellate courts or state supreme courts review lower appellate court decisions. A recent trend has been to develop specialized courts to handle specific justice-related problems. At the federal level, the U.S. district courts are the trial courts of the system while appeals from the district court are heard in one of the intermediate federal courts of appeal. The U.S. Supreme Court is the court of last resort for all cases tried in the various federal and state courts.

The major actors in the court system are the prosecutor, the defense counsel, and the judge. In the Federal system, the chief prosecuting officer is the U.S. attorney who represents the government in federal district courts. At the state level is the district attorney, county attorney, prosecuting attorney, commonwealth attorney, or state's attorney. Prosecutors maintain broad discretion. One of the major discretionary powers is nolle prosequi, the decision not to prosecute a case. Defense attorneys represent the accused in the criminal process and perform a variety of functions. The judge is the senior officer in a court of criminal law. The judge rules on the appropriateness of conduct, settles questions of evidence and procedure, guides the questioning of witnesses, and instructs jury members on which evidence can be examined and which should be ignored. If a defendant is found guilty, the judge decides on the sentence.

There are several methods to select judges in the United States. In some states, the governor may simply appoint judges. In others, judicial recommendations must be confirmed by the state senate, the governor's council, a special confirmation committee, an executive council elected by the state assembly, and an elected review board. Some states employ screening bodies that submit names to the governor for approval. One major way to select judges is the Missouri Plan in which a judicial commission is selected to nominate candidates for the bench, an elected official (usually from the executive branch) makes appointments from the list submitted by the commission, and subsequent nonpartisan, noncompetitive elections in which incumbent judges run on their records.

The pretrial procedures include arrest, charge, arraignment, and bail. Prior to the trial, many defense counsels engage the prosecutors in plea bargaining. The criminal trial begins with jury selection. Prospective jurors can be removed for cause or by peremptory challenges. The primary requirement is that there is an impartial jury. The trial process includes opening statements, the prosecution's case, cross-examination, the defense's case, rebuttal, closing arguments, instructions to the jury, verdict, sentence, and appeal. Defendants have several guaranteed rights in trials. Among them are the right to a speedy and public trial, the right to a jury trial, the right to be free from double jeopardy, the right to legal counsel, the right to be competent at trial, and the right to confront witnesses.

The purposes of sentencing are deterrence, incapacitation, rehabilitation, and desert/retribution. There are five sentencing dispositions including fines, probation, alternative or intermediate sanctions, incarceration, and capital punishment. Judges may impose the sentences to be served concurrently or consecutively. The sentencing structures include indeterminate sentences and determinate sentences. In order to limit judicial discretion in sentencing, many states and the federal government have imposed structured sentences imposed by sentencing guidelines and mandatory sentences. Several states have also imposed truth in sentencing and three strikes laws.

One of the most controversial sentences that can be imposed is the death penalty. There are several arguments for the death penalty: 1) Executions have always been used, and capital punishment is inherent in human nature. 2) The death penalty is sometimes the only real threat available to deter crime. 3) Death is the ultimate incapacitation. 4) The death penalty is cost effective. 5) Despite some allegations of racism, more whites are on death row than minorities. There are several arguments against the death penalty: 1) The death penalty has little deterrent effect. 2) Capital punishment has a brutalization effect. 3) Capital punishment may be tarnished by gender, racial, ethnic, and other biases. 4) Capital punishment may cause more crime than it deters. 5) Abolitionists claim that capital punishment has never been proven to be a deterrent, any more than has life in prison.

STUDENT EXERCISES

Exercise 1

Pick one of your non-criminal justice classes and ask 10 members of that class if they support or do not support the death penalty. Ask each student the primary reason they do or do not support the death penalty. Summarize your findings and analyze how your findings compare with the reasons for support or non-support listed in the textbook.

Exercise 2

Go online to http://www.ncjrs.org/pdffiles1/nij/181942.pdf and read the article, *Efficiency, Timeliness, and Quality:A New Perspective From Nine State Criminal Trial Courts* by Brian J. Ostrom and Roger A. Hanson. Summarize the major findings of the study concerning the right to a speedy trial.

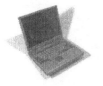

CRIMINOLOGY WEB LINKS

http://www.deathpenaltyinfo.org/
This is the official website of the Death Penalty Information Center, an organization devoted to abolishment of the death penalty.

http://www.ncsconline.org/D_KIS/info_court_web_sites.html
This is the official website of the National Center for State Courts. Through it you can access most every level of court that exists in each of the states.

http://www.ncjrs.org/pdffiles1/ojjdp/204063.pdf
This is document is a study of the access to legal counsel by juvenile offenders. It is published by the Office of Juvenile Justice and Delinquency Prevention.

http://www.supremecourtus.gov/
This is the official website of the United States Supreme Court.

http://www.vera.org/
This is the official website of the Vera Institute, the organization responsible for the changes in judicial policy concerning Release on Recognizance for indigent offenders.

TEST BANK

FILL-IN THE BLANKS

1.   In the state court system, _____ trial courts try felony cases.

2.   State court prosecutors are typically _____ officials.

3.   Lawyers are required to keep their clients' statements confidential: the _____ - _____ privilege.

4.   Some defendants are denied bail because of the danger they present to the community, a practice called _____ _____.

5.   It has been argued that plea bargaining encourages defendants to waive their _____ _____ to a trial.

6.   The verdict in a criminal case is usually required to be _____.

7.   A _____ is usually exacted for a minor crime and may also be combined with other sentencing alternatives, such as probation or confinement.

8.   Under truth in sentencing, _____ eligibility and good-time credits are restricted or eliminated.

9.   Some supporters of the death penalty argue that it is sometimes the only real threat available to _____ crime.

10. Efforts to control _____ _____ include the use of sentencing guidelines, as well as determinate and mandatory sentences.

TRUE/FALSE QUESTIONS

1. T/F A recent trend has been to develop specialized courts to handle specific justice-related problems.

2. T/F The Supreme Court is composed of eight members, appointed for lifetime terms by the president with the approval of Congress.

3. T/F The use of precedent in the legal system gives the Supreme Court power to influence and mold the everyday operating procedures of police agencies, trial courts, and correctional institutions.

4. T/F The ultimate objective of the adversarial system is to seek the best result possible.

5. T/F In the federal system, the chief prosecuting officer is the U.S. attorney.

6. T/F A minority of criminal defendants are indigent people who cannot afford legal counsel.

7. T/F When a jury trial occurs, the judge must instruct jury members on which evidence can be examined and which should be ignored.

8. T/F Bail penalizes the indigent offender who does not have the means to pay the bond.

9. T/F It has been argued that plea bargaining encourages defendants to waive their constitutional right to a speedy trial.

10. T/F At the close of the prosecution's case, the prosecutor may ask the presiding judge to rule on a motion for a directed verdict.

11. T/F Child witnesses could testify via closed-circuit television as long as safeguards were set up to protect the defendant's rights.

12. T/F If a defendant receives an indeterminate sentence, he or she may be released as soon as a parole board concludes he or she is rehabilitated.

13. T/F Despite the widespread acceptance of guidelines, research indicates that judges diverge from the guidelines.

14. T/F It is uncommon for people convicted of similar criminal acts to receive widely different sentences.

15 T/F In 1972, the U.S. Supreme Court, in *Furman v. Georgia,* ruled that use of capital punishment as a penalty was unconstitutional.

MULTIPLE CHOICE QUESTIONS

1. Which of the following is **NOT** a specialty court?
    a. superior court
    b. mental health court
    c. traffic court
    d. drug court

317

2. The trial courts of the federal system are:
   a. U.S. magistrate court
   b. U.S. bankruptcy court
   c. U.S. federal courts of appeal
   d. U.S. district courts

3. The key players in the adversarial process include all of the following **EXCEPT**:
   a. judge
   b. bailiff
   c. prosecutor
   d. defense counsel

4. When a prosecutor attempts to prosecute and then decides to drop a case is known as:
   a. actus reus
   b. nolo contendere
   c. mens rea
   d. nolle prosequi

5. State court prosecutors are typically:
   a. appointed
   b. elected
   c. hired
   d. selected by the State Bar Association

6. Most attorneys who work for prosecutors at state and county levels are:
   a. appointed
   b. elected
   c. hired
   d. selected by the State Bar Association

7. Which form of indigent defense is appointed from a list of private bar members who accept cases on a judge-by-judge, court-by-court, or case-by-case basis?
   a. public defender
   b. assigned counsel
   c. contract
   d. pro bono counsel

8. Which form of indigent defense is usually found in larger urban areas with high case flow rates?
   a. public defender
   b. assigned counsel
   c. contract
   d. pro bono counsel

9. What do we call the charge drawn up by the prosecutor if the crime is a felony and if it is to be considered by a grand jury?
   a. complaint
   b. bill of indictment
   c. information
   d. bail

10. Misdemeanants are charged with what?
    a. complaint
    b. bill of indictment
    c. information
    d. bail

11. At which stage does the judge inform the defendant of the charge, ensure that the accused is properly represented by counsel, and determine whether the accused should be released on bail or handled in some alternative manner pending a hearing or trial?
    a. preliminary hearing
    b. grand jury
    c. bail hearing
    d. arraignment

12. Which plea cannot be used as evidence in subsequent cases?
    a. guilty
    b. not guilty
    c. nolo contendere
    d. All pleas can be used as evidence in subsequent cases

13. Under what is a defendant released on the promise to appear, without any requirement of money bond?
    a. conditional release
    b. release on recognizance
    c. unsecured bail
    d. surety bond

14. Normally the bail bonding agent puts up 90 percent of a bond fee and the defendant the remaining 10 percent; this 10 percent is known as a(n):
    a. conditional release
    b. release on recognizance
    c. unsecured bail
    d. surety bond

15. If a bailee fails to return for trial, the bonding agent may hire whom to track down the fugitive in order to recover the lost bond?
    a. skip tracers
    b. recovery tracers
    c. bail recoverers
    d. U.S. marshals

16. In what decision did the Supreme Court uphold the Bail Reform Act's preventive detention provision on the grounds that its purpose was public safety, that it was not excessive for its stated purpose, and that it contained no punitive intent but was designed to regulate the behavior of accused criminals in a legally permissible way?
    a. *United States v. Salerno*
    b. *Schall v. Martin*
    c. *Batson v. Kentucky*
    d. *Ham v. South Carolina*

17. The process by which all people selected are questioned by both the prosecution and the defense to determine their appropriateness to sit on the jury is called:
    a. venire
    b. voir dire
    c. jury array
    d. peremptory challenge

18. In which case did the Supreme Court rule that the use of peremptory challenges to dismiss black jurors violated the defendant's right to equal protection of the law?
    a. *United States v. Salerno*
    b. *Schall v. Martin*
    c. *Batson v. Kentucky*
    d. *Ham v. South Carolina*

19. Which Supreme Court case overturned the conviction of a man by an all-male jury because a Louisiana statute allowed women but not men to exempt themselves from jury duty?
    a. *Turner v. Murray*
    b. *Taylor v. Louisiana*
    c. *Batson v. Kentucky*
    d. *Ham v. South Carolina*

20. If a person's right to a speedy trial is violated, then a complete dismissal of the charges against him or her is required according to which Supreme Court case?
    a. *Barker v. Wingo*
    b. *Strunk v. United States*
    c. *Duncan v. Louisiana*
    d. *Klopfer v. North Carolina*

21. The right to a speedy trial was made applicable to state courts through the due process clause of the Fourteenth Amendment in the Supreme Court case of:
    a. *Barker v. Wingo*
    b. *Strunk v. United States*
    c. *Duncan v. Louisiana*
    d. *Klopfer v. North Carolina*

22. Which Supreme Court case made the guarantee of a jury trial applicable to the states through the Fourteenth Amendment?
    a. *Baldwin v. New York*
    b. *Benton v. Maryland*
    c. *Duncan v. Louisiana*
    d. *Williams v. Florida*

23. Which Supreme Court case decided that defendants are entitled to a jury trial only if they face the possibility of a prison sentence of more than 6 months?
    a. *Baldwin v. New York*
    b. *Benton v. Maryland*
    c. *Duncan v. Louisiana*
    d. *Williams v. Florida*

24. Which Supreme Court held that a six-person jury fulfilled a defendant's right to a trial by jury?
    a. *Baldwin v. New York*
    b. *Benton v. Maryland*
    c. *Duncan v. Louisiana*
    d. *Williams v. Florida*

25. Which Supreme Court case made the right to be protected from double jeopardy applicable to the states through the Fourteenth Amendment?
    a. *Baldwin v. New York*
    b. *Benton v. Maryland*
    c. *Duncan v. Louisiana*
    d. *Williams v. Florida*

ESSAY QUESTIONS

1. Describe the federal and state court structures.

2. Explain the plea bargaining process.

3. Explain the various forms of sentencing used in the United States.

4. Explain the differences between three strikes laws and truth in sentencing.

5. List five arguments for and five arguments against the death penalty.

MATCHING

1. _____ U.S. District Court
2. _____ Preventive Detention
3. _____ U.S. Supreme Court
4. _____ Writ of Certiorari
5. _____ Precedent
6. _____ Landmark Decision
7. _____ Missouri Plan
8. _____ Nolle Prosequi
9. _____ Peremptory Challenge
10. _____ Adversarial Process

A. Denied bail because of the danger they present to the community.
B. An order issued by the Supreme Court when it decides to hear a case.
C. A decision by the Supreme Court that becomes the law of the land and serves as a precedent for similar legal issues.
D. The prosecutor can also attempt to prosecute and then decide to drop the case.
E. The procedure used to determine truth in the adjudication of guilt or innocence in which the defense is pitted against the prosecution, with the judge acting as arbiter of the legal rules.
F. Trial courts of the federal court system.
G. The court of last resort for all cases tried in the various federal and state courts.
H. Decision by the Supreme Court that must be honored by all lower courts.
I. This three-part approach consists of (1) a judicial commission to nominate candidates for the bench, (2) an elected official to make appointments from the list submitted by the commission, and (3) subsequent nonpartisan, noncompetitive elections in which incumbent judges run on their records.
J. Prosecution and defense can excuse jurors for no particular reason or an undisclosed reason.

CHAPTER 16 ANSWER KEY

Fill In The Blank Answers

1. superior
2. elected
3. attorney-client
4. preventive detention
5. constitutional right
6. unanimous
7. fine
8. parole
9. deter
10. sentencing disparity

True/False Answers

1.	T	6.	F	11.	T
2.	F	7.	T	12.	T
3.	T	8.	T	13.	T
4.	F	9.	F	14.	F
5.	F	10.	F	15.	F

Multiple Choice Answers

1.	A	11.	D	21.	D
2.	D	12.	C	22.	C
3.	B	13.	B	23.	A
4.	D	14.	D	24.	D
5.	B	15.	A	25.	B
6.	C	16.	C		
7.	B	17.	B		
8.	A	18.	C		
9.	B	19.	B		
10.	A	20.	B		

Essay Questions

1. Pages 550 – 558
2. Pages 564 – 565
3. Page 571
4. Page 574
5. Pages 576 – 582

Matching Answers

1.	F	6.	C
2.	A	7.	I
3.	G	8.	D
4.	B	9.	J
5.	H	10.	E

Chapter 17

Corrections

LEARNING OBJECTIVES

1. Be familiar with the early history of punishment.

2. Describe the development of the prison as a means of punishment.

3. Describe the nature of probation and its various services.

4. Discuss the effectiveness of probation and the concept of revocation.

5. Be familiar with the various forms of alternative sanctions.

6. Know the purpose served by the jail, its problems, and what is being done to improve jail conditions.

7. Describe different types of correctional facilities and their level of security.

8. Understand the experience of living in prison.

9. Discuss correctional treatment and the nature of prison violence.

10. Show how the problems of parolees and inmate re-entry have influenced the correctional system.

KEYWORDS AND DEFINITIONS

Corporal punishment: a penalty such as whipping or branding, as a substitute penalty for a fine. (page 593)

Poor laws: developed in the early seventeenth century, they required that the poor, vagrants, and vagabonds be put to work in public or private enterprise. (593)

Walnut Street Jail: at this institution, most prisoners were placed in solitary cells, where they remained in isolation and did not have the right to work. (594)

Auburn system: the philosophy was crime prevention through fear of punishment and silent confinement. (594)

Congregate system: many of its features are still used today. Its innovations included congregate working conditions, the use of solitary confinement to punish unruly inmates, military regimentation, and discipline. (595)

Contract system: officials sold the labor of inmates to private businesses. Sometimes the contractor supervised the inmates inside the prison itself. (595)

Convict-lease system: the state leased its prisoners to a business for a fixed annual fee and gave up supervision and control. (595)

State account system: prisoners produce goods in prison for state use. (595)

Z. R. Brockway: warden at the Elmira Reformatory in New York advocated individualized treatment, indeterminate sentences, and parole. (595)

Offender classification: the probation department will typically evaluate the case, assess the client's personality, and create an appropriate treatment program. This process is used to guide treatment and supervision practice. (598)

Revocation: if the parole rules are violated, a person's probation may be cancelled by the court, and the probationer either begins serving the suspended sentence or, if he or she has not yet been sentenced, receives a prison sentence from the court. (599)

Technical violation: violation of probation rules. (599)

Intermediate sanctions: alternative sanctions include fines, forfeiture, home confinement, electronic monitoring, intensive probation supervision, restitution, community corrections, and boot camps. (599)

Day fines: a concept originated in Europe that gears fines to an offender's net daily income in an effort to make them more equitable. (600)

Forfeiture: involves the seizure of goods and instrumentalities related to the commission or outcome of a criminal act. (601)

Monetary restitution: requiring convicted defendants to repay the victims of crime. (601)

Community service restitution: requiring convicted defendants to serve the community to compensate for their criminal acts. (601)

Split sentencing: in a number of states and in the federal criminal code, a jail term can actually be a condition of probation. (601)

Shock probation: involves resentencing an offender after a short prison stay. The shock comes because the offender originally receives a long maximum sentence but is then eligible for release to community supervision at the discretion of the judge (usually within 90 days of incarceration). (601)

Intensive probation supervision (IPS): involve small caseloads of fifteen to forty clients who are kept under close watch by probation officers. (601)

Home confinement (HC): requires convicted offenders to spend extended periods in their own homes as an alternative to incarceration. (603)

Electronic monitoring (EM): devices to manage offender obedience to home confinement orders. (603)

Residential community corrections (RCC): these programs have been defined by the National Institute of Corrections as a freestanding nonsecure building that is not part of a prison or jail and houses pretrial and adjudicated adults. The residents regularly depart to work, to attend school, and/or to participate in community corrections activities and programs. (604)

Boot camps (Shock incarceration (SI)): programs typically include youthful, first-time offenders and feature military discipline and physical training. The concept is that short periods (90 to 180 days) of high-intensity exercise and work will shock young criminals into going straight. (605)

Jail: a secure institution used to (1) detain offenders before trial if they cannot afford or are not eligible for bail and (2) house misdemeanants sentenced to terms of 1 year or less, as well as some nonserious felons. (596)

New generation jails: are being built that use modern designs to improve effectiveness. Some contain a cluster of cells surrounding a living area or "pod," which contains tables, chairs, TVs, and other material. A correctional officer is stationed within the pod. The officer has visual observation of inmates and maintains the ability to relate to them on a personal level. (607)

Prison (Penitentiary): state and federal governments maintain closed correctional facilities to house convicted felons. (607)

Super-max prison: these high-security institutions can be independent correctional centers or locked wings of existing prisons operating under such names as the "secure housing unit" or "maximum control unit." (608)

The hole: those who flout prison rules may be segregated, locked in their cells, or put in solitary confinement. (610)

Inmate subculture: the loosely defined culture that pervades prisons and has its own norms, rules, and language. (611)

Social code: unwritten guidelines that express the values, attitudes, and types of behavior that the older inmates demand of younger inmates. Passed on from one generation of inmates to another, the inmate social code represents the values of interpersonal relations within the prison. (611)

Prisonization process: the inmate's assimilation into the prison culture through acceptance of its language, sexual code, and norms of behavior. Those who become the most prisonized will be the least likely to reform on the outside. (611)

Importation model: inmate culture is affected by the values of newcomers. (611)

Surrogate family: one common form of adaptation to prison employed by women. This group contains masculine and feminine figures acting as fathers and mothers; some even act as children and take on the role of either brother or sister. Formalized marriages and divorces may be conducted. Sometimes multiple roles are held by one inmate, so that a "sister" in one family may "marry" and become the "wife" in another. (613)

Therapeutic communities (TCs): an approach to substance abuse uses a psychosocial, experiential learning process that relies on positive peer pressure within a highly structured social environment. (614)

Free-venture programs: developed in the 1980s in Minnesota, Kansas, and other areas with the aid of the federal government, the programs involve businesses set up by private entrepreneurs off prison grounds that contract with state officials to hire inmates at free-market wages and produce goods that are competitively marketed. Inmates can be fired by being sent back to the general prison population. (614)

Parole: the planned release and community supervision of incarcerated offenders before the expiration of their prison sentences. (614)

Parole grant hearing: where the decision is made in states where discretionary parole is used. (621)

CHAPTER OUTLINE

I. History of punishment and corrections
    A. The middle ages
        1. Little law or governmental control existed during the early Middle Ages
        2. The word *felony* comes from the twelfth century, when the term *felonia* referred to a breach of faith with one's feudal lord
        3. If in the heat of passion or in a state of intoxication a person severely injured or killed a neighbor
            a. Free men in the area would gather to pronounce judgment and make the culprit do penance or
            b. Make a payment to the injured party called wergild
        4. The inability of lower-class offenders to pay a fine led to the development of corporal punishment
    B. Punishment in the seventeenth and eighteenth centuries
        1. The punishment of criminals changed to meet the demands of the times
        2. Poor laws, developed in the early seventeenth century, required that the poor, vagrants, and vagabonds be put to work in public or private enterprise
        3. Houses of correction were developed to make it convenient for petty law violators to be assigned to work details
        4. The constant labor shortage in the colonies also prompted authorities to transport convicts overseas
        5. Transportation to the colonies waned as a method of punishment with the increase in colonial population

6. The American Revolution ended transportation of felons to North America

C Corrections in the late eighteenth and nineteenth centuries
1. Correctional reform in the United States was first instituted in Pennsylvania under the leadership of William Penn
   a. Penn revised Pennsylvania's criminal code to forbid torture and the capricious use of mutilation and physical punishment
   b. These devices were replaced by the penalties of imprisonment at hard labor, moderate flogging, fines, and forfeiture of property
   c. The widely used public forms of punishment included stocks, pillories, the gallows, and the branding iron
2. Under pressure from the Quakers, the Pennsylvania legislature renovated the prison system
   a. The ultimate result was the creation of Philadelphia's Walnut Street Jail
   b. Most prisoners were placed in solitary cells, remained in isolation, and did not have the right to work
   c. Overcrowding undermined the goal of solitary confinement of serious offenders
3. The Auburn system
   a. The Auburn prison design became known as the tier system
   b. Cells were built vertically on five floors of the structure
   c. Referred to as the congregate system because most prisoners ate and worked in groups
   d. The philosophy of the Auburn system was crime prevention through fear of punishment and silent confinement
   e. Prison officials sought to overcome the side effects of total isolation while maintaining the penitentiary system
      1) The solution was to keep convicts in separate cells at night but allow them to work together during the day under enforced silence
      2) Hard work and silence became the foundation of the Auburn system
      3) Silence was the key to prison discipline
4. The new Pennsylvania system
   a. A prison that placed each inmate in a single cell with no work to do
   b. Classifications were abolished because each cell was intended as a miniature prison
   c. It was built in a semicircle, with the cells positioned along its circumference
      1) Built back-to-back, some cells faced the boundary wall while others faced the internal area of the circle
      2) Its inmates were kept in solitary confinement almost constantly
   d. Supporters believed that the penitentiary was truly a place to do penance
   e. The congregate system eventually prevailed
5. Post-civil war developments
   a. The prison of the late nineteenth century was similar to that of today
   b. The congregate system was adopted in all states except Pennsylvania
   c. Prison industry developed and became the predominant theme around which institutions were organized
      1) Contract system – officials sold the labor of inmates to private businesses
      2) Convict-lease system – the state leased its prisoners to a business for a fixed annual fee and gave up supervision and control
      3) State account system – had prisoners produce goods in prison for state use

        d.   The development of prison industry quickly led to abuse of inmates

        e.   During the 1880s, opposition by trade unions

            1)   Sparked restrictions on interstate commerce in prison goods

            2)   Ended their profitability

        f.   Reforms in prison operations

            1)   Z. R. Brockway advocated

                a)   Individualized treatment

                b)   Indeterminate sentences

                c)   Parole

            2)   The reformatory program initiated by Brockway included

                a)   Elementary education for illiterates

                b)   Designated library hours

                c)   Lectures by local college faculty members

                d)   A group of vocational training shops

            3)   Cost to the institution's operations was to be held to a minimum

            4)   Significance of his contribution was the injection of a degree of humanitarianism into the industrial prisons of the day

D.   Corrections in the twentieth century

    1.   The early twentieth century was a time of contrasts in the U.S. prison system

        a.   Prison reform groups proposed better treatment for inmates

        b.   Opposed were conservative prison administrators and state officials

    2.   In time, some of the more rigid prison rules gave way to liberal reform

    3.   A more important trend was the development of specialized prisons designed to treat particular types of offenders

    4.   Prison industry also evolved

    5.   Despite these changes and reforms, the prison in the mid-twentieth century remained a destructive total institution

E.   The modern era

    1.   The modern era has witnessed change and turmoil in the nation's correctional system

        a.   Between 1960 and 1980, a great deal of litigation was brought by inmates seeking greater rights and privileges

        b.   Violence within the correctional system became a national scandal

        c.   The alleged failure of correctional rehabilitation has prompted many penologists to reconsider the purpose of incapacitating criminals

    2.   The inability of the prison to reduce recidivism has prompted the development of alternatives to incarceration

F.   Contemporary corrections

    1.   Correctional treatment can be divided today into community-based programs and secure confinement

    2.   Treatment in the community is viewed as a viable alternative to traditional correctional practices

        a.   It is significantly less expensive to supervise inmates in the community than to house them in secure institutional facilities

        b.   Community-based corrections are necessary if the prison system is not to be overwhelmed by an influx of offenders

        c.   Community-based treatment is designed so that first-time or nonserious offenders can avoid the stigma and pain of imprisonment and be rehabilitated in the community

    3.   In secure confinement

        a.   Jails

      b.   State and federal prisons

      c.   Parole and aftercare

II.   Probation
    A.   General
        1.   Probation usually involves the suspension of the offender's sentence in return for the promise of good behavior in the community under the supervision of a probation department
        2.   Probation involves a contract between the court and the offender
        3.   If the rules are violated, probation may be revoked
        4.   Probation may also be revoked simply because its rules and conditions have not been met
        5.   *Gagnon v. Scarpelli* – Supreme Court ruled that before probation can be revoked
            a.   Offender must be given a hearing before the sentencing court
            b.   Offender must be provided with counsel if there is a substantial reason for him or her to require legal assistance
    B.   Probationary sentences
        1.   Juries can recommend probation
        2.   The judge has the final say
        3.   Almost all offenders are eligible for probation
        4.   Only mandatory sentencing laws that require incarceration preclude the probation option
        5.   Misdemeanor probation usually extends for the entire period of the jail sentence
        6.   Felons may receive probationary periods shorter than a corresponding prison sentence
    C.   Probation services
        1.   Investigation
            a.   After a person is convicted of a crime, the probation department investigates the case to determine if the defendant is a suitable candidate for probation
            b.   Based on this presentence investigation, the department makes a sentencing recommendation to the judge
        2.   Treatment
            a.   Offender classification, is used to guide treatment and supervision practice
            b.   Probation officers help their clients cope with the personal problems that have put them at risk for criminal activity
        3.   Supervision
            a.   Probation departments are charged with monitoring offenders while they are in the community
            b.   Some communities are now experimenting with innovative supervision programs
    D.   Probation rules and revocation
        1.   Each offender granted probation is given a set of rules to guide his or her behavior
        2.   Most jurisdictions have a standard set of rules that must be followed
        3.   Sometimes an individual probationer is given specific rules that relate to his or her particular circumstances
        4.   Probationers may also be required to give up some of their legal rights and protections
        5.   *United States v. Knights* – Supreme Court upheld the legality of a warrantless search of a probationer's home for the purposes of gathering criminal evidence
        6.   If rules are violated, a person's probation may be revoked by the court
            a.   For violation of probation rules

        b.   For committing another offense

   E.   Success of probation
      1.   Most revocations occur for technical violations that occur during the first 3 months of the probation sentence
      2.   There are some studies that have found a lower recidivism rate among particular classes of probationers

III. Intermediate sanctions
   A.   General
      1.   Alternative sanctions are viewed as a new form of corrections that falls somewhere between probation and incarceration
      2.   The development of these sanctions can be tied to a number of different sources
          a.   The need to develop alternatives to prisons
          b.   The need to develop punishments that are fair, equitable, and proportional
   B.   Fines
      1.   Fines are monetary payments imposed on an offender
      2.   Some jurisdictions are experimenting with day fines
      3.   It is far from certain that fines are an effective sanction
      4.   They remain one of the most commonly used criminal penalties
   C.   Forfeiture
      1.   Forfeiture is not a new sanction
      2.   Use of forfeiture was reintroduced in American law with the passage of
          a.   Racketeer Influenced and Corrupt Organizations (RICO) Act
          b.   Continuing Criminal Enterprises Act
   D.   Restitution
      1.   Types
          a.   Monetary restitution
          b.   Community service restitution
      2.   Restitution programs offer convicted offenders a chance to avoid jail or prison sentences or lengthy probation
      3.   Restitution is inexpensive
   E.   Split sentencing and shock probation
      1.   Alternative sanctions that allow judges to grant offenders community release only after they have sampled prison life
      2.   Split sentencing – a jail term can actually be a condition of probation
      3.   Shock probation – involves resentencing an offender after a short prison stay
   F.   Intensive probation supervision
      1.   Involve small caseloads of fifteen to forty clients who are kept under close watch by probation officers
      2.   The primary goal of IPS is diversion
      3.   The form and structure of IPS programs vary a great deal
      4.   The failure rate in IPS caseloads is quite high
   G.   Home confinement/electronic monitoring
      1.   Requires convicted offenders to spend extended periods in their own homes as an alternative to incarceration
      2.   There is a great deal of variation in HC initiatives
      3.   There are no definitive data that indicate that HC effectively deters crime
      4.   There is insufficient evidence to conclude that it lowers recidivism rates
      5.   Electronic monitoring (EM) devices manage offender obedience to home confinement orders
      6.   Growth in the number of electronically monitored offenders has been explosive

H. Residential community corrections
   1. A more secure intermediate sanction is a sentence to a residential community corrections (RCC) program
   2. Defined by the National Institute of Corrections as a freestanding nonsecure building that is not part of a prison or jail and houses pretrial and adjudicated adults
   3. The traditional concept of community corrections has expanded recently
I. Boot camps/shock incarceration
   1. These programs typically include youthful, first-time offenders and feature military discipline and physical training
   2. There is wide variety in the programs now operating around the United States
      a. Some programs include educational and training components, counseling sessions, and treatment for special needs populations
      b. Others devote little or no time to therapeutic activities
      c. Some receive program participants directly from court sentencing
   3. The results so far have not been encouraging
   4. Mackenzie's extensive evaluations of the boot camp experience generate little evidence that they can significantly lower recidivism rates
J. Can alternatives work?
   1. There is little evidence that alternative sanctions can
      a. Prevent crime
      b. Reduce recidivism
      c. Work much better than traditional probation or prison
   2. They often produce some "small victories"

IV. Jails
   A. The jail is a secure institution used to
      1. Detain offenders before trial if they cannot afford or are not eligible for bail
      2. House misdemeanants sentenced to terms of 1 year or less, as well as some nonserious felons
   B. Jail populations
      1. There has been a national effort to remove as many people as possible from local jails
      2. Jail inmates
         a. Tend to be troubled people
         b. Many were sexually abused as children (about half the female inmates)
         c. Grew up in a single-parent household
   C. Jail conditions
      1. Jail conditions have become a national scandal
      2. Jails are marked by
         a. Violence
         b. Overcrowding
         c. Deteriorated physical conditions
         d. Lack of treatment or rehabilitation efforts
      3. Numerous jails are under court order to improve
      4. New generation jails
         a. Are being built that use modern designs to improve effectiveness
         b. Some contain a cluster of cells surrounding a living area or "pod"
         c. Research shows that they may help reduce postrelease offending in some situations

V. Prisons
   A. General
      1. State and federal governments maintain closed correctional facilities to house convicted felons
      2. The prison population has continued to rise for the past decade
      3. Most rapid increase in the offender population has been for violent offenses
      4. The declining crime rate has ended the rapid increase in the prison population experienced during the 1980s and 90s
   B. Types of prisons
      1. Categorized according to their level of security and inmate populations
         a. Maximum-security
            1) Surrounded by high walls
            2) Have elaborate security measures and armed guards
            3) House inmates classified as potentially dangerous
            4) Inmates engage in closely controlled activities
         b. Medium-security
            1) Similar protective measures as maximum but usually contain less violent inmates
            2) More likely to offer a variety of treatment and educational programs to their residents
         c. Minimum-security
            1) Operate without armed guards or walls
            2) House the most trustworthy and least violent offenders
            3) White-collar criminals may be their most common occupants
            4) Inmates may be transferred to these nonrestrictive institutions as a reward for good behavior prior to their release
            5) A great deal of personal freedom is allowed inmates
            6) Often considered country clubs
            7) Yet they remain prisons
            8) The isolation and loneliness of prison life deeply affects the inmates at these facilities
      2. Super-max prisons
         a. More than thirty states now operate super-max prisons or units
         b. The 484-bed federal facility in Florence, Colorado, is the model for the super-max prison
         c. Getting out of the prison seems impossible
         d. Civil rights watchdog groups charge that these super-maximum prisons violate the United Nations standards for the treatment of inmates
      3. Farms and camps
         a. This type of facility is found primarily in the South and the West
         b. Ranches are primarily a western phenomenon
      4. Private prisons
         a. Private facilities span the full range of correctional institutions
         b. Some private prisons are stand-alone institutions
         c. Some correctional institutions outsource services such as medical care or food supply to private for-profit companies
      5. Legal issues
         a. *Correctional Services Corp. v. Malesko* – this decision shields the private prison corporation from suits brought under the federal civil rights statute
         b. Private correctional enterprise may be an attractive alternative to a costly correctional system

B. Prison inmates: male
   1. Prisoners reflect the same qualities that are found in samples of arrestees
   2. Prison is not a new experience for many inmates – over 60 percent have been incarcerated before
   3. Inmates are educational and vocational underachievers
C. Living in prison
   1. Inmates quickly learn what the term total institution really means
   2. Inmates in large, inaccessible prisons find themselves physically cut off from
      a. Families
      b. Friends
      c. Former associates
   3. A totally new world with its own logic, behavior, rules, and language
   4. Prisoners have no privacy
   5. Those obeying rules are given choice work assignments, privileges, and educational opportunities
   6. Those who flout prison rules may be segregated, locked in their cells, or put in solitary confinement (the hole)
   7. The inmate must learn to deal with sexual exploitation and violence in the prison
   8. To avoid victimization, inmates must learn to adopt a lifestyle that shields them from victimization
   9. Becoming familiar with and perhaps participating in the hidden, black market economy of the prison—the hustle
   10. Inmates must also learn to deal with daily racial conflict
   11. Prisoners must learn to deal with their frustrations over getting a "rotten deal"
D. Prison inmates: female
   1. Women make up between 5 and 6 percent of the adult prison population
   2. The percentage of women in prison is increasing at a faster pace than men's
   3. Female inmates are usually housed in minimum-security institutions
   4. Women in prison tend to be of three basic types
      a. "The square"
      b. "The life"
      c. "The cool"
   5. Like men, female inmates must adjust to the prison experience
   6. First go through a period in which they deny the reality of their situation
   7. Then comes a period of anger over the circumstances that led to their incarceration
   8. A third stage finds female inmates greatly depressed
   9. Many female inmates eventually find reason to hope that their lives will improve
   10. Daily life in the women's prison community is also somewhat different from that in male institutions
      a. Women usually do not present the immediate physical danger to staff and fellow inmates that many male prisoners do
      b. Few female inmates experience the violent atmosphere common in male institutions
      c. Confinement for women may produce severe anxiety and anger
      d. Low self-esteem is a major problem among female inmates
   11. One common form of adaptation to prison employed by women is the surrogate family
      a. This group contains masculine and feminine figures acting as fathers and mothers
      b. Some even act as children and take on the role of either brother or sister
      c. Formalized marriages and divorces may be conducted

        d.   Sometimes multiple roles are held by one inmate
   12. Helping the female inmate
        a.   The special needs of female inmates must be addressed by correctional authorities
        b.   Health care is an issue
        c.   Helping women to adjust after they leave the institution is another goal
        d.   Many women display psychological problems including serious psychopathology

E.   Correctional treatment
   1.   Correctional treatment has been an integral part of prison life since Z. R. Brockway introduced it
   2.   There are many approaches to treatment
   3.   Therapy and counseling
        a.   The most traditional type of treatment in prison involves psychological counseling and therapy
        b.   Counseling programs exist in almost every major institution
        c.   It is more common for group methods to be used
   4.   Various innovative psychological treatment approaches have been used in the prison system
        a.   Behavior therapy uses tokens to reward conformity and help develop positive behavior traits
        b.   Reality therapy is meant to help satisfy individuals' needs to feel worthwhile to themselves and others
        c.   Transactional analysis encourages inmates to identify the different aspects of their personalities and to be their own therapists
        d.   Milieu therapy uses the social structure and processes of the institution to influence the behavior patterns of offenders
   5.   Therapeutic communities
        a.   Used because drug abuse is so prevalent among inmates
        b.   Uses a psychosocial, experiential learning process that relies on positive peer pressure within a highly structured social environment
        c.   The community itself becomes the primary method of change
        d.   The approach encourages personal disclosure rather than the isolation of the general prison culture
   6.   Educational programs
        a.   The first prison treatment programs were educational
        b.   Most correctional institutions (90 percent) provide some type of educational experience
        c.   Some prisons provide college courses
   7.   Vocational rehabilitation
        a.   Most prisons operate numerous vocational training programs
        b.   Today programs stress marketable skills
        c.   Unfortunately, prisons often have difficulty obtaining the necessary equipment to run meaningful programs
        d.   Several state correctional departments also have instituted prerelease and postrelease employment services
   8.   Private industry in prison
        a.   A new version of vocational rehabilitation
        b.   This can take many different forms
             1)   Private citizens sitting on prison industry boards
             2)   Private vendors marketing goods from prison industry

3) Inmates manufacturing and marketing their own goods
   c. Another approach is the free-venture programs developed in the 1980s
   d. On paper, private industry in prison is quite attractive
   e. Questionable whether they could be applied to the general prison population
9. Elderly inmates
   a. Research indicates that older prisoners tend to be "loners"
   b. May experience symptoms of depression or anxiety
   c. Suffer from an assortment of physical and health problems associated with aging
   d. Some correctional systems have created elderly facilities tailored to their needs
10. Inmate self-help
    a. Inmates have attempted to organize self-help groups to provide the psychological tools needed to prevent recidivism
    b. Some are chapters of common national organizations such as Alcoholics Anonymous
    c. Other groups are organized along racial and ethnic lines
    d. Those developed specifically to help inmates find the strength to make it on the outside
11. Does rehabilitation work?
    a. Martinson and his associates found that rehabilitative efforts seemed to have no appreciable effect on recidivism
    b. Some criminologists continue to challenge the "nothing works" philosophy
    c. Treatment seems to be most effective if it is matched with the needs of inmates
F. Prison violence
   1. Conflict, violence, and brutality are sad but ever-present facts of institutional life
   2. One common threat is sexual assault
   3. One of the more significant problems facing prison administrators is the constant fear of interpersonal and collective violence
   4. There is no single explanation for either collective or individual violence
      a. One position holds that inmates are often violence-prone individuals who have always used force to get their own way
      b. A second view is that prisons convert people to violence by their
         1) Inhumane conditions, including overcrowding
2) Depersonalization
         3) Threats of rape
      c. Third view is that prison violence stems from
         1) Mismanagement
         2) Lack of strong security
         3) Inadequate control by prison officials
   5. Prison riots – sometimes prison violence takes the form of large-scale rioting
G. Corrections and the rule of law
   1. Freedom of speech and press
      a. *Procunier v. Martinez* – the court ruled that an inmate's mail could be censored only if there existed substantial belief that its contents would threaten security
      b. *Saxbe v. Washington Post* – the right of an inmate to grant press interviews was limited

2. Medical rights
    a. *Estelle v. Gamble* – stated that deliberate indifference to serious medical needs of prisoners constitutes the "unnecessary and wanton infliction of pain,' and is proscribed by the Eighth Amendment
    b. *Pennsylvania Department of Corrections v. Yeskey* – Supreme Court found that the ADA's protections extended to cover prison inmates as well as any other citizen
H. Cruel and unusual punishment
    1. *Rhodes v. Chapman* – the Supreme Court upheld the practice of double-bunking two or more inmates in a single-person cell
    2. *Hope v. Pelzer* – the Supreme Court ruled that correctional officials who knowingly violate the Eighth Amendment rights of inmates can be held liable for damages

VI. Parole
A. The parolee in the community
    1. The offender is supervised by a trained staff of parole officers
    2. Parolees are subject to strict standardized or personalized rules that guide their behavior and limit their activities
    3. Parole can also be revoked if the offender commits a second offense and the offender may be tried and sentenced for this crime
    4. Parole is viewed as an act of grace on the part of the criminal justice system
B. How effective is parole?
    1. Parole decision making relies on human judgment
    2. The evaluation of parole effectiveness has produced some disturbing results
    3. A majority return to prison shortly after their release
    4. Prisons may do little to help inmates to adjust on the outside
    5. Inmates themselves may have a long history of criminal behavior
    6. Those most likely to avoid recidivating
        a. Have had a good employment record in the past
        b. Maintain jobs after their release
    7. Many parolees are returned to prison for technical violations

CHAPTER SUMMARY

Correctional reform in the United States was first instituted in Pennsylvania under the leadership of William Penn. Penn revised Pennsylvania's criminal code to forbid torture and the capricious use of mutilation and physical punishment. Under pressure from the Quakers, the Pennsylvania legislature renovated the prison system and the ultimate result was the creation of Philadelphia's Walnut Street Jail. The Auburn prison design became known as the tier system in which cells were built vertically on five floors of the structure. It is referred to as the congregate system because most prisoners ate and worked in groups. Hard work and silence became the foundation of the Auburn system and silence was the key to prison discipline. A new system called the Pennsylvania system developed. Supporters believed that the penitentiary was truly a place to do penance. The congregate system was adopted in all states except Pennsylvania.

Reforms in prison operations, led by Z. R. Brockway, advocated individualized treatment, indeterminate sentences and parole. The significance of his contribution was the injection of a degree of humanitarianism into the industrial prisons of the day. The early twentieth century was a time of contrasts in the U.S. prison system. Prison reform groups proposed better treatment for inmates while those opposed were conservative prison administrators and state officials. Between 1960 and 1980, a great deal of litigation was brought by inmates seeking greater rights and privileges.

Today, correctional treatment can be divided into community-based programs and secure confinement. Probation involves the suspension of the offender's sentence in return for the promise of good behavior in the community under the supervision of a probation department. It involves a contract between the court and the offender. Juries can recommend probation, but the judge has the final say. Almost all offenders are eligible for probation and only mandatory sentencing laws that require incarceration preclude the probation option. Misdemeanor probation usually extends for the entire period of the jail sentence, while felons may receive probationary periods shorter than a corresponding prison sentence. Each offender granted probation is given a set of rules to guide his or her behavior. Probationers may also be required to give up some of their legal rights and protections. Most revocations occur for technical violations that occur during the first 3 months of the probation sentence.

Alternative sanctions are viewed as a new form of corrections that falls somewhere between probation and incarceration. Among the more common alternative or intermediate sanctions are fines, forfeiture, restitution, split sentencing and shock probation, intensive probation supervision, home confinement/electronic monitoring, residential community corrections, and boot camps/shock incarceration.

The jail is a secure institution used to detain offenders before trial if they cannot afford or are not eligible for bail and house misdemeanants sentenced to terms of 1 year or less, as well as some nonserious felons. State and federal governments maintain closed correctional facilities to house convicted felons. Prisons are classified as maximum-security, medium-security, and minimum-security. Prison is not a new experience for many inmates as over 60 percent have been incarcerated before. Prisoners have no privacy. Those obeying rules are given choice work assignments, privileges, and educational opportunities. Female inmates are usually housed in minimum-security institutions. Daily life in the women's prison community is also somewhat different from that in male institutions because women usually do not present the immediate physical danger to staff and fellow inmates that many male prisoners do.

Correctional treatment has been an integral part of prison life since Z. R. Brockway introduced it. The most traditional type of treatment in prison involves psychological counseling and therapy. Various innovative psychological treatment approaches have been used in the prison system such as behavior therapy, reality therapy, transactional analysis, and milieu therapy. Another program is the use of therapeutic communities. The first prison treatment programs were educational; in fact, most correctional institutions (90 percent) provide some type of educational experience and some prisons provide college courses. Most prisons operate numerous vocational training programs and stress marketable skills.

Parole is the planned release and community supervision of incarcerated offenders before the expiration of their prison sentences. Parolees are subject to strict standardized or personalized rules that guide their behavior and limit their activities. Parole can also be revoked if the offender commits a second offense and the offender may be tried and sentenced for this crime. Parole is viewed as an act of grace on the part of the criminal justice system. The evaluation of parole effectiveness has produced some disturbing results. A majority return to prison shortly after their release. Many parolees are returned to prison for technical violations.

STUDENT EXERCISES

Exercise 1

Go online to http://www.ojp.usdoj.gov/bjs/pub/pdf/llgsfp.pdf and read the article, *Lifetime Likelihood of Going to State or Federal Prison* by Thomas P. Bonczar and Allen J. Beck. Summarize the major findings of the study concerning the likelihood of going to prison. Note that although the study is dated 1997, the data in the study have been updated to include 2001 data.

Exercise 2

Go online to http://www.ncjrs.org/pdffiles1/nij/197018.pdf and read the article, *Correctional Boot Camps: Lessons from a Decade of Research* by Dale G. Parent. Summarize the major findings of the study concerning the research on boot camps.

CRIMINOLOGY WEB LINKS

http://www.bop.gov/
This is the official website of the United States Bureau of Prisons.

http://www.hrw.org/prisons/
This is the official website of Human Rights Watch. The material in this website concerns information on prison conditions, prison abuses, human rights protections for prisoners, and related issues in the United States.

http://www.usdoj.gov/uspc/
This is the official website of the United States Parole Commission.

http://www.ojp.usdoj.gov/bjs/pandp.htm
This website contains information on probation and parole statistics in the United States.

http://www.corrections.com/aja/index.shtml
This is the official website of the American Jail Association.

TEST BANK

FILL-IN THE BLANKS

1. The inability of lower-class offenders to pay a fine led to the development of
_____ _____.

2. The Auburn prison design was sometimes also referred to as the _____
system because most prisoners ate and worked in groups.

3. In most jurisdictions, juries can recommend probation, but the _____ has
the final say.

4. _____ are a direct offshoot of the early common-law practice requiring
compensation to the victim and the state for criminal acts.

5. A more advanced method of control for home confinement has been the introduction of
_____ _____ devices to manage offender obedience to
home confinement orders.

6. State and federal governments maintain closed correctional facilities to house
_____ felons.

7. Those who flout prison rules may be segregated, locked in their cells, or put in solitary
confinement in the _____.

8. Female inmates are usually housed in _____-_____
institutions.

9. Recognizing that the probability of failure on the outside is acute, inmates have attempted to
organize _____-_____ groups to provide the psychological
tools needed to prevent recidivism.

10. _____ is the planned release and community supervision of incarcerated
offenders before the expiration of their prison sentences.

TRUE/FALSE QUESTIONS

1. T/F During the feudal period, the main emphasis of criminal law and punishment lay in
arresting criminals.

2. T/F The Pennsylvania system eventually prevailed and spread throughout the United States;
many of its features are still used today.

3. T/F Misdemeanor probation usually extends for the entire period of the jail sentence.

4. T/F Revocation for violation of probation rules is called a technical violation.

5. T/F Forfeiture is not a new sanction.

6. T/F The primary goal of intensive probation supervision is treatment.

7. T/F A residential community corrections program can be both a sole sentence and a halfway house.

8. T/F Jail conditions have become a national scandal.

9. T/F Prison farms and camps are found primarily in the North and the East.

10. T/F The inmate social code represents the values of interpersonal relations within the prison.

11. T/F Female offenders are more likely than males to be convicted of a nonviolent crime and incarcerated for a low-level involvement in drug offenses.

12. T/F Research indicates that older prisoners tend to be "players" but may experience periodic symptoms of depression or anxiety.

13. T/F Conflict, violence, and brutality are sad but ever-present facts of institutional life.

14. T/F The Supreme Court ruled that the ADA's protections did not extend to cover prison inmates.

15. T/F Fear of a prison stay has less of an impact on behavior than ever before.

MULTIPLE CHOICE QUESTIONS

1. Physical pain inflicted on the offenders for the purposes of punishment is known as:
   a. shock incarceration
   b. house arrest
   c. shock probation
   d. corporal punishment

2. 17th century laws in England that bound out vagrants, abandoned and neglected children as indentured servants are known as:
   a. forfeiture
   b. day fines
   c. poor laws
   d. intermediate sanctions

342

3. Under pressure from the Quakers, the Pennsylvania legislature in 1790 called for the renovation of the prison system. The ultimate result was the creation of the:
   a. Auburn system
   b. Elmira Reformatory
   c. Walnut Street Jail
   d. Cumberland County Jail

4. The prison system developed in New York during the nineteenth century that stressed congregate working conditions is known as the:
   a. Auburn system
   b. Elmira Reformatory
   c. Walnut Street Prison
   d. Cumberland County Jail

5. A system used to lease inmates out to private industry to work is known as:
   a. convict-lease system
   b. state account system
   c. contract system
   d. probation

6. A system used where the state leased inmates to a business for a fixed annual fee and the state gave up supervision and control is known as:
   a. contract system
   b. probation
   c. convict-lease system
   d. state account system

7. The system where prisoners produce goods in prison for state use is known as:
   a. probation
   b. convict-lease system
   c. state account system
   d. contract system

8. The first warden of Elmira Reformatory in New York was:
   a. Travis Hirschi
   b. Edwin Sutherland
   c. Z. R. Brockway
   d. John Augustus

9. A sentence of release into the community under the supervision of the court subject to certain conditions is known as:
   a. parole
   b. house arrest
   c. shock incarceration
   d. probation

10. Punishments falling between probation and prison including house arrest and intensive supervision are known as:
    a. intermediate sanctions
    b. probation
    c. parole
    d. prison

11. A judicial order by a court removing a person from parole or probation in response to a violation on the part of the parolee or probationer is known as:
    a. day fines
    b. home confinement
    c. revocation
    d. shock incarceration

12. Process where probation department diagnoses offender's personality and treatment needs is known as:
    a. offender classification
    b. electronic monitoring
    c. shock incarceration
    d. intensive probation supervision

13. Violations of the rules of probation or parole are known as:
    a. split sentencing
    b. technical violations
    c. day fines
    d. boot camps

14. A fine geared to an offender's net daily income collected in an effort to make punishment more equitable is known as:
    a. restitution
    b. probation
    c. day fines
    d. monetary restitution

15. Seizure of personal property by the state as a civil or criminal penalty is known as:
    a. forfeiture
    b. monetary restitution
    c. community service restitution
    d. day fines

16. A direct payment to the victim as a form of compensation is known as:
    a. forfeiture
    b. community service restitution
    c. day fines
    d. monetary restitution

17. Work in the community by the offender in lieu of more severe criminal penalties is known as:
   a. monetary restitution
   b. forfeiture
   c. community service restitution
   d. day fines

18. A sentence which includes a jail term as a condition of probation is known as:
   a. split sentencing
   b. shock probation
   c. intensive probation supervision
   d. home confinement

19. A sentence in which offenders serve a short prison term to impress them with the pains of imprisonment before they begin probation is known as:
   a. home confinement
   b. split sentencing
   c. shock probation
   d. intensive probation supervision

20. A type of immediate sanction involving small probation caseloads and strict monitoring is known as:
   a. home confinement
   b. split sentencing
   c. shock probation
   d. intensive probation supervision

21. A program in which convicted offenders are required to spend extended periods of time in their own homes as an alternative to incarceration is known as:
   a. home confinement
   b. split sentencing
   c. shock probation
   d. intensive probation supervision

22. The program whereby a convicted offender is required to wear a device under the home confinement penalty is known as:
   a. intensive probation supervision
   b. house arrest
   c. split sentencing
   d. electronic monitoring

23. A short prison sentence served in boot-camp type facilities is known as:
   a. split sentencing
   b. electronic monitoring
   c. shock incarceration
   d. intensive probation supervision

24. A short-term military style correctional facility in which inmates undergo intensive physical conditioning and discipline is known as:
   a. shock incarceration
   b. split sentencing
   c. electronic monitoring
   d. boot camps

25. A place to detain people awaiting trial, hold drunks and disorderly individual, and confine convicted misdemeanants serving sentences of less than one year is known as:
   a. prison
   b. walnut street prison
   c. boot camp
   d. jail

ESSAY QUESTIONS

1. Describe the nature of probation and its various services.

2. Describe purpose of the jail, its problems, and what is being done to improve the jail.

3. Describe the different types of correctional facilities and their level of security.

4. Discuss correctional treatment and the nature of prison violence.

5. Explain how problems of parolees and inmate reentry have influenced the correctional system.

MATCHING

1. _____ Revoke
2. _____ Offender Classification
3. _____ Technical Violation
4. _____ Day Fines
5. _____ Forfeiture
6. _____ Monetary Restitution
7. _____ Community Service Restitution
8. _____ Split Sentencing
9. _____ Shock Probation
10. _____ Intensive Probation Supervision

A.   Probation department diagnoses offender's personality and treatment needs.
B.   A fine geared to an offender's net daily income in an effort to make them more equitable.
C.   A direct payment to the victim as a form of compensation.
D.   Sentence which includes a jail term as a condition of probation.
E.   Type of immediate sanction involving small probation caseloads and strict monitoring.
F.   Judicial order by a court removing a person from parole or probation in response to a violation on the part of the parolee or probationer.
G.   Violation of rules of probation or parole.
H.   The seizure of personal property by the state as a civil or criminal penalty.
I.   Work in the community by the offender in lieu of more severe criminal penalties.
J.   Sentence in which offender's serve a short prison term to impress them with the pains of imprisonment before they begin probation.

CHAPTER 17 ANSWER KEY

Fill In The Blank Answers

1. corporal punishment
2. congregate
3. judge
4. fines
5. electronic monitoring
6. convicted
7. hole
8. minimum-security
9. self-help
10. parole

True/False Answers

1.	F	6.	F	11.	T
2.	F	7.	T	12.	F
3.	T	8.	T	13.	T
4.	T	9.	F	14.	F
5.	T	10.	T	15.	T

Multiple Choice Answers

1.	D	11.	C	21.	A
2.	C	12.	A	22.	D
3.	C	13.	B	23.	C
4.	A	14.	C	24.	D
5.	C	15.	A	25.	D
6.	C	16.	D		
7.	C	17.	C		
8.	C	18.	A		
9.	D	19.	C		
10.	A	20.	D		

Essay Questions

1. Pages 596 – 598
2. Pages 605 – 606
3. Pages 607 – 609
4. Pages 613 – 618
5. Pages 620 – 623

Matching Answers

1.	F	6.	C
2.	A	7.	I
3.	G	8.	D
4.	B	9.	J
5.	H	10.	E